OXFORD HANDBOOKS IN EMERGENCY MEDICINE
Series Editors   R. N. Illingworth, C. E. Robertson, and A. D. Redmond

1. The Management of Major Trauma
COLIN ROBERTSON AND ANTHONY D. REDMOND

2. Accidents and Emergencies in Children
ROSEMARY J. MORTON AND BARBARA M. PHILLIPS

OXFORD HANDBOOKS IN EMERGENCY MEDICINE

This series will cover topics of interest to all Accident and Emergency staff. The books are aimed at junior doctors and casualty nurses. Each book starts with an introduction to the topic, including epidemiology where appropriate. The clinical presentation and the immediate practical management of common conditions is described in detail, so that the casualty officer or nurse is able to deal with the problem on the spot. A specific course of action is recommended for each situation, and alternatives discussed.

Accidents and Emergencies in Children

Rosemary J. Morton MRCP, FRCS
Consultant in Accident and Emergency Medicine,
Manchester Royal Infirmary, Manchester

and

Barbara M. Phillips FRCP
Consultant Paediatrician in Accident and Emergency,
Booth Hall Children's Hospital, Manchester

Oxford • New York • Tokyo
OXFORD UNIVERSITY PRESS
1992

Oxford University Press, Walton Street, Oxford OX2 6DP
Oxford New York Toronto
Delhi Bombay Calcutta Madras Karachi
Petaling Jaya Singapore Hong Kong Tokyo
Nairobi Dar es Salaam Cape Town
Melbourne Auckland
and associated companies in
Berlin Ibadan

Oxford is a trade mark of Oxford University Press

Published in the United States
by Oxford University Press, New York

A catalogue record for this book is available from the British Library

Library of Congress Cataloging in Publication Data
Morton, Rosemary J.
   Accidents and emergencies in children / Rosemary J. Morton and Barbara
M. Phillips.
      (Oxford handbook in emergency medicine)
   Includes index.
   1. Pediatric emergencies–Handbooks, manuals, etc. 2. Children's
accidents–Handbooks, manuals, etc. I. Phillips, Barbara M.
II. Title. III Series.
   [DNLM: 1. Accidents–in infancy & childhood–handbooks.
2. Emergencies–in infancy & childhood–handbooks. WS 39 M889a]
RJ370.M67 1992   618.92'0025–dc20   91–32093
ISBN 0–19–262222–6 (h'bk)   ISBN 0–19–261929–2 (p'bk)

Set by Footnote Graphics, Warminster, Wiltshire
Printed in Great Britain by
Biddles Ltd, Guildford & King's Lynn

For Bryony and Robert
and
for Ruth and Rachel

Preface

We have written this book to help Accident and Emergency Senior House Officers, who may have no postgraduate paediatric experience, to manage the wide variety of paediatric patients who attend their departments.

Emphasis has been placed on the emergency management of serious illness and injury and on the management of common problems.

Indications for referral to paediatric and other specialists are clearly made. However, in many instances further management is also described both for readers studying for the Accident and Emergency Fellowship examination and in case paediatric help is otherwise occupied!

Although efforts have been made to ensure the accuracy of drug dosage, readers should consult the *British National Formulary* before prescribing.

Our thanks go to our teachers over years of medical practice and to our many colleagues, patients, and families from whom we have learnt how to care for children. Particular thanks are offered to our paediatric colleagues who have contributed helpful criticisms from their own specialist expertise– Tim David, Jon Couriel (also permission to use Table 16.1), David Evans, Mike Clarke, John Keen, Raine Roberts, Frank Bamford, Victor Miller, Peter Davenport, and Sheila Stainthorpe (permission to modify Table 2.2).

The guidance of Robin Illingworth, the series editor, and the support of Oxford University Press were invaluable.

Finally, we thank John Coffey for the drawings, Jennifer Loxley for her patience with countless manuscript revisions, and our families for tolerating the time spent away from them.

1991
Manchester

R.J.M.
B.M.P.

Contents

CHAPTER 1

Children in the Accident and Emergency department

Facilities for children and their families

Between 20 and 30 per cent of attenders at District General Hospital Accident and Emergency (A & E) departments are children under 16 years old. In England and Wales there are more than two million child attenders at A & E departments annually. There is a disproportionately high number of attenders under five years of age.

It is sometimes considered that because children are small they require a smaller provision of space in hospital buildings than do adults. In fact the opposite is true. Children attending A & E departments are usually accompanied by at least one adult, and often siblings, prams, or push-chairs.

Box 1.1 Minimum requirements for children in A & E:
- Separate waiting area with play facilities.
- Separate treatment area suitably decorated and equipped.
- Private room for distressed parents.
- At least one RSCN trained nurse on the staff.
- A consultant paediatrician to have responsibility for liaison with the consultant in Accident and Emergency medicine concerning general arrangements for children.
- A liaison health visitor to facilitate communication between the department and the community.

The requirements in Box 1.1 are supported by the joint statement on children's A & E attendances produced in 1988 by the British Paediatric Association, the British Association of Paediatric Surgeons, and the Casualty Surgeons Association (now the British Association for Accident and Emergency Medicine).

A separate resuscitation area for children is not appropriate for most A & E departments but equipment and drugs for children should be easily identifiable and available.

Categories of paediatric problems in A & E

- Trauma Medical Surgical Behavioural/psychiatric problems

Trauma

Injured children account for the majority of attendances (60–70 per cent). Most will have relatively minor injuries, but a few will have suffered major blunt or, more rarely, penetrating injury, severe burns or scalds, or will have been seriously poisoned.

Accidents are the commonest cause of death in children over 1-year-old in the United Kingdom. Each year, about 700 children die as a result of accidents, and about 10 000 become permanently disabled. About 20 per cent of children's admissions to hospital are the result of accidents.

Medical

Fifteen to twenty per cent of attenders have medical problems. These will range from the seriously ill child with convulsions, collapse, or respiratory difficulty, to patients who have conditions usually treated by their general practitioner (GP). In this latter group are children who have been treated by their GP but whose parents want a 'second opinion', children whose illness is not improving as quickly as their parents expect, and children whose parents fear they are seriously ill. Children under five years old and especially children under two predominate in the medical attenders.

Surgical

A smaller percentage of patients have non-traumatic surgical problems, such as irritable hip, Perthe's disease, appendicitis, hernia, etc.

Behavioural/psychiatric problems

A small number of children, usually adolescents, attend with symptoms related to drug, alcohol, or solvent abuse, or following self-poisoning attempts.

The problem of **child abuse** may be found throughout the whole spectrum of A & E child attenders.

The child in the A & E department

- **Triage   The importance of play   The approach to the child and parents   Treatment and procedures   Information   Liaison with other departments**

Triage

In most A & E departments patients are assessed on arrival by an experienced nurse who decides if they require urgent treatment or can safely wait. Children are usually given a high priority. It is important to remember that seriously ill babies can be presented in their parents' arms as apparently 'walking wounded'. All infants should be seen by the triage nurse as soon as they enter the department.

The importance of play

A & E attendance when acutely injured or ill is a frightening introduction to hospital for a child. Play reduces anxiety in an unfamiliar situation, as it is through play that children learn and express themselves. Children's cooperation can be more easily secured if, while waiting, they are distracted by playing and, when examined or undergoing procedures, the element of play is introduced.

The approach to the child and parents

When first meeting a family, introduce yourself, know the child's name and ascertain if the accompanying adults are the child's parents. Talk to the child even if he is not old enough to understand—even babies love being talked to. A little flattery often helps; for example admiring clothing or a toy. Praise encourages cooperation during the examination, for example 'how good you are being' or 'you are very grown-up'.

The examination of children, especially young ones, often

does not proceed in an ordered fashion and one must be opportunistic while examining. Leave unpleasant procedures, such as throat or rectal examination, until last.

Treatment and procedures

To minimize anxiety both for the child and parent it is most important that the parent accompanies the child through all treatments and procedures. In some cases this may even include treatment in the resuscitation room, for example, in a child who has frequent convulsions and whose parent is experienced in managing them. A parent who has not accompanied the child to the resuscitation room, must be brought back to be with the child again as soon as the emergency situation is under control. Children should be given a clear explanation appropriate to their age before the start of any procedure.

Information

Leaflets detailing instructions for parents, problems to look out for, and information on who to contact in the event of concern are very useful for parents of children who are discharged from the department. Leaflets should be available on wound care, burns care, management of plaster of Paris, observations for head injury, and management of gastroenteritis. Appropriate translations should be available for non-English speaking families.

Liaison with other departments

Close liaison is needed between the A & E department and the paediatric, anaesthetic, orthopaedic, and surgical departments in particular. This liaison will be facilitated if there is feedback from other departments on the progress of children who have been admitted to hospital and if joint audit meetings can be held.

Ideally, general practitioners should receive information on all of their patients who have attended the local A & E department.

Recognition of children with potentially serious illness

It is often difficult in the early stages of illness to differentiate the child with serious illness from one with a mild self-limiting disease. Two small groups of children need to be differentiated from the larger group with benign self-limiting disease:

1. the child with a severe form of a common, often benign disease, for example gastroenteritis, pneumonia, and
2. the child with early serious disease always requiring hospital treatment, for example meningitis, pyloric stenosis.

In addition to history and examination the clinical assessment of children includes observation to assess whether they look 'ill' or not. There are four steps in the initial assessment of the unwell child:

- History
- Observation
- Examination
- Investigation.

1. History—In addition to disease-specific symptoms, such as cough, breathing difficulties, vomiting, diarrhoea, convulsions, cyanosis, etc., the history of an infant's alertness, interaction with his environment, and overall activity is important when assessing the presence of serious illness. Other useful non-specific symptoms are taking less than half the usual amount of fluid and passing less urine than usual in the previous 24 hours. These general symptoms are often not mentioned by the parent who will usually concentrate on the more graphic symptoms, such as cough, vomiting, or diarrhoea. Careful questioning of the parent is necessary to elicit this aspect of the history.

2. Observation—Before a systematic examination of the patient there should be a period of observation (often while taking the history) for evidence as to whether the child looks 'ill' or not. The child should be on the parent's lap, or

wherever he seems happy, and observation should be made of:

- Alertness—a well child will look around at his environment but an ill child will be disinterested or irritable.
- Interaction with parents—does he respond to his parents, playing if happy, or is he easily distracted when crying? A child who is ill will be less easily interested or distracted than one who is well.
- Interaction with the doctor—a baby will respond to eye contact, smile if he is old enough, or reach out for a proffered toy, but the unwell baby will show a lack of interest.
- State of wakefulness—the well baby will wake up quickly when stimulated if asleep, and if awake will stay alert. The unwell baby takes a while to wake up and becomes drowsy easily.

3. Examination—specific physical signs of disease are referred to in the relevant chapters.

4. Investigations—recommended investigations can be found in the relevant chapters.

Recently, a score called 'Baby Check' has been devised and tested for use in babies under 6-months-old. It has been designed to help both parents and doctors with little paediatric experience to differentiate between the non-specific symptoms of mild disease and early serious disease by means of 19 scored symptoms and signs (see Further reading, Reference 5).

The febrile child

The infant or child with a fever is often presented for medical attention early in the disease when specific clinical diagnosis is difficult.

First, assess the child's overall condition. *Seek urgent paediatric help with the febrile child who is drowsy, unresponsive, pale, or has a purpuric rash.* He may have septicaemia (p. 38), meningitis (p. 257), pyelonephritis (p. 237), or a severe episode of a more common infection such as gastroenteritis (p. 223).

The history may be helpful in suggesting a focus for the illness, for example there may have been diarrhoea, a cough, a painful throat, or earache.

Thorough examination will reveal the infectious focus in some children: common causes of fever are:

- Colds (p. 196)
- Tonsillitis (p. 199)
- Pharyngitis (p. 199)
- Otitis media (p. 197)
- The exanthems, e.g. measles (p. 277)

The following causes are less common but should be actively sought, clinically, in a child with unexplained fever:

- Meningitis (p. 257)
- Septicaemia (p. 38)
- Urinary tract infection (p. 237)
- Pneumonia (p. 206)
- Peritonitis (p. 231)
- Osteomyelitis/septic arthritis (p. 134)

The white cell count is generally unhelpful in the assessment of the febrile child although occasionally it may point to a specific diagnosis, for example atypical mononuclear cells in glandular fever.

Do not forget infectious diseases not endemic in the UK in febrile recent travellers.

Children for whom no cause for fever can be found and those who are unwell should be referred to the paediatric team.

Further reading

1. British Paediatric Association, British Association of Paediatric Surgeons, Casualty Surgeons Association (1988). *Joint statement on children's attendances at Accident & Emergency departments*. British Paediatric Association, London.
2. Royal College of Nursing (1989). *Nursing children in Accident & Emergency Departments; guidelines for children and the family*. Royal College of Nursing, London.

3. National Association for the Welfare of Children in Hospital (1990). *NAWCH quality review: setting standards for children in health care*. National Association for the Welfare of Children in Hospital, London.
4. Child Accident Prevention Trust (1989). *Basic principles of child accident prevention: a guide to action*. Child Accident Prevention Trust, London.
5. Morley, C. J., Thornton, A. J., Cole, T. J., and Hewson, P. H. (1991). Interpreting the symptoms and signs of illness in infants. In *Recent advances in paediatrics*, No. 4. (ed. T. J. David), pp. 137–55. Churchill Livingstone, Edinburgh [Description of 'Baby Check' score].

CHAPTER 2

Cardiopulmonary resuscitation and the seriously ill child

Key points in cardiopulmonary resuscitation

1 Respiratory and/or circulatory failure are the usual causes of cardiac arrest in children.

2 Airway control and ventilation with 100% oxygen are of prime importance.

3 Venous access must be gained as soon as possible for circulatory support and administration of drugs.

4 Earlier recognition and treatment of imminent respiratory and circulatory failure will improve outcome.

5 Overwhelming infection is a frequent precursor of collapse especially in infancy. After initial resuscitation early consideration should be given to the use of intravenous broad spectrum antibiotics.

Introduction

- **Aetiology of cardiac arrests   Outcome**
  Cardiopulmonary resuscitation   Summoning help

Aetiology of cardiac arrests

Cardiac arrests in children are rarely due to primary cardiac problems. Most cardiac arrests are the result of hypoxia and some are caused by circulatory failure (see Figure 2.1). The mode of death in Sudden Infant Death syndrome (p. 320) is unknown.

The important initial goals of cardiopulmonary resuscitation (CPR) in children are, therefore, oxygenation of the

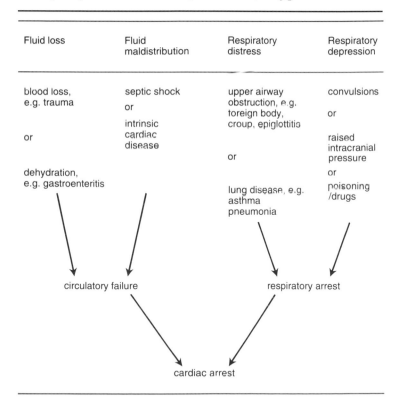

Fig. 2.1 • Disease pathways which may end in cardiac arrest in childhood.

lungs, and the restoration of a normal cardiac rhythm and circulating blood volume.

Outcome

The outcome of respiratory arrest alone should initially be good and long-term survival depends on the underlying pathology. However, the outcome of cardiac arrest in children is less good than that in adults. Many cardiac arrests in adults result from ventricular fibrillation; the heart rhythm and output can often be restored by prompt defibrillation. However, in children most cardiac arrests are caused by hypoxia or shock and the cardiac rhythm is usually asystole. In children, the heart is usually healthy and withstands hypoxia and acidosis for longer than the brain. By the time cardiac arrest has occurred, the injury to the brain and other organs may be too severe to permit recovery even if the heart is restarted.

The worst outcome is in children who arrive apnoeic and pulseless at an Accident and Emergency department. These children have a poor chance of intact neurological survival. There has often been a prolonged period of hypoxia and ischaemia before the start of adequate cardiopulmonary resuscitation. Earlier recognition of seriously ill children and paediatric CPR training for ambulancemen and the public could improve the outcome for these children.

Cardiopulmonary resuscitation

Cardiopulmonary resuscitation has three aims:

1. Restoration of flow of oxygenated blood to vital organs, especially the heart and brain, by external chest compression and artificial ventilation.

2. Restoration of satisfactory, spontaneous cardiac output and ventilation by drug treatment and by reversing the processes leading to cardiac arrest, for example hypoxia, hypovolaemia, acidosis.

3. Initial management of the underlying condition.

Summoning help

When a child with a suspected respiratory or cardiac arrest is brought into the A & E department, an immediate emergency call should be made for the paediatrician and the anaesthetist. The A & E staff must start resuscitation. Table 2.1 gives a list of suggested personnel and their initial tasks. One member of the team must assume leadership. A rapid history should be obtained from parents or ambulancemen and relayed to the resuscitation team. Such information is vital to the resuscitation effort, for example if the child has had profuse diarrhoea, volume replacement is especially important.

Table 2.1 • Arrest team personnel

Personnel	Suggested initial task
Anaesthetist	airway and breathing management
A & E SHO	cardiac compression
Paediatric SHO and/or Registrar	i.v. access and drugs
Nurse 1	assist anaesthetist with airway and breathing
Nurse 2	drug and i.v. fluid preparation
Nurse 3	monitors and charts
Nurse 4	liaison with parents

Airway and breathing management, cardiac compression, and i.v. access and drug administration must proceed simultaneously. Patient observations and drugs must be documented.

Table 2.2 shows sizes of equipment needed and doses of drugs to be used in CPR.

Paediatric resuscitation procedure

- **Assessment   Airway management   Breathing management   Circulation management   Arrhythmias Drugs in CPR and post-resuscitation management Fluids in CPR   Monitoring in CPR**

Assessment

1. Time—make a mental note.

Table 2.2 •

			Prem.	Newborn
Age				
Average wt	kg		2 kg	3 kg
	lb		4.5 lb	7 lb
ETT diameter			2.5–3 mm	3 mm
Oral ETT length cm			8.5 cm	9.5 cm
Nasal ETT length cm			10 cm	11 cm
Chest drain F (Ch) gauge			8	8
Urinary catheter F gauge			3.5	5
Minimum Artificial Ventilation rate/min			40/min	40/min
Defibrillator charge				
1st and 2nd 2 J/kg			4 J	6 J
3rd–4 J/kg			8 J	10 J

Drug	Dose	Concentration	Route		
Atropine	20 μg/kg	600 μg/ml	i.v. or ETT	0.17 ml	0.17 ml
Adrenalin	10 μ/kg	1:10 000	i.v. or ETT	0.2 ml	0.3 ml
Sodium bicarbonate	1 mmol/kg	8.4% (1 mmol/ml)	i.v.	2 ml	3 ml
Lignocaine	1 mg/kg	1%	i.v. or ETT	0.2 ml	0.3 ml
Calcium chloride	10 mg/kg	10%	i.v.	0.2 ml	0.3 ml
Frusemide	1 mg/kg	20 mg/2 ml	i.v.	0.2 ml	0.3 ml
Mannitol	500 mg/kg	10%	i.v.	10 ml	15 ml
		20%	i.v.	5 ml	7.5 ml
Dopamine	2 μg/kg/min	Dissolve 60 mg Dopamine in 500 ml	i.v. dextrose 5%	2 ml/h	3 ml/h
Dopamine	10 μg/kg/min	Dissolve 300 mg of Dopamine in 500 ml	i.v. dextrose 5%	2 ml/h	3 ml/h
		Age		Prem.	Newborn
		Average wt		2 kg	3kg

Note: Equipment sizes are only a guide. A size larger or smaller may be required.

2. Colour—blue, pale, pink. If the skin is pigmented look inside the mouth.

3. Respiration—feel, listen, and look for air movement at the nose and mouth, chest, and abdomen. If this is:

- adequate—check circulation;
- poor, absent, or obstructed—proceed to airway management.

1m	2m	3m	6m	1yr	2yr	3yr	5yr	7yr	10yr	15yr
4kg	4.5kg	5kg	8kg	10kg	13kg	15kg	18kg	23kg	30kg	40+
9lb	10lb	12lb	17lb	22lb	29lb	33lb	40lb	50lb	66lb	88+
3mm	3mm	3.5mm	4mm	4mm	4.5mm	5mm	5mm	6.5mm	7.5mm	7.5mm
10cm	10cm	10.5cm	11cm	12cm	13cm	13.5cm	14cm	16cm	18.5cm	19cm
11.5cm	11.5cm	12cm	12.5cm	14.5cm	15cm	16cm	16.8cm	18cm	19cm	20cm
8	8	10	10	10	12	14	16	18	20	24
5	5	8	8	8	10	10	12	12	16	16
40/min	40/min	40/min	30/min	30/min	30/min	30/min	30/min	25/min	25/min	25/min
8J	9J	10J	15J	20J	25J	30J	40J	50J	60J	100J
16J	18J	20J	30J	40J	50J	60J	80J	100J	120J	200J
0.17ml	0.17ml	0.2ml	0.25ml	0.35ml	0.5ml	0.5ml	0.6ml	0.8ml	1ml	1ml
0.4ml	0.45ml	0.5ml	0.7ml	1ml	1.3ml	1.5ml	2ml	2.5ml	3ml	4ml
4ml	4.5ml	5ml	8ml	10ml	13ml	15ml	18ml	23ml	30ml	40ml
0.4ml	0.5ml	0.5ml	0.7ml	1ml	1.3ml	1.5ml	2ml	2.5ml	3ml	4ml
0.4ml	0.5ml	0.5ml	0.7ml	1ml	1.3ml	1.5ml	2ml	2.5ml	3ml	4ml
0.4ml	0.4ml	0.6ml	0.7ml	1ml	1.3ml	1.5ml	2ml	2.5ml	3ml	4ml
20ml	22ml	25ml	35ml	50ml	66ml	75ml	100ml	125ml	150ml	200ml
10ml	11ml	12ml	17ml	25ml	32ml	37ml	50ml	62ml	75ml	100ml
4 ml/h	4.5 ml/h	5 ml/h	8 ml/h	10 ml/h	13 ml/h	15 ml/h	18 ml/h	23 ml/h	30 ml/h	40 ml/h
4 ml/h	4.5 ml/h	5 ml/h	8 ml/h	10 ml/h	13 ml/h	15 ml/h	18 ml/h	23 ml/h	30 ml/h	40 ml/h
1m	2m	3m	6m	1yr	2yr	3yr	5yr	7yr	10yr	15yr
4kg	4.5kg	5kg	8kg	10kg	13kg	15kg	18kg	23kg	30kg	40+

4. Circulation— feel for brachial pulse (not cardiac impulse), note volume and approximate rate.
5. Neurological status—response to painful stimulation.

The whole assessment should take a few seconds only.

Airway management

1. Clearing the airway. The airway may be obstructed with

Table 2.3 • Equipment for the paediatric resuscitation area

1. Airway
   - Oropharyngeal airway sizes 000, 00, 0, 1, 2, 3, 4
   - Endotracheal tubes sizes 2.5, 3.0, 3.5, 4.0, 4.5, 5.0, 5.5, 6.0, 6.5, 7.0, 7.5 uncuffed and 7.5 cuffed
   - Oxygen masks for facial oxygen
   - Laryngoscopes
     neonatal, e.g. Wisconsin type
     intermediate, e.g. Robertshaw
     adult, e.g. Macintosh
   - Inflating bag, e.g. Laerdal, Ambu (with reservoirs)
     240 ml infant size
     500 ml child size
     1600 ml adult size
   - Transparent cuffed masks for inflating bags
     infant—circular 01, 1, 2
     child—shaped to nose 2, 3
     adult—shaped to nose 4, 5
   - Connections—e.g. Portex type
   - Magill forceps
   - Yankauer sucker
   - Tracheal catheters
   - Ayre's T-piece anaesthetic circuit
   - Needle cricothyrotomy set
2. e.c.g. monitor with defibrillator (with paediatric paddles)
3. Automatic blood pressure monitor (with infant and child-sized cuffs)
4. Pulse oximeter (with infant and child-sized probes)
5. Intravenous access requirements, e.g.
   - Jelco   18–24 gauge
   - Venflon   18–24 gauge
   - Medicut   18–24 gauge
   - Butterfly   18–25 gauge
   - Intraosseous infusion needles 16–18 gauge
   - Graduated burette
   - Intravenous giving sets
   - Syringes 1–50 ml sizes
6. Intravenous drip monitoring device, e.g. Imed
7. Cut-down set
8. Dextrostix or BM stix
9. Chest drain set 8–28 F (Ch) sizes
10. Urinary catheters 8–18 F sizes
11. Seldinger percutaneous cannulation set
12. Nasogastric tubes 3.5–16 F sizes

fluid, for example saliva, blood, vomit. Remove fluids by suction with a rigid, angled sucker (for example Yankauer). 2. Opening the airway. The airway is opened by head tilt and chin lift. The neck should be moderately extended and the chin lifted by a finger under the mandible. The same effect can be achieved with jaw thrust in which the mandible is pushed forward by two fingers behind both angles of the jaw. Do not over-extend the neck.

In an unconscious child, an oropharyngeal airway should then be inserted into the mouth concave side up, then when it is over the tongue, turned over to slide into place. This will maintain an open airway by preventing the tongue pressing back on the posterior pharyngeal wall.

Breathing management

If breathing is now adequate, maintain the airway position and give oxygen, in high concentration, at 6–10 litres per minute by mask—not via a self-inflating bag (this may impede spontaneous ventilation).

If breathing is inadequate with an open airway, proceed to assisted ventilation with oxygen by a self-inflating bag and mask with an oxygen reservoir. The appropriate sized inflating bag should be used (Table 2.3). Bag and mask ventilation can be very satisfactory in ventilating infants and children, but an oxygen reservoir is necessary for high oxygen concentration. It is important to ensure a good airtight seal between the mask and the child's face. Watch for chest expansion and improvement in colour.

Proceed to oral endotracheal intubation if you are trained in the technique.

Endotracheal intubation This should be preceded by bag and mask ventilation with 100 per cent oxygen for at least one minute to pre-oxygenate the patient. The tube should be cut to the recommended length for the child's age (see Table 2.2). There is no need for lubrication of the tube. When you pass the laryngoscope an assistant should stand at the child's right-hand side with a wide bore suction catheter and prepared endotracheal tube. Upward thyroid cartilage pressure may improve the view of the larynx. The laryngoscope is used to lift the base of the tongue forward to expose and illuminate the epiglottis and vocal cords. The tube is passed between the vocal cords. Intubation attempts should be limited to 30 seconds, then the child should be re-oxygenated by bag and mask before the next attempt. When the endotracheal tube is in place connect the bag and ventilate. Check the tube's position and adequacy of ventilation by looking for chest movement and by listening for air entry with a stethoscope on both sides of the chest. The ventilation rate is 40/min for infants, 30/min for young children, and 25/min for older children.

Estimated tidal volume is 10–15 ml/kg, but use sufficient tidal volume to ensure chest movement. It is wise to use a small tidal volume for the first few inflations and to increase the volume if necessary rather than to be too vigorous and cause a pneumothorax. Both the rate of ventilation and the tidal volume may need to be increased depending on the patient's response. In respiratory arrest there should now be clinical improvement, the child's colour should improve and the heart rate, if previously low, increase.

Endotracheal drug administration Once the endotracheal tube is in position the route can be used for drugs if venous access has not been obtained. Atropine, adrenalin, and lignocaine may all be given this way. The speed of onset is similar to that following central venous administration. Use double the recommended intravenous dose. The drug should be injected quickly down a narrow bore suction catheter beyond the tracheal end of the ET tube. Ventilation should then continue.

In patients with pulmonary disease or prolonged asystole, pulmonary oedema and intrapulmonary shunting may make the endotracheal route for drugs less effective. If there has been no clinical effect, further doses should be given intravenously once venous access has been secured. The intracardiac route for adrenalin is no longer recommended.

Circulation management

Chest compression Chest compression must begin immediately in the pulseless child. External chest compression, when properly performed, is thought to produce a cardiac output of approximately one-third of the healthy state. The site of compression is at the junction of the lower and middle third of the sternum. In infants this is one finger's breadth below the inter-nipple line. The index and middle fingers should be used to compress the chest. In children the heel of the hand should be placed two fingers' breadth above the bottom of the sternum. The patient must lie on a firm surface. Compression should be smooth and firm and not jabbing. The rate is 100–120/min in infants and 80–100/min in children, with a depth of compression of 2–3 cm in infants and 3–5 cm in children. In small infants chest compression can be achieved by encircling the child's thorax with both hands and compressing the sternum with the thumbs. In infants with a large occiput there may be a dead space behind the upper thorax; therefore a towel should be placed there to ensure adequate compression against the resuscitation trolley surface. Until adequate cardiac output is established chest compression must not be interrupted for more than 15 seconds for the implementation of other procedures, such as chest radiograph or chest drain placement.

The adequacy of chest compression must be monitored by feeling for a pulse in a peripheral artery, such as the brachial.

If the child is being ventilated by bag and mask, there should be five chest compressions to each lung inflation. Allow one second for each lung inflation. If the child is intubated there is no need to stop chest compression to allow ventilation.

Intravenous access Attempts to obtain venous access should be started as soon as possible.

1. Try a visible vein first, including antecubital fossa, external jugular, and scalp veins.
2. If, after two minutes, i.v. access is not secured, try more invasive methods. The simplest is an intraosseous infusion (see procedures p. 329), then a percutaneous cannulation of the femoral vein (p. 328). A cut-down on the saphenous vein will take several minutes and is, therefore, less useful. In small children emergency cannulation of the subclavian is

difficult and should only be undertaken by those who are experienced in the technique.

Always use a giving set with a measuring burette in children under 30 kg.

Arrhythmias (see Figures 2.2, 2.3)

Asystole This is the commonest arrhythmia in pulseless children. As discussed earlier, it is often associated with a poor outcome. In adult CPR, defibrillation is recommended in apparent asystole in case the commoner and more treatable rhythm, ventricular fibrillation, is present, but not seen on the e.c.g. This manoeuvre is not recommended in children, but, especially in older, or cold, or poisoned children (in whom ventricular fibrillation may be more common), make sure that apparent asystole is not due to a technical e.c.g. problem by checking leads and connections and turning up the gain on the e.c.g. monitor.

In asystole, adrenalin at 10 µg/kg should be given intravenously preferably through a central line if one is in place. The drug should be flushed in with dextrose saline. If venous access has not been secured, then the adrenalin may be given intratracheally at twice the dose. CPR should be continued.

After one minute, atropine should be given intravenously (0.02 mg/kg) or intratracheally (0.04 mg/kg).

Children with asystole are usually profoundly acidotic as their cardiac arrest has usually been preceded by respiratory arrest or shock. Adrenalin is poorly effective in acidosis; therefore sodium bicarbonate 1 mmol/kg should precede further doses of adrenalin.

Ventricular fibrillation This arrhythmia is uncommon in children but should be sought in children who are recovering from hypothermia, those poisoned by tricyclic antidepressants, and those with cardiac disease.

Electrical defibrillation should be carried out immediately. Paediatric paddles (4.5 cm) should be used for children under 10 kg. One electrode is placed just below the right clavicle and the other in the left mid-clavicular line at the level of the xiphoid. If only adult paddles are available for an infant

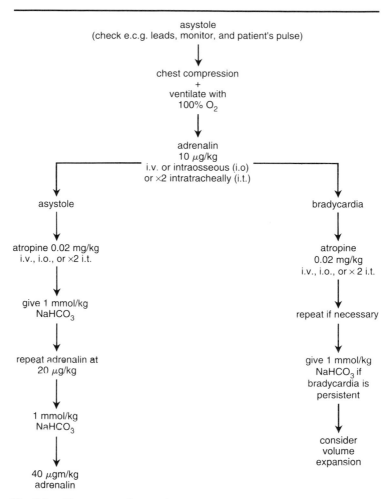

Fig. 2.2 • Treatment of asystole.

under 10 kg, one may be placed on the infant's back and one over the left lower part of the chest at the front.

The initial shock should be 2 J/kg. If two attempts are unsuccessful, a third attempt should use 4 J/kg. If three shocks fail to produce defibrillation the patient should be hyperventilated (to increase pH), given adrenalin 10 µg/kg intravenously, and the shock (4 J/kg) repeated. Following

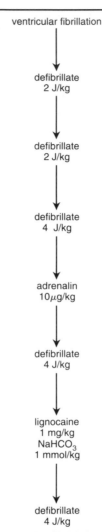

Fig. 2.3 • Treatment of ventricular fibrillation.

this a fifth shock should be preceded by lignocaine 1 mg/kg and sodium bicarbonate 1 mmol/kg intravenously. Then different paddle positions or another defibrillator may be tried. Finally, the antiarrhythmic agent bretylium tosylate may be used with further defibrillation attempts.

Electromechanical dissociation (EMD) This is an apparent absence of a palpable pulse with QRS complexes seen on the e.c.g. monitor. The commonest cause in children is profound shock, making the pulse difficult to feel. It should be treated with rapid volume expansion (see Shock p. 37). In patients with trauma, cardiac tamponade or pneumothorax should be considered and treated if necessary.

After shock or mechanical obstruction have been excluded or treated, persistent EMD should be treated like asystole, with adrenalin.

Very occasionally, intravenous calcium may be required in a patient with EMD due to hypocalcaemia, hyperkalaemia, hypermagnesaemia, or calcium channel blocker overdose.

Drugs in CPR and post-resuscitation management

Oxygen All patients undergoing CPR initially require 100 per cent oxygen. Potential adverse effects of high oxygen concentration are not a consideration in these circumstances. Face masks with differing oxygen concentration capability are available, varying from 25 per cent to 60 per cent. However, concentration masks are not appropriate for CPR. It is unlikely that the higher percentage ones really deliver 60 per cent oxygen accurately. Bag and mask devices

Table 2.4 • Drugs for the paediatric resuscitation area

Drugs	Presentation
Adrenalin	1:10 000
Atropine	600 µg/ml
Sodium bicarbonate	8.4%
Dopamine	40 mg/ml
Lignocaine	1%
Dextrose	25% + 50%
Calcium chloride	10%
Frusemide	20 mg/ml
Mannitol	10% + 20%
Antibiotics—penicillin, chloramphenicol, gentamicin, ampicillin, ceftazidime, cefotaxime	

give up to 60 per cent with oxygen connected and up to 100 per cent if an oxygen reservoir is added. An Ayre's T-piece bag will deliver 100 per cent oxygen, however, the T-piece circuit is difficult to handle by the inexperienced and is probably best left for the anaesthetist.

Adrenalin Adrenalin has both α- and β-adrenergic stimulatory effects. The α effect results in vasoconstriction while the β effect increases cardiac rate and contractility and dilates coronary and cerebral vasculature. Adrenalin is used primarily in the treatment of asystole.

The initial dose of adrenalin is 10 μg/kg and this should be doubled and then quadrupled in subsequent doses. Acidosis renders adrenalin less effective. It is inactivated by sodium bicarbonate, so a saline flush should first be used if adrenalin injection follows sodium bicarbonate. The drug is safe in children, although occasionally it may produce ventricular tachycardias.

Atropine Atropine increases the heart rate by increasing the rate of discharge from the sinoatrial node and increasing conduction through the atrioventricular node. The indication for atropine is bradycardia with a poor cardiac output despite adequate ventilation. It is also given following adrenalin in asystole. The minimum dose is 0.1 mg.

Sodium bicarbonate Sodium bicarbonate is used for the correction of metabolic acidosis. Acidosis may be demonstrated by analysis of an arterial blood gas sample, or can be assumed to be present in a patient who has had circulatory arrest for more than a few minutes. Sodium bicarbonate is an irritant and hyperosmolar drug which contains a high concentration of sodium. It produces carbon dioxide which may cause problems in the unventilated patient. In addition, it can cause intracellular acidosis as it releases carbon dioxide, though it will temporarily raise the intravascular pH. If the patient is being ventilated, the excess carbon dioxide may be removed by hyperventilation while the bicarbonate is being infused.

The drug is now used more sparingly than in the past. However, children in cardiac arrest are likely to be very acidotic from preceding respiratory or circulatory failure and it is appropriate to use bicarbonate earlier in paediatric than in adult CPR. The dose for children is 1 mmol/kg (1 ml/kg of 8.4 per cent bicarbonate), and it should be administered by a doctor or nurse with a syringe and not run in through a burette. Sodium bicarbonate must *not* be given in the same intravenous line as calcium as precipitation will occur. Sodium bicarbonate inactives adrenalin and dopamine and therefore the line must be flushed with saline if these drugs are subsequently given. Bicarbonate may not be given by the intratracheal route.

Glucose Young, sick infants have poor glycogen stores and glucose may be given during the course of cardiopulmonary resuscitation even without clear evidence of hypoglycaemia. The dose is 0.5 g/kg intravenously. A 25 per cent or 50 per cent solution is available, but a 10 per cent solution should be used in the neonatal period because the stronger solutions are more likely to damage tiny veins.

Dopamine Dopamine has a similar cardiac action to adrenalin, but it increases peripheral vascular resistance more effectively. It is indicated for the patient who has cardiac activity and output but hypotension and inadequate renal perfusion despite adequate volume replacement. Dopamine is given by infusion. At a dose of 2–10 µg/kg/min, dopamine increases blood flow to renal and mesenteric blood vessels and will improve renal perfusion and, therefore, urine output in a patient with poor urine flow. Following cardiopulmonary resuscitation, however, a dose of 10–15 µg/kg/min is required to increase blood pressure in a hypotensive patient. If 60 mg of dopamine is added to 100 ml of infusion solution (such as dextrose 5 per cent) the infusion of 1 ml/kg/h will deliver 10 µ/kg/min to the patient. Therefore, at this dilution the rate in millilitres per hour is equal to the patient's body weight. Dopamine can produce tachycardia and ectopic cardiac beats, hence careful monitoring of the blood pressure is necessary. As extravasation of the drug into subcutaneous tissues may cause damage, it should, therefore, be given through a central line whenever possible and monitored with a drip counter. Dopamine is inactivated by bicarbonate.

Lignocaine Lignocaine is rarely used in paediatric resuscitation. Ventricular fibrillation is a relatively uncommon event and is usually treated with cardioversion. However, if repeated defibrillation is unsuccessful, even after a dose of adrenalin, lignocaine at a dose of 1 mg/kg may be given intravenously before a further defibrillation attempt.

Calcium Calcium is rarely used in resuscitation. It is occasionally needed for treating hyperkalaemia or hypocalcaemia. It is probably of no use in asystole. Calcium chloride is given at 10 mg/kg and calcium gluconate at 30 mg/kg intravenously. Calcium may have serious toxic effects, particularly causing bradycardia, coronary artery spasm, and myocardial irritability. It causes severe local tissue necrosis if injected outside a vein.

Frusemide This diuretic is occasionally used following cardiopulmonary resuscitation after the patient has established cardiac output and if there is no urine production in the face of acute pulmonary oedema. The initial dose is 1 mg/kg intravenously. However, hypovolaemia or poor cardiac contractility are also causes of poor urine output and should also be addressed in patients with anuria. Following resuscitation a urine output of 2 ml/kg/h in infants and 1 ml/kg/h in children is adequate.

Mannitol This osmotic diuretic is used when there is evidence of life-threatening raised intracranial pressure, as shown by dilating pupils, slowing pulse, and increasing blood pressure or a decrease in level of consciousness not caused by hypoxia, hypovolaemia etc.

Steroids There remains controversy over the indication for steroids. There is no evidence that they are beneficial in CPR. However if cerebral oedema or septic shock are present then dexamethasone 1 mg/kg intravenously may be given following the initial use of first line drugs. The use of steroids in CPR is not a priority.

Fluids in CPR

Requirements for intravenous fluids will vary depending on the cause of cardiac or respiratory arrest and on the patient's response to initial treatment. Three guidelines should be followed:

1. In cardiac arrest possibly caused by or associated with hypovolaemia a plasma expander such as plasma or a colloid should be given at an initial volume of 10 ml/kg as rapidly as possible. This may be repeated up to four times. At 40 ml/kg almost half of the child's circulating volume will have been transfused. If at this stage there is a cardiac output but poor perfusion, assessment will need to be made as to whether further fluid is required intravenously (as the patient is still hypovolaemic), or whether inotropic cardiac support from infused dopamine would be more appropriate (see post-resuscitation management p. 30).

2. In a patient who has had only a respiratory arrest, maintenance fluid at 4 ml/kg/h should be given unless there are circulatory problems.

3. In a patient whose arrest has been precipitated by raised intracranial pressure, once circulation has been restored, fluid restriction should be maximal and the patient nursed in the 30 degree head-up position. Consideration should be given to the use of mannitol.

Table 2.5 • Intravenous fluids for the paediatric resuscitation area

0.9% Saline
4% Dextrose and 0.18% saline
5% Dextrose
Hartmann's solution or Ringer's lactate
Colloid, e.g. Haemaccel
Plasma
5% human albumin

Monitoring in CPR

1. E.c.g.—leads should be attached at the periphery of the chest or on limbs so as not to obscure any X-ray appearances.

2. Core temperature—a continuously-reading rectal temperature probe should be used. A low-reading thermometer is

also needed for small infants who may easily become hypothermic.

3. Oxygen saturation—a pulse oximeter should be attached to a digit or foot in the case of a small infant. You should aim for a saturation over 95 per cent. The instrument is inaccurate when circulation is poor.

4. Non-invasive blood pressure—a blood pressure monitoring device should be recording at two minute intervals on a limb not needed for i.v. access. Ensure that the correct sized cuff is used. The width of the cuff should be two thirds of the length of the child's upper arm.

5. Urine output—following the resumption of effective cardiac action a urinary catheter should be inserted and all output measured.

Post-resuscitation management

- **Airway and breathing** **Circulation** **Cerebral management** **Investigations and further treatment following CPR** **Hypothermia** **Transport** **When to stop resuscitation**

The survivors of resuscitation vary from those, usually with a respiratory arrest only, who are apparently fully recovered, to the unconscious child with multisystem failure. Again, a systematic approach is necessary to maximize the patient's outcome. Management of this stage is a paediatric and anaesthetic responsibility. Monitoring of e.c.g., blood pressure, and oxygen saturation should continue.

Airway and breathing

Many post-resuscitation patients will have an impaired level of consciousness or depressed gag reflex. In most cases the child should remain intubated and the decision to extubate should be made by senior paediatric or anaesthetic staff.

Adequate oxygenation is vital; an arterial blood-gas will give information on this, pCO_2, and acid–base status. Ventilation with a concentration of oxygen sufficient to keep the patient's oxygen saturation, as measured on a pulse oxi- meter, above 95 per cent should be continued if there are any doubts about the patient's ventilatory status.

Circulation

There is often poor cardiac output following resuscitation. This may result both from the underlying illness or injury and also from the damaging effects of hypoxia and ischaemia on the heart and circulation. If there is poor cardiac output, as shown by hypotension and poor peripheral perfusion, an initial bolus of 20 ml/kg of plasma or a colloid should be given and its clinical effect noted. A further 20 ml/kg may be given if the first had no useful effect, and if there is no evidence of fluid overload, such as distended neck veins. At the same time a central venous pressure (CVP) line should be placed, the external jugular or femoral vein (p. 328) being the usual sites for cannulation. This will usually be performed in the intensive care unit but may occasionally be necessary in the A & E department. The procedure should only be undertaken by a skilled person.

The CVP is principally a measure of right ventricular func- tion and of the effect of venous return on preload. The CVP is best utilized in assessing the response to a fluid challenge. The CVP of a hypovolaemic patient will change little in re- sponse to an initial fluid bolus, but the CVP of a patient who is euvolaemic, hypervolaemic, or in cardiogenic shock will have a large, sustained increase with a fluid challenge. A CVP of less than 10 mmHg indicates the need for further volume replacement. Above this level, the need is probably for inotropic cardiac support and an intravenous infusion of 10 μg/kg/min of dopamine should be started through the central line.

If it is not possible to obtain a CVP line, and hypotension with poor perfusion continues, the dopamine infusion should be started, through a peripheral vein, at the same time as a third fluid challenge of 10 ml/kg of colloid.

Transfer should be made to intensive care where more invasive monitoring of cardiac output may be necessary to ensure optimum treatment.

A urinary catheter should be passed and all urinary output measured and charted. A rate of 2 ml/kg/h in an infant and 1 ml/kg/h in a child is evidence of reasonable renal perfusion and function.

Cerebral management

In some cases the brain will have suffered damage from hypoxia and ischaemia before and during CPR. It is important to avoid further insult during the post-resuscitation period by the following strategies:

- Ensure good oxygenation.
- Avoid hypo- and hypertension.
- Keep the patient normothermic.
- Avoid hypo- and hyperglycaemia.
- Treat acid–base abnormalities.
- Help to reduce raised intracranial pressure by hyperventilation (arterial pCO_2 of 28–30 mmHg).
- Nurse the patient in the 30 degree head-up position.
- Avoid painful or unpleasant procedures, which cause surges in arterial blood pressure, without adequate pain relief.
- If there is evidence of falling conscious level, the development of neurological signs such as sixth nerve palsy, or a slowing pulse, intravenous mannitol may be used.

Investigations and further treatment following CPR

The most important investigation is an arterial blood gas to determine oxygenation, ventilatory adequacy, and acid–base balance. Sodium bicarbonate may be needed if there is a pronounced metabolic acidosis and should be given initially as a slow bolus (over 5 min) of 1 mmol/kg. Blood may be taken for serum electrolyte and urea estimations, as well as for a haemoglobin and a blood film.

A blood culture should be taken, and if there is any suggestion that infection is a possible cause of the child's collapse, antibiotics should be given (see p. 38).

A chest radiograph is needed to show the position of the ET tube and any pulmonary pathology.

Hypothermia

Sick children, especially very young ones, can become hypothermic when exposed to cold for even short periods. Try to prevent this by keeping the child covered or under an overhead heater without compromising access or observation. Monitor rectal temperature.

Transport

Once resuscitation has achieved cardiorespiratory stability most patients will require intensive care. This may be in the receiving hospital or may require transfer to another hospital. Patients should be transferred in either circumstance:

• with endotracheal intubation and ventilatory support
• with appropriately trained personnel in attendance, for example an anaesthetist, and
• with drugs and equipment for further resuscitation on the journey (see Tables 2.3, 2.4).

If the patient is to be transferred to another hospital it is wise to discuss transport needs with the receiving team; some intensive care units have a mobile team who will come to transport the patient back to their unit.

When to stop resuscitation

If an initially apnoeic, pulseless patient has had no detectable signs of cardiac output and no evidence of cerebral activity despite 30 minutes of CPR it is reasonable to stop resuscitation. The decision to stop CPR is taken by the team leader but it is appropriate to ensure that all team members are in agreement.

The exception to the above is the hypothermic patient in whom resuscitation must continue until the patient has a core temperature of 35 °C (see p. 43).

Laryngeal or tracheal obstruction management

If foreign body aspiration has been witnessed or is strongly suspected and the child is coughing forcefully, encourage him to continue trying to dislodge the obstruction himself and give oxygen in high concentration. As long as the child is able to move air there is only partial obstruction. Attempts to dislodge the foreign body should not be undertaken at this stage as this may convert the partial obstruction into a complete one. *A senior anaesthetist and ENT surgeon should be urgently called to the child.* The ENT surgeon will probably remove the obstruction by direct laryngoscopy but operative intervention may be necessary.

A lateral radiograph of the neck may reveal a radiopaque foreign body in the upper airway or oesophagus. A child in

Fig. 2.4 • Emergency management of upper airway obstruction in infants and young children.

respiratory distress should not be X-rayed but should proceed to laryngoscopy by an experienced person. If radiography is arranged, an experienced doctor should accompany the child.

However, if the child is blue, or there is no evidence of air movement, emergency management in the A & E department is necessary. First remove any obvious foreign body by a careful oral finger sweep, making sure that the procedure does not traumatize the mucosa or push the foreign body further down.

Infants less than 1 year should be placed prone with the head dependent over the operator's knees and 6–10 back blows given in rapid succession while the airway is opened (see Fig. 2.4). If this is not successful, place the infant supine on a firm surface and give 4 chest thrusts. Small children aged 1–5 years should be placed supine on a firm surface and given 6–10 midline abdominal thrusts in the upper abdomen.

For children over five years of age the Heimlich manoeuvre should be performed. In this the patient's abdomen is grasped from behind and a sharp upward squeeze in the sub-diaphragmatic area is given (see Figure 2.5). This may be accompanied by back blows. The Heimlich manoeuvre can be performed with the patient supine.

If these manoeuvres are unsuccessful and there is still no air movement, rapid direct laryngoscopy should be attempted to see if the foreign body is removable with forceps. If it is not then an emergency cricothyrotomy should be performed (see p. 341).

Recognition of the seriously ill child

- **Imminent respiratory failure   Signs of early circulatory failure**

As described earlier, cardiac arrest in childhood is usually secondary to respiratory or circulatory failure. Recognition of the early stages of these problems allows early management which may avert deterioration.

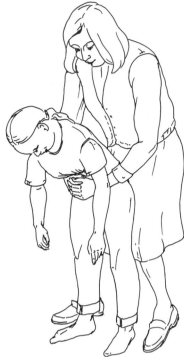

Fig. 2.5 • The Heimlich manoeuvre for upper airways obstruction in children five years and over.

Imminent respiratory failure

Box 2.1 **Signs suggestive of imminent respiratory failure**

- Severe chest retraction, tachypnoea, and use of accessory muscles of respiration (these signs diminish as the patient either improves with treatment or worsens with fatigue).
- Decreased or absent breath sounds on auscultation.
- Decreased level of consciousness or restlessness and agitation.
- Hypotonia.
- Cyanosis.

Children with signs as shown in Box 2.1 require a high concentration of oxygen at 6–10 litres/min by mask and specific treatment of the underlying respiratory complaint should be given. *Paediatric and anaesthetic help should be sought urgently.* If the respiratory rate is falling because the child is exhausted then artificial ventilation with oxygen via a bag and mask will be necessary until intubation can be performed, preferably by an experienced person.

Signs of early circulatory failure

Shock can develop rapidly in children because the loss of relatively small amounts of fluid may comprise a high percentage of their intravascular volume. Children have approximately 80 ml of blood per kilogram body weight. In addition, children initially compensate well for fluid loss with few physical signs until more than one-third of the circulating volume is lost. Shock then develops rapidly.

Box 2.2 **The signs of circulatory failure are:**

1. Rapid thready pulse (compensation for diminished stroke volume)
2. Rapid deep breathing (acidosis from peripheral ischaemia).
3. Agitation or depressed conscious level (caused by poor cerebral perfusion).
4. Skin pallor and coldness with poor capillary refill (vasoconstriction to preserve essential organs)— capillary refill after cutaneous pressure for five seconds should occur within two to three seconds. A refill time of greater than five seconds is clearly abnormal.
5. Hypotension—this is a late sign of circulatory failure. Expected systolic blood pressure can be estimated by the formula:
   blood pressure = 80 + (age in years × 2).

Treatment of children in circulatory failure Intravenous access must be secured immediately and 20 ml/kg of plasma,

Table 2.6 • Acceptable upper limits for physiological parameters in awake children

Age group	Respiratory rate	Pulse rate
Infant	50	160
Toddler	35	140
School-age	25	120
Adolescent	20	110

colloid or normal saline infused. Oxygen must be given and an arterial blood gas estimation performed.

Some specific problems

- **Septicaemia   Meningococcal septicaemia   Reye's syndrome   Diabetic ketoacidosis   Haemolytic uraemic syndrome   Hypothermia   Drowning   Anaphylactic shock   Heat stroke   Supraventricular tachycardia (SVT)**

The following are serious illnesses and conditions, which, while not exclusive to childhood, are especially encountered in this age group. Other life-threatening conditions, which are largely confined to one organ system, are described in the appropriate chapters, for example epiglottitis (p. 202), meningitis (p. 257). *Urgent senior paediatric help should be sought in each instance.*

Septicaemia

There should be a high index of suspicion for the possibility of bacterial infection in children who become rapidly and seriously ill, especially in the under 2-year-olds. Unless there is clear evidence of a specific alternative diagnosis, very ill children with shock should be treated with intravenous antibiotics, as well as receiving supportive therapy. A blood culture should first be taken.

The commoner bacterial pathogens are *Haemophilus*

influenzae, Neisseria meningitidis and *Streptococcus pneumoniae*. Less frequently, infection with *Staphylococcus sp., E. coli, Salmonella* sp. and *Shigella* sp. occur. In neonates, Gram-negative organisms are more common and beta haemolytic streptococcus is an important pathogen. In addition to oxygen, intravenous colloid and the correction of any significant metabolic acidosis, septicaemic children should be given intravenous penicillin, and a broad-spectrum antibiotic, such as gentamicin or cefotaxime, active against Gram-negative organisms.

Meningococcal septicaemia

Meningococcal septicaemia is the most fulminant infectious disease. The interval from first symptom to death can be less than 12 hours. Some patients complain of a sore throat at the onset of the disease, others are simply febrile and ill. The cardinal sign of meningococcal septicaemia is a purpuric rash in an ill child. At the onset, the rash is not florid and a careful search should be made for purpura in any unwell child. In about 10 per cent of patients with meningococcal septicaemia an initial blanching erythematous rash precedes a purpuric one, and in some cases no rash occurs.

Purpura is caused by vasculitis and disseminated intravascular coagulation (DIC), both of which are the result of endotoxins produced by the organism *Neisseria meningitidis*. Although the majority of patients who survive have no long-term sequelae, a few have skin or limb loss as a result of vasculitis and DIC.

Management If meningococcal septicaemia is suspected a blood culture and full blood count should be taken, and intravenous benzyl penicillin 50 mg/kg up to a maximum of 2 g given immediately. The antibiotics should be given over five to ten minutes, as more rapid infusion of such a high dose could cause convulsions. If the patient is showing signs of shock, intravenous colloid should be given at 10–20 ml/kg initially. These patients should be urgently referred to the paediatrician and many will need transfer to an intensive care unit. A poor prognosis is associated with those who present with a low white cell count or shock. If the patient is allergic to penicillin, intravenous erythromycin or aztreonam can be given. However 'penicillin allergy' is considerably overdiagnosed on the strength of a rash fortuitously occurring during the course of an illness in which a penicillin was used. One would wish to be fairly sure of penicillin allergy before omitting the use of penicillin in meningococcal infection.

Reye's syndrome

This relatively uncommon condition is characterized by a rapidly progressive encephalopathy with hypoglycaemia and fatty changes in the liver. Some cases follow varicella or influenza infection. These children appear to improve from their first illness and then become unwell again with profuse vomiting and progressive drowsiness. Other children do not appear to have a prodromal illness. An alleged association with aspirin has led to the banning of aspirin for general use in children less than 12 years of age.

Children with Reye's syndrome present to the A & E department with vomiting, drowsiness, convulsions, or coma. The liver is palpably enlarged and firm. The blood sugar is very low and liver enzymes and serum ammonia are raised.

Although the condition is relatively uncommon, a high index of suspicion should be maintained for Reye's syndrome in patients presenting with profuse vomiting, neurological changes, or hypoglycaemia. Patients can make a good recovery if the disease is recognized early and vigorous treatment instituted rapidly.

The mainstays of treatment are management of the hypoglycaemia and the raised intracranial pressure. For the latter the patient needs to be transferred to a paediatric intensive care unit for intracranial pressure monitoring and treatment of raised intracranial pressure. While awaiting transfer the patient should be kept in a head-up position and fluids restricted. If there is continuing deterioration, intubation and ventilation should be instituted and intravenous mannitol given.

Diabetic ketoacidosis

Ketoacidosis is found at presentation in 30 per cent of newly diagnosed diabetic children. Patients may present at A & E departments with:

- A history of polyuria and polydipsia.
- Weight loss and dehydration.
- Abdominal pain and vomiting (sometimes mis-diagnosed as appendicitis).
- Rapid respiration (sometimes mis-diagnosed as pneumonia or asthma).
- Coma.

On examination children with diabetic ketoacidosis are dehydrated and acidotic with rapid acidotic breathing. The conscious level may be decreased, and in severe cases there may be signs of shock with a rapid pulse and cold extremities.

The initial treatment is to correct dehydration. Intravenous access should be secured and 10–20 ml/kg of normal saline infused over the first hour unless shock requires a more rapid infusion of colloid. Blood should be taken for measurement of glucose, urea, and electrolytes, and an arterial sample for acid–base status. The paediatric team should have taken over the patient's care at this stage and will probably infuse insulin at the rate of 0.1 unit/kg/h once the blood sugar result is known as well as starting potassium replacement. Despite metabolic acidosis, intravenous sodium bicarbonate is rarely indicated, as replacement of fluid and electrolytes usually corrects the acidosis. The patient's neurological status should be carefully monitored as a few diabetic children (even mildly affected ones) may develop fatal cerebral oedema.

Haemolytic uraemic syndrome

This relatively uncommon condition affects approximately 150 children each year in the UK. It comprises a micro-angiopathic haemolytic anaemia, thrombocytopenia, and acute renal failure. Most cases follow a diarrhoeal illness (often with bloody stools) caused by *Escherichia coli* or *Shigella* sp. and it is thought that a toxin produced by these organisms initiates the disease.

The patient presents to the A & E department with

diarrhoea, pallor, or anuria. On examination the patient is unwell and pale, some petechiae may be seen, and some patients are hypertensive. The diagnosis is suspected on examination of a blood film which will show anaemia, red blood cell fragmentation, and thrombocytopenia. The blood urea level will be raised. It is important to restrict fluids in these patients as their renal function is compromised. They usually need dialysis.

Hypothermia

Profound hypothermia rarely occurs in children with the exception of the near-drowned patient. Mild hypothermia (temperature usually over 32 °C) occurs in small babies often in association with an infection. It may also occur in those handicapped children who are undernourished and immobile.

In all cases of mild hypothermia, the patient should be warmed by wrapping with warmed blankets in a warm draught-free room, or with an overhead radiant heater in the case of infants. Infants warmed by radiant heat may be covered in 'bubble' polythene to insulate and reduce convection losses while allowing radiant heat to penetrate the covering. Continuous rectal temperature and e.c.g. monitoring are needed. Admission, screening, and treatment for infection will be necessary.

Drowning

Most drowning incidents in this country are in freshwater canals and lakes, domestic swimming pools, and in infants, the domestic bath.

Two main problems in the drowned patient are hypoxia and hypothermia. Hypoxia is caused in 15 per cent of cases by laryngospasm which prevents water from entering the lung—'dry drowning'. In the other 85 per cent flooding of fresh water into the lungs causes profuse alveolar damage and pulmonary oedema.

Hypothermia leads to bradycardia and asystole with circulatory shutdown and the development of acidosis.

However, hypothermia may have a minor protective effect

in some cases of near-drowning. In addition there is a small protective effect from the 'dive reflex'. This is a reflex, weak in humans, which, following sudden immersion in cold water, causes peripheral and splanchnic vasoconstriction shunting blood primarily to the brain and heart and giving those organs a few more minutes perfusion.

Haemolysis or electrolyte problems caused by the inhalation or ingestion of large amounts of water are unusual.

Management of the near-drowned patient All victims must be hospitalized for at least 24 hours even if they seem well, as late respiratory sequelae may occur. It is important to find out if the patient has a history of epilepsy, diabetes or drug abuse problems which may have precipitated the near-drowning episode.

For those patients who are admitted in asystole or respiratory arrest, cardiopulmonary resuscitation should be immediately initiated and carried on in the usual way. After resuscitation, the patient must be examined for additional trauma, such as a head or neck injury which may have occurred before or during the near-drowning episode.

The patient's core temperature should be measured using a low reading thermometer which can read down to 15 °C. Warming procedures should be instituted. If the core temperature is above 30 °C then external re-warming with blankets or radiant heaters is usually sufficient.

For a core temperature below 30 °C, active core warming in addition to warmed blankets or radiant heaters is necessary. Core warming can be carried out by:

- Gastric and rectal or urinary bladder lavage with saline warmed to 40 °C.
- The use of warmed humidified inspired gases via the ventilator.
- Warmed intravenous fluids (40 °C).
- Peritoneal lavage with saline at 40 °C.

Extra-corporeal blood warming may be available in a few centres but is unlikely to be easily applicable in most hospitals.

Intravenous fluids should be 5 per cent dextrose and 0.18 per cent saline infused at 4 ml/kg/h initially until the circulatory status and electrolyte status are ascertained.

Resuscitation should be continued in the hypothermic patient until the patient's core temperature has been at or near normal for 15 minutes. Occasional cases have been recorded where complete recovery has resulted despite cardiac arrest due to submersion in water for periods exceeding one hour.

Patients recovering from near-drowning may develop ventricular fibrillation. This is best treated with DC shock, and is often refractory to the use of lignocaine.

Whether or not resuscitation has been required, the near-drowned patient should be given oxygen. A chest radiograph should be taken and the patient should have continuous e.c.g. monitoring.

Blood should be taken for arterial blood gas, urea, electrolytes, and glucose estimations; the blood gas results should be corrected for the patient's temperature if he is still hypothermic. Patients with biochemical or radiographic abnormalities or respiratory symptoms or signs should be considered for admission to an intensive care unit as 'secondary drowning' is very likely.

Anaphylactic shock

This is a severe and occasionally life-threatening generalized allergic reaction. The main causes are:

- Injection of drugs, e.g. penicillin.
- Injection of foreign proteins, e.g. horse serum blood products.
- Bee, wasp, hornet stings.
- Hyposensitization injections—this treatment is now virtually abandoned for hay fever because of the risk of fatal anaphylactic reaction.
- X-ray contrast injections.
- Foods, especially peanuts.

Anaphylactic shock occurs rapidly within minutes of the cause. The condition usually starts with urticaria and angioneurotic oedema (swelling of the face, eyelids, and lips). The patient may have sneezing and wheezing leading to stridor, shock, collapse, and death. Sometimes vomiting, abdominal pain, and loose stools occur, especially when the cause has been an ingested allergen.

Management of anaphylactic shock

1. The first essential is to ensure a patent airway and to give oxygen. *Anaesthetic help should be urgently sought.* If there is obstruction of the airway, intubation, or if this is impossible, cricothyrotomy is necessary.
2. Intramuscular adrenalin should be given at a dose of 0.1 ml/kg of 1:10 000 adrenalin. If a patient is collapsed and has poor peripheral circulation then intravenous adrenalin is necessary. If venous access is difficult and the patient is intubated then the adrenalin may be given down the endotracheal tube, otherwise an intramuscular dose should be given or try the intraosseous or femoral vein route (see p. 329). In the face of a poor response, repeated doses of adrenalin should be given every 10 minutes.
3. General cardiorespiratory support will also be necessary with intravenous colloid and ventilation with oxygen.
4. Intravenous steroids (hydrocortisone 2 mg/kg) and antihistamines (for example chlorpheniramine 2–4 mg) can be given but their effect, if any, is delayed.

Heat stroke

Heat stroke occurs occasionally in infants who are too warmly wrapped during a febrile illness. It may occur if children are left unattended in a closed car in direct sunlight.

There is a suggestion that overheating is associated with the Sudden Infant Death syndrome (see p. 320) and with the uncommon haemorrhagic encephalopathy syndrome which shows similar pathological changes to heat stroke.

The core temperature is usually above 41 °C in infants with heat stroke. The infant usually has circulatory collapse, may convulse, and may have diarrhoea and vomiting.

The infant must be cooled rapidly. This is usually quickly achieved by wetting and fanning the exposed skin. Rectal paracetamol should be given.

Supportive care with oxygen, ventilation, and intravenous colloid is often necessary. The paediatrician should be called urgently. Infection is usually associated with the hyperthermia and should be treated appropriately (see p. 38).

The infant will usually require intensive care as brain swelling and clotting disorders often develop.

Supraventricular tachycardia (SVT)

This condition is uncommon but may be fatal especially in early infancy. Most babies with SVT present in congestive cardiac failure with poor feeding, tachypnoea, and an enlarged liver.

The diagnosis is suggested by noting the extremely rapid heart rate. Occasionally it can be difficult to distinguish clinically between supraventricular tachycardia and sinus tachycardia in an ill infant. A rate of 250 beats per minute is a supraventricular tachycardia, but rates between 200 and 240 per minute may be a sinus tachycardia in an infant. An e.c.g. should clarify this and allow the heart rate to be measured accurately.

The baby should be given oxygen in high concentration by mask, and urgent paediatric help sought.

The best treatment for supraventricular tachycardia in early infancy is to elicit the 'diving reflex' which produces an increase in vagal tone, slows atrioventricular conduction, and interrupts the tachycardia. The baby should be attached to an electrocardiographic monitor, wrapped in a towel, and his whole face immersed in iced water for about five seconds. There is no need to obstruct the mouth or nostrils as the baby will be temporarily apnoeic. The tachycardia will usually stop immediately, but may be delayed for a few seconds. There may be bradycardia for a short while until normal sinus rhythm returns. If this technique fails, the infant should receive a synchronized DC shock of an initial dose of 1J/kg. Adenosine is a safe antiarrhythmic drug which may be used as an alternative to DC shock. Urgent paediatric advice should be sought and a paediatric cardiologist contacted.

Note: Verapamil is no longer considered safe to give to the paediatric age group and especially to infants, although the drug is effective in stopping supraventricular tachycardia it has caused asystole in a number of patients.

Further reading

1. Evans, T. R. (ed.) (1990). *ABC of resuscitation*, (2nd edn). *British Medical Journal*, London.
2. Levin, D. C. and Morris, F. C. (ed.) (1990). *Essentials of Paediatric Intensive Care*. Quality Medical Publications. St. Louis.
3. Chameides, L. (ed.) (1988). *Textbook of Advanced Paediatric Life Support*. American Heart Association. Dallas, Texas.

CHAPTER 3

Major trauma

Key points in major trauma

1 The first priority is to ensure a patent airway and adequate ventilation with 100% oxygen.

2 Intravenous access should be obtained with two large cannulae. A child can sustain a relatively large blood loss with initial compensation. Shock then develops rapidly.

3 A detailed history of the accident will help to anticipate the nature and severity of injuries.

4 Suspect internal chest injury if there is continuing hypoxia in a ventilated patient. Children often have severe chest cavity injuries despite intact ribs.

5 Abdominal and pelvic injury are especially common and difficult to detect in children. Repeated abdominal examination, CT and US scan and peritoneal lavage will all help in assessment. The patient with suspected abdominal injury who cannot be made haemodynamically stable with ventilation and transfusion must go for urgent surgical exploration. Exact pre-operative diagnosis is unnecessary.

6 The management of head injuries should focus on prevention of secondary damage from hypoxia, hypotension and raised intracranial pressure.

Introduction

Accidents cause about 700 deaths a year in children in England and Wales. Fifty-five per cent of these are the result of road traffic accidents (RTA), and 29 per cent from accidents in the home. The main cause of death is head injury (with brain swelling).

Most RTA deaths in children occur in pedestrians (250 per year) and about 70 deaths per year occur in cyclists (mainly from head injuries). Ejection from a car causes particularly serious injuries.

Most home fatalities are due to burns, and about 60 deaths a year are the result of falls in the home.

Many of these deaths are potentially avoidable. Firstly, by preventing the accident: children should be well-supervised and dangerous situations avoided. Design of the urban environment and of vehicles should be with safety in mind. Homes should be equipped with smoke alarms. Safety glass should be installed in doors and windows and child-proof tops used for drugs and household products. Secondly, the injury caused by an accident can be minimized by the use of safety devices such as seat belts and cycle helmets. Thirdly, prompt and effective treatment of the injured child will improve the outcome. However, at present in the UK, many doctors treating children with major trauma are relatively inexperienced as most hospitals treat only two or three severely injured children per year.

The early management of the multiply injured child is crucial, not only for the immediate problems but also for long-term rehabilitation. Untreated hypoxia and shock will have adverse short- and long-term effects. The first hours after the accident are the most important in this regard. A major difficulty is how to assess the severity of the child's injuries quickly. Trauma scores have been used in the assessment of adults with major trauma for some time; however, the disadvantage of a trauma score is that it can give a falsely benign result if calculated very soon after the injury. Additional difficulties in children are unfamiliarity with the score due to infrequent use and a lack of verification

Table 3.1 • Paediatric trauma score

Score	+2	+1	−1
Size	> 20 kg	10–20 kg	< 10 kg
Airway	normal	oral or nasal airway	intubated
Systolic BP	> 90 mmHg	90–50 mmHg	< 50 mmHg
Level of consciousness	fully awake	drowsy	unconscious
Open wound	none	minor	major/penetrating
Fractures	none	minor	open or multiple

of its widespread applicability in the UK. Table 3.1 shows a paediatric trauma score adapted from the Advanced Trauma Life Support (ATLS) course.

A score of less than 8 is used in the United States to indicate to on-scene paramedics that the child should be admitted to a Paediatric Trauma Unit. *When faced with a child with severe or multiple trauma call for senior help immediately. An anaesthetist is the person most urgently needed as airway management and intravenous access are the two first requirements.* While awaiting the anaesthetist the A & E staff must of course start resuscitation. Many hospitals have a 'trauma team' consisting of an anaesthetist and one or more surgeons. The surgeon will take over the patient's care and call in specialist surgeons for neurosurgery, orthopaedics, etc. as appropriate and if they are available.

The management of major trauma has been improved by training doctors with the Advanced Trauma Life Support Course. The method approved is to follow the following scheme of management:

- Primary survey.
- Initial resuscitation.
- Secondary survey (total evaluation of the patient).
- Definitive care.

In the primary survey the 'ABCDE' of priorities is followed:

- Airway with cervical spine control.

- Breathing.
- Circulation with haemorrhage control.
- Disability—brief neurological evaluation.
- Exposure—completely undress the patient.

If the above plans are followed then the resuscitation will take place in an ordered and rational way.

There are several differences between children and adults which will affect the impact that trauma has on them and that have implications for treatment. Children are smaller than adults, therefore they are a smaller target if hit, for instance by a car. The energy of impact is dissipated over a smaller mass so that a greater force is applied to a small area, thus more severe injuries are likely to be caused. Children have less body fat, less elastic connective tissue, and closer proximity of multiple organs than adults. There is a high frequency of multiple organ injury. The skeleton of the child is incompletely calcified and has many active growth centres. A child's bones often bend rather than break and so there may be significant organ damage without overlying bony fracture; for example in the chest the ribs may be intact but there could be underlying pulmonary contusion, haemorrhage, or pneumothorax.

The ratio between the child's body surface and the body volume is highest at birth and decreases during infancy and childhood. This relatively large surface area increases heat loss. It is important to ensure that any fluids or gases that are given are warmed, if time permits, and that the child is covered with a blanket and/or an overhead heater is used. An additional difficulty is that frightened children may not cooperate. Reassurance and, if possible, a parent's presence are very important.

Initial assessment and management

- **Airway   Breathing   Circulation   Disability**

Airway

Always assume that there is an injury to the cervical spine although these injuries are less common than in adults. The child should have a rigid cervical collar applied until spinal damage is excluded. If the collar needs to be removed then someone should remain responsible for holding the neck completely still and straight.

The child will need to lie on his back for most of the examination and for treatment to be carried out. Therefore great care must be taken to prevent aspiration of stomach contents by protecting the airway and using suction if the child seems to be retching.

Ask the child to speak. If words are spoken this usually means the airway is patent, oxygenation is adequate, and the brain is working. A child crying is always a good sign in this respect. If the child cannot cry or speak, open his mouth. Be prepared with a sucker to remove any vomit, blood, or debris. Check for a gag reflex. If this is absent then intubation will definitely be required. Infants are obligate nose breathers and have narrow air passages. They are more likely than adults to have airway problems. Open the airway (see p. 17). Jaw thrust is preferable to chin lift and neck extension if there is suspected cervical spine injury. An airway may be needed.

Breathing

If the child is breathing spontaneously, attach a mask giving high concentration oxygen.

Count the respiratory rate and watch the movements of the chest. Check that the trachea is central. If not, this indicates mediastinal shift, for example from a tension pneumothorax. Auscultate both sides of the chest. Note the child's colour and, if available, attach a pulse oximeter to check oxygenation.

If there are facial injuries precluding intubation or the use of a mask then a cricothyrotomy should be considered (see p. 341). This will allow oxygenation until a tracheostomy is performed.

Before intubation, preoxygenate the child using a bag with reservoir and mask and 100 per cent oxygen. Ensure there is a good seal between the mask and the face. Extend the neck and keep the child's chin up to open the airway.

Box 3.1 **Indications for intubation:**

- Apnoea.
- Moderate or severe respiratory distress or hypoxia.
- Obstruction of the upper airway.
- Absent gag reflex—intubation protects the lower airway from aspiration of vomit.
- Severe head injury—hyperventilation may be needed to lower intracranial pressure, and control of ventilation to prevent hypoxia and hypercapnia is vital.
- Severe facial or oral injuries, e.g. burns.

Insert an oral airway. The child can be oxygenated for several minutes in this way. However, the stomach may fill with air and the airway is not protected against aspiration. Proceed with intubation. Except in an emergency, intubation should be preceded by rapid induction anaesthesia performed by a skilled person. Rapid sequence induction of anaesthesia with thiopentone and suxamethonium is necesary if the child is not unconscious. This should be done by someone suitably trained. Select the correct tube size (see Table 2.2). Use either a straight bladed laryngoscope (most suitable for babies) or a curved blade laryngoscope which is easier to use. An assistant should apply cricoid pressure to prevent aspiration of the stomach contents. Keep the neck straight in case of cervical spine fracture. Once the tube has been inserted attach a self-inflating bag with reservoir and ventilate with oxygen. Auscultate the chest to check for adequacy of ventilation and to ensure the tube has not entered the right main bronchus. If there is air entry on the right side only, shorten the tube. Use a pulse oximeter or check blood gases. The PaO_2 should be above 9 kPa and the saturation 95 per cent or above. Indrawing of the chest indicates respiratory difficulty. Agitation, poor cooperation or decreased conscious level all may indicate hypoxia.

Once the airway is secure and assisted ventilation is being performed, there may still be problems with oxygenation. This may be apparent by the failure of the patient to 'pink-up' or there may be continuing respiratory distress. Examination of the chest may show decreased air entry or other chest problems.

Box 3.2 **Causes of inadequate ventilation after intubation**:

- ET tube in wrong place.
- Obstruction of the ET tube by blood or vomit.
- Pneumothorax.
- Haemothorax.
- Lung contusion.
- Flail segment.

A chest drain may need to be inserted immediately (see p. 331).

Circulation

Make a brief initial assessment to see whether the child is shocked or has had a major external bleed. Control major external haemorrhage by pressure.

Initially put up an intravenous infusion. Use the widest bore cannula practicable. If the child is obviously seriously injured then a second cannula in another limb is necessary. It is preferable to cannulate an arm as an infusion in the leg may not reach the central circulation if, for instance, there is pelvic or abdominal bleeding. If peripheral venous access fails then there are several alternatives:

- Intraosseous infusion (see p. 329).
- Central venous cannulation (see p. 328).
- Venous cut-down.

The method chosen will depend on the experience of the doctor. It is unwise to use the upper central veins unless you are experienced in doing so and are aware of the potential complications. Cannulation of the femoral vein is relatively safe for inexperienced practitioners.

Assess hypovolaemia Children have a good ability to constrict the vascular bed. Therefore they may have a normal blood pressure, despite over 25 per cent of their blood volume being lost. However, once the blood pressure does fall, circulatory failure is imminent. Try to be aware of the pulse rates and blood pressure and other parameters which are normal for children of different ages (Table 3.2).

Table 3.2 • Physiological parameters in childhood

	Pulse rate	Systolic BP (mmHg)	Respiratory rate (rate/min)
Infants	< 160	80	50
Preschool	< 140	90	35
Schoolchild	< 120	100	25

Weight = 2 × age (yr) + 8 kg

Blood volume approximately 80 ml/kg

Blood pressure systolic 80 mmHg + 2 × age (yr)

Urine output—2 ml/kg/h in infants
              —1 ml/kg/h over 2 years of age

Assess the child for hypovolaemia using the following criteria:

1. Confusion, drowsiness, and coma—as the child becomes shocked his mental state will alter. The child may become agitated and refuse to lie still or cooperate. As he becomes more shocked he will eventually become comatose.
2. Increased capillary refill time—press the great toe for five seconds then release. A delay of five seconds or more in return of colour to the skin is abnormal.
3. Skin pallor—catecholamines are released due to shock. These cause skin vasoconstriction and, therefore, the skin looks pale and feels cool or clammy to the touch.
4. Tachycardia—this is associated with hypovolaemia. Note

that the child's resting pulse rate is usually higher than an adult's. A tachycardia can also be due to other factors, i.e. crying and being upset by the accident.

5. Tachypnoea—the patient will become acidotic and, therefore, the respiratory rate will be raised.

6. Hypotension—this is almost always due to loss of blood or fluid. Note the difference from the normal blood pressure for the child's age.

7. Reduced urine output—due to reduced kidney perfusion (this cannot be assessed immediately but is important later).

The volume of blood lost needed to produce the above signs varies with the age and size of the child (Table 3.3). The total blood volume is approximately 85 ml/kg at 1 yr, dropping to 70 ml/kg in an older child.

Treatment of shock Start by giving the child a bolus infusion of 20 ml/kg of intravenous fluid. Reassess the child. If there is no improvement give another 20 ml/kg (that will be 50 per cent of the intravascular volume). If the child is still showing signs of shock an initial 10 ml/kg of whole blood

Table 3.3 • Systemic responses to blood loss in children

	Early (< 25% blood volume loss)	Prehypotensive (25% blood volume loss)	Hypotensive (40% blood volume loss)
Cardiac	increased heart rate	increased heart rate, weak pulse volume	frank hypotension, tachycardia to bradycardia
CNS	lethargic irritable confused argumentative	decrease in level of consciousness, dulled response to pain	unconscious
Skin	cool, clammy	cyanotic decreased capillary refill cold extremities	pale cold very slow capillary refill
Kidneys	decreased urinary output increased specific gravity	increased blood urea	no urinary output

must be given. Continuous assessment is essential. It is useful to insert a urine catheter so urine output can be checked. If there is no external haemorrhage and the child is still shocked then major internal bleeding must be suspected and the appropriate measures taken (see below). There may still be internal bleeding even if the shock improves with treatment.

The following infusion fluids can be used:

1. Colloid—e.g. Gelofusine / Haemaccel / albumin / plasma / HPPF. These replace intravascular loss and will rapidly restore haemodynamic variables to normal. They persist in the circulation for several hours. They do not replace interstitial loss. They are infused in a volume roughly equivalent to the volume of blood lost. Artificial colloids have a similar electrolyte content to plasma (Gelofusine has less potassium). There is a low risk of anaphylactic reactions.

2. Crystalloid solutions—0.9 per cent saline or Hartmann's solution (Ringer's lactate) can be used, but at least double the volume of blood lost is required as the crystalloid is rapidly distributed throughout the extracellular space. These solutions are more suitable for smaller blood losses.

3. Blood—fresh, warm whole blood is the ideal fluid to replace blood loss and must be used if over 30 per cent of blood volume is lost. O-negative blood can be used in an emergency but it is preferable to use grouped or cross-matched blood if time allows.

There is no consensus about which is the best fluid to start with. Our practice is to start with colloid in clearly shocked patients. In mildly shocked patients, we start with crystalloid and change to colloid if a second 20 ml bolus is required.

Assessment of adequacy of resuscitation Pulse rate and blood pressure should be recorded at least every five minutes initially. (An automatic cuff if available is invaluable.) Check the patient's mental state. Use a pulse oximeter if available to check the PO_2. Urine output should be measured, and a rate of 1 ml/kg/h achieved to ensure adequate renal perfusion. The child should feel warmer, become less sweaty, and be more alert.

Disability

A rapid assessment of the child's conscious level (Glasgow coma scale), pupillary reactions, and spinal cord function must be made. Check the child can talk or cry and assess movement of all four limbs (Table 3.4).

Analgesia—the amount and type of analgesic drug varies with the individual clinical problem. In the absence of head injury small aliquots of morphine are recommended together with an anti-emetic. Even with head injury morphine may be used as its sedative effects may be reversed with naloxone but codeine phosphate given intravenously is more frequently used.

Entonox (50% nitrous oxide with 50% oxygen) is useful for short painful procedures in patients with no ventilatory problems.

Secondary survey and treatment of injuries

- **Chest injuries   Abdominal injuries   Genitourinary injuries   Head injuries   Spinal injuries   Limb injuries   Crush injuries   Amputations   Continuous assessment**

Once the initial steps of immediate resuscitation have been checked and acted upon, then a more careful and less hurried examination of the patient should be made.

History Much of this can be obtained from the ambulancemen during resuscitation. Obtain as accurate details as possible of the exact events surrounding the accident and the mechanism of injury, i.e. crush injury, high or low velocity impact, penetrating trauma. Certain types of accident are likely to produce a particular pattern of injuries which must be looked for, for example if the child is thrown over the handlebars of a cycle then duodenal injuries may occur. The severity of the trauma should indicate the possibility of serious injuries, i.e. in an RTA where there has been a fatality, persons in the same vehicle are also likely to be badly hurt. It is helpful to know the child's condition at the scene, i.e.

Table 3.4 • Primary survey—Action check list

	Examine	Procedures
Airway	vocalization obstruction gag reflex	suction bag and mask intubation cricothyrotomy
Breathing	respiratory rate respiratory effort auscultation mental state PaO2	oxygen 100% ventilation chest drain
Circulation	pulse rate capillary refill time mental state blood pressure	stop external haemorrhage intravenous lines × 2 infusion cross-match blood

conscious or unconscious, palpable pulse present, an estimate of blood loss. If the parents are available they should be asked about the child's previous medical history (for example a bleeding disorder or diabetes which will affect management). Note whether the child is allergic to any particular drugs (for example penicillin) and check the immunization status.

Examination The patient should be examined completely. This means totally undressing the child. Cover him with a blanket so that he does not get cold during the assessment. This is particularly important in small children who become cold very quickly. The patient should be turned over (with spine and neck straight) and checked for back injuries.

Investigations When siting the i.v. infusion take blood for a full blood count, grouping, and cross-matching. The number of units requested will depend on the age of the child and an initial rapid assessment of the type of injuries sustained. Blood gas levels need to be obtained.

Taking radiographs is time-consuming so it is important to order relevant views only. *Radiographs should not take the place of thorough physical examination.* Whilst being X-rayed the child should be accompanied by a trained nurse or doctor who must ensure that regular observations are continued and infusions monitored so that any problems can be detected. If possible the radiographs should be taken in the resuscitation area. The first radiograph to take is a lateral cervical spine. Once this is shown to be normal, and if the patient has no clinical evidence of spinal damage he can be more easily moved. This should be followed by a chest radiograph which should always be done even if there is no clinical evidence of a chest problem, as potentially fatal conditions, for example lung contusion, are often clinically undetectable. A radiograph of the pelvis should also be taken even if there are no clinical signs of a fracture, as again this is often clinically undetectable and frequently occurs in road traffic accidents. This should be followed by skull radiographs. Other radiographs depend on the clinical state of the patient.

Chest injuries

After initial resuscitation of the patient examine the chest thoroughly. The aim is to detect life-threatening conditions and institute appropriate treatment, for example obstruction of the airway, open chest wound, tension pneumothorax, massive haemopneumothorax, cardiac tamponade.

Examination
1. Look at the child—is he a good colour? Does he appear cyanosed or well-oxygenated?
2. Look at the chest—is there any bruising or marks indicating direct trauma?
3. Look for open wounds (front and back). These will need to be covered immediately.
4. Look for movements of the chest wall—do both sides of the chest expand equally? Is there any indrawing indicating respiratory difficulty?
5. Look for evidence of a flail chest—part of the chest will be seen to move inwards on inspiration rather than outwards as in normal respiration.
6. Count the respiratory rate.
7. Feel for the trachea—is it central? (If not this indicates mediastinal shift, probably from a tension pneumothorax.)
8. Palpate the chest—feel for crepitus indicating surgical emphysema which would indicate an air leak or pneumothorax.

9. Feel along the ribs for any tenderness indicating rib damage.
10. Squeeze the sides of the chest to detect rib and/or cartilage damage.
11. Auscultate both sides of the chest listening for differences in air entry on either side.
12. Listen for the heart sounds—if muffled may indicate cardiac tamponade.
13. Attach a cardiac monitor to the child. This will give the pulse rate and show any arrhythmias which may indicate cardiac damage.

Note: Children's ribs are very flexible so that they rarely fracture. Often severe underlying damage is present without any evidence of external rib injury.

Investigations
1. A chest X-ray should be taken early, but certain conditions will need urgent treatment before X-ray, for example tension pneumothorax, respiratory obstruction, cardiac tamponade, massive haemorrhage, profound hypoxia. If the patient can sit up or be propped up then a better picture is achieved which shows fluid levels or air under the diaphragm, etc. However, if the child is ill a supine picture will suffice. Look carefully for evidence of a pneumothorax by examining the lung markings to the periphery of the lung fields. Look at the mediastinum for evidence of widening which might indicate aortic rupture. Look at the cardiac shadow. If enlarged it may indicate cardiac tamponade. If bowel is seen in the chest there is a diaphragmatic rupture. Look for areas of opacity which would suggest blood in the chest or pulmonary contusion.
2. Arterial blood gases—should always be taken as these may give early evidence of more serious chest damage, and repeated estimations may indicate deterioration in the patient's condition before it becomes clinically apparent. A pulse oximeter can be used to give frequent estimations of PaO_2. Blood gases still need to be taken to assess pH and CO_2 levels.
3. E.c.g.—If there has been significant trauma to the chest, then an e.c.g. should be done. This occasionally shows

changes similar to that of a myocardial infarction which would indicate cardiac muscle damage. Frequently in children the e.c.g. is normal even if there is some degree of underlying damage, therefore it is always important to act on clinical evidence of malfunction, rather than to rely on e.c.g. changes.

Management *Respiratory obstruction*—the child will be cyanosed, have absent or reduced respirations or may be trying to breathe against the obstruction. There may be grunting or indrawing of the chest wall. There will be decreased or absent air entry. Start by lifting the child's chin and insert an oral or nasal airway using a bag and mask with oxygen. The child should be intubated as soon as possible and oxygenated using 100 per cent oxygen. If the obstruction is high (for example facial injuries) cricothyrotomy may need to be performed. Once mechanical ventilation is instituted the child should recover quickly.

Tension pneumothorax—the child may be cyanosed and will have a tachycardia. There may be unexplained hypotension. The trachea may be shifted to the side away from the pneumothorax. There will be absent air entry on that side. Immediately insert a wide-bore needle or cannula into the second intercostal space in the mid-clavicular line. Air will escape and should be easily aspirated via a syringe. This should give enough time to prepare and put in a chest drain (see Chapter 17). This must precede a radiograph. Smaller pneumothoraces, detected on the chest radiograph also need chest drainage.

Open chest wound—this will be obvious on examination (but ensure you have looked at the back of the chest). Cover the wound with several layers of dressing with lots of adhesive tape over to provide a seal. Check afterwards that the air leak is now sealed and that you have not created a tension pneumothorax. A chest drain must be inserted if there is a pneumothorax.

Massive haemothorax—the child will appear shocked. He will have a low BP, tachycardia, tachypnoea, and be restless with cold clammy peripheries. If there is no external evidence of bleeding then the likely source is the chest or the abdomen. Ensure that you have two fast flowing peripheral lines and give blood and colloid. Ventilate on 100 per cent oxygen. Insert a chest drain in the side of obvious trauma and decreased breath sounds. Relieving the haemothorax will allow better ventilation. Another drain may be needed on the other side. Refer the child immediately to the cardiothoracic or general surgeons for a possible thoracotomy.

Haemopneumothorax—in most cases of internal chest trauma there is both air and blood in the pleural cavity. There will be free air and a fluid level on the erect chest X-ray. Insert a chest drain. Make sure that you have an adequate peripheral line to transfuse the volume lost.

Cardiac tamponade—this impedes the function of the heart. The peripheral circulation will be poor with low volume peripheral pulses. The patient will be restless and sweaty. The jugular veins will be engorged. The heart sounds may be muffled. Immediate pericardiocentesis should be undertaken using a wide-bore needle of suitable length. Insert the needle just below the xiphisternum. Point towards the left nipple at an angle of about 45 degrees, continuously aspirating as you do so. The child should be attached to an e.c.g. monitor. You should be able to feel the needle enter the pericardium and be able to aspirate blood (if the needle is in the ventricles there will be e.c.g. changes on the monitor). Aspirate as much as possible until the child's condition improves. If immediately available, portable ultrasonography can help with this procedure. The pericardium is likely to refill with blood so the child should be referred immediately to the cardiothoracic or general surgeons.

Flail chest—this will show as a segment of chest wall which moves inwards instead of outwards on inspiration. Its main effect is on ventilation. A small segment may need no treatment. With a large segment the child will need mechanical ventilation. Ensure adequate analgesia and check blood gases to gauge its effect on ventilation. If there is bony injury there will almost certainly be underlying lung injury. Refer the child to the cardiothoracic surgeons.

Abdominal injuries

Injuries to the abdomen may need urgent treatment and should be assessed after examination of the chest. Repeated examination should be carried out as abdominal injuries are often difficult to detect, and in 25–50 per cent of cases no clinical sign of injury is apparent initially.

Examination

1. Look at the abdomen—are there any external signs of injury, i.e. bruising, tyre marks, abrasions, etc. These would herald serious internal injuries; in order to cause bruising the anterior abdominal wall must be pressed against the spine and thus may have damaged any intervening organs. As the child's abdomen is relatively larger than the limbs compared with an adult, the abdomen often bears the brunt of the injury.

2. Look for any wounds which might indicate penetrating trauma. Try and assess their depth but do not probe the wound. Leave any penetrating foreign body in situ. Refer any child with wounds that penetrate deeper than the skin for surgical assessment.

3. Assess distension—initially there will be gastric and intestinal distension due to ileus and swallowed air. Once this is decompressed using a nasogastric tube, the abdomen should return to normal. The abdominal cavity can accommodate a large volume of blood before becoming distended, so abdominal distension should not be relied upon as a sign of bleeding.

4. Palpate for tenderness, rebound or guarding—any signs of peritonism should be taken as an indication for surgical referral and possible laparotomy. The abdomen is often difficult to assess if the child is ventilated or unconscious.

5. Auscultate for bowel sounds—they are often absent even if there is no intra-abdominal trauma as the child will have gastric and intestinal ileus.

6. Rectal examination—look for bleeding. Feel for rectal damage and sphincter tone (spinal trauma may affect the sphincter) and palpate gently for evidence of a pelvic fracture.

7. If there are any signs of injury to the lower ribs suspect a liver or spleen injury.

8. Always suspect an abdominal injury if there are also chest and pelvic injuries.

9. Shoulder tip pain on lying down might indicate irritation of the phrenic nerve from abdominal injuries.

Investigations

1. Abdominal radiograph—a plain radiograph does not offer much useful information. A lateral decubitus view may show air in the peritoneum which would indicate a burst viscus. This is not needed if it is already clear that the child requires a laparotomy.

2. Peritoneal lavage—is an investigation which may help in the diagnosis of intra-abdominal injury. It should not be performed if there is obvious abdominal bleeding (for example shock in the presence of peritonism or external evidence of abdominal trauma) as it wastes time when the child needs to go to theatre immediately.

Indications for lavage:

• Equivocal abdominal examination; fractured lower ribs, pelvic and lumbar spine fractures may obscure findings.

• Unreliable examination due to head injury, paraplegia, anaesthesia, etc.

• Unexplained hypotension or blood loss.

Lavage should usually be carried out by the surgeon who will decide whether to proceed to laparotomy. *Lavage confuses later abdominal examination by producing peritoneal irritation, and so should be authorized by the surgeon who is to have ongoing responsibility for the patient.* A positive result does not necessarily indicate the need for surgery as children's solid viscus injuries are sometimes treated conservatively. A negative result does not exclude abdominal injury as the bleeding may be localized or retroperitoneal.

3. CT scan—in hospitals which have the facility, a CT scan is useful as it can detect intra-abdominal injury quite accurately (but do not waste time doing this if a laparotomy is needed).

4. Ultrasound imaging is useful for detecting intraperitoneal fluid.

Management In abdominal trauma the exact diagnosis is not important in the initial management. The main decision

is whether the child needs a laparotomy. If surgery is antici-
pated then the patient must be transferred to theatre as soon
as possible. It is dangerous to transfer a patient with a severe
intra-abdominal bleed to another hospital or to delay surgery,
for example for a CT scan of the head.

1. Insert a nasogastric tube—this will decompress an ileus
and allow easier assessment of the abdomen. If the abdomen
is distended with air then it will splint the diaphragm and
compromise ventilation. It can also cause vomiting and
aspiration. An orogastric tube should be inserted if there is a
suspicion of a basal skull fracture.
2. Insert a urinary catheter (but see p. 69). A distended
bladder will interfere with assessment of the abdomen. Urinary output needs to be calculated and the bladder must be
catheterized before peritoneal lavage and surgery.

Box 3.3 **Indications for surgical referral:**
- External wounds or bruising to the abdomen.
- Abdominal distension after nasogastric tube
  deflation.
- Unexplained hypotension or evidence of
  haemorrhage.
- Abdominal tenderness or guarding.
- Rectal bleeding.
- Lower rib fractures.
- Stab wounds—examine (do not probe). If the wound
  is deeper than the skin the patient needs referral for
  a surgical opinion.

Genitourinary injuries

These are often associated with abdominal injuries. They
may not be easily detected immediately but can cause problems with recovery.

Examination
1. Examine the urethral meatus for bruising and bleeding.
2. Look for bruising of the scrotum.

3. Feel for a bladder—if palpable it may indicate obstruction due to a clot of blood or a blocked urethra due to injury.
4. Palpate the renal angles for tenderness. Feel for any renal masses (an abnormally shaped or placed kidney is more likely to be traumatized).

Investigations and management

1. Catheterization—if there is no bruising or bleeding at the urethral meatus insert a urinary catheter of a size appropriate for the child (see Table 2.2). If a urethral injury is suspected then suprapubic drainage must be considered.
2. Obtain a urine sample—test for blood. If blood is present an intravenous urogram should be performed.
3. Intravenous urogram—if there is any evidence of damage to the renal tract an intravenous urogram should be done. This can be performed in A & E. This will show if both kidneys are functioning and the state of the urinary tract. It is also useful prior to abdominal surgery to check the patient has two functional kidneys. The X-ray can also be done on the operating table if surgery is urgent.
4. X-ray of the pelvis—if the pelvis is fractured look for associated urinary tract damage. A CT scan will show a fractured pelvis well. Severe, concealed retroperitoneal bleeding may occur with a fractured pelvis.

Box 3.4 **Indication for referral to the GU surgeons:**

- Inability to pass urethral catheter.
- Urethral bleeding or bruising.
- Macroscopic haematuria.
- Fractured pelvis.
- Abnormal IVP.

Head injuries

Head injury is the most common cause of death in injured children. The damage to the brain after an accident can be primary, as a direct result of the trauma, or secondary to other factors, especially hypoxia, hypotension, and raised intracranial pressure. The main aim in the A & E department is to prevent and treat these secondary conditions in order to minimize brain damage.

Primary damage can be caused by direct contact between the surface of the brain and the skull as the brain can move within its bony shell. There are also shearing forces as the brain moves and twists.

Focal damage occurs at the site of a fracture, especially if depressed, as the bone fragment enters the brain. Skull fractures are less common in children as their skulls are more elastic than in adults. A fracture indicates an increased risk of an intracranial bleed. Secondary damage is caused by:

1. Extradural haematoma.
2. Subdural haematoma.
3. Hypoxia and ischaemia—if the systolic blood pressure is reduced by 20–40 mmHg the cerebral perfusion drops. Areas of ischaemic brain damage will occur after a few minutes. In multiply injured patients shock and respiratory obstruction often lead to periods of hypoxia with the associated risk of brain hypoxia and CO_2 retention.
4. Raised intracranial pressure—this reduces cerebral perfusion and 'coning' may occur. Raised intracranial pressure is caused by haematoma, or more frequently in children by cerebral oedema.

Examination Remember first the importance of the basic checks on airway, breathing, and circulation. Brain damage is exacerbated by shock and hypoxia.

1. Conscious level—in children over 4 years of age use the Glasgow Coma Scale (Table 3.5). In younger children, there is no consensus as to the best score in the acutely injured child. Our practice is to itemize the child's response to each of the three assessments of eye opening, motor, and verbal response.
2. Pupils—look at the size and reaction of the pupils. A unilateral dilated pupil may indicate raised intracranial pressure with coning possibly due to intracranial haematoma, this would need immediate action. Local trauma to the eye may also cause a dilated pupil.
3. Examine the eyes themselves for trauma—also look for

Table 3.5 • Glasgow coma scale

		Score
Eye opening		
	spontaneously	4
	to speech	3
	to pain	2
	nil	1
Best motor response		
	obeys commands	6
	localizes stimuli	5
	withdraws	4
	abnormal flexion	3
	extensor responses	2
	nil	1
Verbal response		
	orientated	5
	confused	4
	inappropriate words	3
	incomprehensible words	2
	nil	1
Verbal response modified for small children		
	appropriate words or social smile,	
	fixes and follows	5
	cries but consolable	4
	persistently irritable	3
	restless and agitated	2
	none	1

subhyloid haemorrhage or a scleral haemorrhage without a posterior border which might indicate a fractured base of the skull.

4. Look at the fundi—papilloedema does not occur immediately with raised intracranial pressure, but examination of the fundi may show other abnormalities, such as fundal haemorrhages, which might indicate non-accidental injury.
5. Look around the eyes—bilateral periorbital haematomas (racoon eyes) indicate a fractured base of the skull or direct trauma and facial injury.
6. Look behind the ears for Battle's sign (bruising over the mastoid process)—this indicates a fractured base of the skull.

7. Look for CSF leak from the nose or ears—this may be mixed with blood and is difficult to differentiate from traumatic extracranial bleeding. Blood mixed with CSF will not usually clot. (It will form two rings if allowed to drop on to the sheet.) Again, this indicates a basal skull fracture.

8. Examine the scalp—feel for haematomas or areas of depression indicating a skull fracture. Look for lacerations. If a laceration is present, feel inside it with a gloved finger for a fracture.

9. Examine the limbs—for movement, tone, and reflexes.

Investigations

1. Blood gases or pulse oximetry—the importance of hypoxia has already been stated. PCO_2 measurements will also need to be taken if the patient is being ventilated, or is unconscious.

- Blood glucose—if the patient is unconscious.
- Indications for skull X-ray:
  - neurological symptoms or signs,
  - cerebrospinal fluid or blood from nose or ear,
  - suspected penetrating injury, and/or
  - pronounced bruising or swelling of the scalp.
- X-ray the cervical spine, ensure C7 is on the film.

2. Computerized tomography—the CT scan will be interpreted by the neurosurgical team so it would be appropriate to discuss the child with them first. The main indications for scanning and neurosurgical consultation are impaired conscious level or localized neurological signs with or without a skull fracture or a depressed skull fracture. The child often needs to be anaesthetized with controlled ventilation for the scan.

Management The aim of management is to protect the brain from hypoxia and ischaemia and to prevent secondary brain damage. The child must be continuously assessed to see if the condition has deteriorated, which would indicate the need for further action.

The first priority is always to ensure adequate ventilation and oxygenation and to restore the circulation. Competent anaesthetic help should be requested immediately.

Airway—the neck should still be immobilized in a cervical collar. The patient may require intubation. Indications for intubation are:

1. Unconscious patient. G.C.S. of eight or less.
2. Protection of the airway, for example facial injuries, oropharyngeal bleeding.
3. Poor ventilation—this will be assessed clinically, but in addition intubation should be carried out if oxygen saturation is less than 90% when breathing air or less than 95% when receiving oxygen or $PaCO_2 > 45$ mmHg.
4. To allow hyperventilation when the patient's condition is deteriorating because of raised intracranial pressure. Rapid sequence induction of anaesthesia, with thiopentone and suxamethonium should be used. An anaesthetist or experienced senior A & E doctor should undertake this. Intubation should be performed immediately if the child is in extremis and there is no time to give anaesthetic drugs.

If the child does not need ventilation then a high concentration oxygen mask must be used.

Sedation and analgesia—avoid drugs which cause clouding of consciousness and respiratory depression (for example opiates). Paracetamol or codeine phosphate may be given.

Immediate complications associated with head injury
Seizures—fits need to be controlled as quickly as possible as they may lead to further hypoxic brain damage and raised intracranial pressure. The preferred drug to stop the fits is phenytoin as it does not depress conscious level. Give a bolus of 15 mg/kg intravenously over 20 minutes (with e.c.g. control as this drug can cause cardiac arrythmias). Intravenous diazepam can be given but it will cause respiratory depression. Alternatively, ask the anaesthetist to give thiopentone and ventilate the child.

Intracranial haematoma—this should be suspected if there is a deterioration in consciousness. An ipsilateral dilated pupil due to stretching of the third nerve is a late sign. This will be followed by bilateral dilated pupils. Intracranial haematomas are more likely in the presence of a skull fracture but can still occur without a fracture due to the shearing force of tearing blood vessels. The child should be referred immediately to the neurosurgeons. Most neurosurgeons would prefer to do a CT scan prior to operation as this localizes the bleeding area and eliminates other causes of deterioration, for example brain swelling. Methods to reduce intracranial pressure (see below) may help the child to recover temporarily to allow for scanning.

Raised intracranial pressure—this is likely in any child with significant head injury. The first sign is deterioration in consciousness. Raised systemic blood pressure and bradycardia occur late. The patient should be hyperventilated to decrease $PaCO_2$, to about 28–30 mmHg. If the $PaCO_2$ is high this causes cerebral vasodilation which increases the intracranial pressure. It is very important to keep the patient well-oxygenated. Intravenous mannitol can be given to temporarily reduce the intracranial pressure by its osmotic effect (Table 2.2). This should be given over a period of 20 minutes.

There are several causes of deterioration in conscious level:

1. Hypoxia—check blood gases (or pulse oximeter), respiratory rate, and look for chest injuries.
2. Ischaemia—check pulse, blood pressure, etc. Treat shock.
3. Post-seizure—there is often a deterioration in consciousness after a fit. This should recover in less than an hour (but do not delay seeking neurosurgical help).
4. Hypoglycaemia—check the blood sugar and give i.v. glucose if necessary.
5. Intracranial complications—if the above have been excluded an urgent CT scan should be performed.

Infection—many neurosurgeons no longer give prophylactic antibiotics if there is a CSF leak (indicating a fractured base of skull) or a compound vault fracture. Local policies vary.

Interhospital transfer Children with head injuries may need transfer to another hospital which has a neurosurgical unit. It is important that they are in a stable condition before transfer and major haemorrhage needing immediate abdominal or chest surgery would contraindicate transfer. *The child should always be accompanied by an experienced doctor.* Ensure the airway is protected. *The child should be intubated prior to transfer.* A portable ventilator will assist in giving the correct ventilation. Make sure there is a secure line for intravenous access. Take all relevant documentation with you (including radiographs). Ask the receiving doctor's advice about transport requirements.

Spinal injuries

Always assume the patient has a spinal injury until proved otherwise. They can be easily overlooked if the child is unconscious or has other major injuries. Always use a rigid collar and preferably this should have been put on before arrival in hospital. When moving the child remember the possibility of thoracolumbar injury, and log roll with the whole spine in the neutral position.

Examination

1. Airway and breathing—breathing is often compromised if there is damage to the spinal cord due to partial or complete intercostal paralysis, partial phrenic nerve palsy, inability to expectorate, and ventilation–perfusion mismatch. There may also be associated chest injuries.

2. Circulation—spinal cord injuries will cause hypotension and bradycardia due to reduced sympathetic outflow. Associated injuries may also cause hypotension.

3. Neurological examination—look for movement in all four limbs with response to pain. Power can be tested in the conscious patient. Test all reflexes. Spinal injuries are often incomplete and may give equivocal signs. Test for anal reflexes and tone. Priapism in the male indicates spinal cord injury.

4. Local examination—examine the neck and back (log roll the patient) for open wounds, bruising, swelling, and localized tenderness. Feel for any bony deformity of the spine.

5. Abdominal examination—in a spinal cord injury the abdominal wall is flaccid and an ileus will develop. Peritoneal lavage may be necessary to exclude abdominal bleeding.

6. Urinary system—acute retention will develop and the bladder should be catheterized under aseptic conditions.

Investigations Radiographs must be taken and should include a lateral and AP of the cervical spine and an open mouth odontoid view. The X-rays must show C7. This may require someone to pull down on the child's arms to drop the shoulders to get the required view. Look at the bones themselves and their alignment. Look for a prevertebral haematoma which would indicate trauma. The retrotracheal space (C6) should not exceed 14 mm, the retropharyngeal space (C2) should not exceed 6 mm, the retropharyngeal space widens if the child cries. The atlanto–odontoid gap should not exceed 4 mm, and if increased this indicates rupture of the transverse ligaments of the atlas. Flexion, extension, or oblique views may all be needed. Radiographs may be normal even with severe spinal cord injury. X-ray the thoracolumbar spine as indicated clinically.

Management

1. Airway and ventilation—the indications for intubation are the same as in any multiple injury. Intubation should be performed by the most experienced person present with the patient's neck held in a neutral position to prevent movement. Assisted ventilation may be necessary.

2. Circulation—if the child's pulse falls below 50 then atropine should be given at a dose of 15 μg/kg stat i.v. Hypotension could be due to spinal shock or blood loss, if it is associated with bradycardia it is likely to be due to spinal shock rather than blood loss. Give a fluid challenge of 20 ml/kg of colloid i.v. Spinal hypotension should recover with this.

3. Management of the fracture—the neck should remain immobilized in a stiff cervical collar with the patient lying flat (the airway may need the protection of intubation). Refer to the orthopaedic or the surgical department. Most neck injuries will be treated with traction using skull callipers, for example Gardner–Wells calliper or halo traction. If there is a thoracolumbar injury the child should remain on his back. The child may be referred to a spinal injury centre.

Limb injuries

Unless there is profuse bleeding or evidence of arterial damage then limb injuries can be left until the potentially life-threatening injuries have been dealt with.

Examination

1. Look at both arms and legs for evidence of bruising, wounds, or deformity.

2. Gently palpate for crepitus or abnormal movement.

3. If the patient is conscious check voluntary movement at all joints.

4. Feel for the pulse distal to any possible fracture site.

5. Examine the skin overlying the fracture—check for viability by noting its colour and whether the skin blanches on pressure.

6. If the fracture is compound examine the wound for soft tissue damage and foreign bodies.

7. Test for function of the part distal to the fracture (there may be associated nerve or tendon damage).

Investigations If a fracture is suspected the limb should be X-rayed in two planes, including the joint above and the joint below. These X-rays are a low priority, and chest, abdominal, and head injuries must all be dealt with first.

Management If a fracture is suspected clinically then splint the limb. This helps reduce pain, prevent blood loss, and prevent fat embolism.

Check arterial pulses before and after any manoeuvre, i.e. X-ray or reduction. If a distal pulse is absent call for urgent orthopaedic help. The fracture must be reduced immediately by traction with analgesia.

All compound injuries should be covered. A saline or betadine soaked gauze is ideal as this helps stop the wound drying out. Alternatively, use clingfilm as this allows the wound to be viewed without contamination. If bleeding is profuse apply a pressure bandage, but monitor the distal circulation and do not allow the patient to leave the department without ensuring someone in the surgical team knows that a pressure bandage has been applied.

If the injury is compound, give tetanus toxoid if the patient has not received a booster within ten years. Also give intravenous antibiotics, for example flucloxacillin and ampicillin or a cephalosporin. Refer the patient to the orthopaedic department.

Crush injuries

The crush syndrome develops when muscle has been crushed for a length of time, for example if a child is buried under fallen masonry. Muscle breakdown occurs which releases acid myoglobin. When the crush or pressure is released this is carried in the circulation throughout the body. Renal failure is the consequence. Immediately after the pressure is released the child may become shocked and urine output decreases. The limb itself will appear swollen, red, and blistered. Crush syndrome is often fatal. If a crush injury is suspected then an intravenous line should be started and normal saline (20 ml/kg) given to initiate a diuresis. Give i.v. morphine as the limb will be very painful. Monitor e.c.g. for hypercalcaemia. Sodium bicarbonate (1 mmol/kg) may need to be given. If the limb has been ischaemic for greater than six hours it may be necessary to perform an amputation. Sepsis is often associated with a more serious prognosis so give prophylactic antibiotics (for example flucloxacillin and ampicillin) and be meticulous about wound care.

Amputations

Type of amputation Clean amputations are the most suitable for reimplantation, but some degloved amputations of fingers, and some crush or avulsion amputations, can be reimplanted with good functional result. Partial amputations may also benefit from microsurgical procedures.

Care of the amputated part for transfer The amputated part should be put in a dry polythene bag, and placed on top of a bowl of ice with several layers of gauze between the ice and the part. Do not place the part under ice and do not allow direct contact between the part and the ice. Do not put the part and the ice in the same polythene bag. If the amputated part freezes reimplantation is not possible.

Care of the patient Resuscitate the patient if necessary. Wrap the stump in a sterile dressing and elevate to stop the bleeding. Try to avoid using artery clips to achieve haemostasis as these will damage the vessels. (Use local pressure to stop bleeding with elevation of the limb.) Refer to the nearest plastic surgery centre for reimplantation.

Continuous assessment

During the secondary survey, while different systems are being assessed, it is important to continue to review the child's condition as a whole, in case of further deterioration.

Many severely injured children's lives would be saved by:

1. *Getting experienced senior help early.*
2. *Avoiding hypoxia—intubate and ventilate early.*
3. *Treating hypovolaemia vigorously.*

Further reading

1. American College of Surgeons (1988). *Advanced trauma life support course core course manual.* American College of Surgeons, Chicago, Illinois.
2. Mayer, T. A. (ed.) (1985). *Emergency management of paediatric trauma.* W. B. Saunders, Philadelphia.
3. Coran, A. G. and Harris, B. H. (ed.) (1990). *Paediatric trauma: proceedings of the 3rd national conference.* J. B. Lippincott, Philadelphia.
4. Alpar, E. K. and Owen, R. (ed.) (1988). *Paediatric trauma.* Castle House Publications, Tunbridge Wells.

Minor trauma

Wound management

- **History   Examination   Management of wounds**

One of the commonest reasons for a child attending an Accident and Emergency department is a wound. The treatment given will vary with the type of wound. The main points to be considered are:

- Is the wound suitable for primary suture?
- Is there any damage to deep structures?
- Are there foreign bodies in the wound?
- Is the wound dirty?
- Is the wound suitable for management in the A & E department?

If possible the parents should be allowed to accompany the child throughout all procedures.

History

1. Time elapsed since injury—ideally, wounds should be sutured within six hours of having been sustained. After six hours, the skin cells at the edge of the wound may be non-viable. The wound edge will require trimming if primary suture is to be successful. The exception is a scalp wound in which there is usually an excellent blood supply.
2. Cause and mechanism of the injury—i.e. knife wound, glass, etc. Think about how the wound was caused and what implications this may have. For instance, glass or knife wounds, although insignificant on the surface, often penetrate into deeper tissues causing nerve, vessel, or tendon damage. Wounds inflicted with some force may have caused a deeper injury, such as a broken bone.
3. Possibility of a foreign body—wounds inflicted by glass may contain glass fragments. Other materials, for example thorns, wood splinters, etc., may cause infection later if not removed.
4. Medical history—for example a bleeding disorder. Specific treatment will be required (see Chapter 13).
5. Drug history—for example patients on steroids may have a higher incidence of wound breakdown and infection.

Examination

1. Examine the wound. Decide whether it is clean and suitable for suture, or dirty (see p. 87). Look for areas of skin loss. Gently open the wound for an approximate assessment of its depth. Think what deeper structures may be involved.
2. Palpate the wound for presence of a foreign body.
3. Check movement distal to the wound. Any loss of movement may indicate tendon or nerve damage. This problem usually needs to be referred to the orthopaedic department for further treatment.
4. Assess sensation distal to the wound. A moderately sharp instrument, i.e. an opened up paperclip, can be used rather than a needle which might frighten the child. If you suspect any loss of nerve function refer the child to a plastic surgeon (even very distal wounds may warrant repair).
5. Feel for the distal pulse and assess circulation. A laceration of an artery may need repair and, therefore, should be referred to the vascular, general, or plastic surgeons. Digital arteries and nerves run closely adjacent to each other, so if there is digital arterial bleeding also suspect nerve damage.
6. All wounds caused by glass should be X-rayed, but a full wound assessment must also be made. All glass is relatively radio-opaque, but whether or not glass fragments show on the radiograph depends on various factors, i.e, the size and orientation of the foreign body, the X-ray exposure, and the radiodensity of the tissues. Glass may easily be obscured by overlying bones. In order to show a glass foreign body it is often necessary to ask for soft tissue and/or tangential views. If a glass foreign body is present it should be removed unless it is extremely small and difficult to access.

Management of wounds

Abrasions These are wounds which have removed the surface of the skin but have not penetrated into the deep tissues. They should be very thoroughly cleansed as any residual dirt will leave tattoo marks. Lignocaine gel, 2 per cent, applied 15 minutes before cleaning, will produce some analgesia. Smaller abrasions may have lignocaine infiltrated beneath them before cleaning. (Beware of toxicity from lignocaine, calculate maximum dose first, see p. 334.) Extensive or facial abrasions will usually need to be cleaned under general anaesthesia. Use forceps and a small brush to remove embedded dirt. When the wound is completely clean apply a dressing (except on the face). Very clean wounds should have a non-adherent dressing such as paraffin gauze applied. Wounds which were very dirty or those caused in a dirty area (for example in the garden) may have an antiseptic added to them, i.e. spray with povidone–iodine or cover with a paraffin gauze impregnated with chlorhexidine or povidone–iodine. The parents should be advised to leave the dressing on for about a week (earlier removal would be painful and may remove new tissue) and to keep the dressing clean and dry. Patients with minor abrasions can usually be discharged to the care of the general practitioner.

Lacerations Do not attempt any repair unless you are entirely confident to do so. The following wounds are not suitable for suture in the A & E department:

1. Extensive wounds—may need general anaesthetic.
2. Deep wounds with tendon, nerve, or arterial damage—refer to the appropriate surgical team.
3. Facial wounds—consider referral to the plastic surgeons. Wounds involving foreheads and chins can usually be sutured in the A & E department. Refer large wounds and wounds involving the red margins of the lips and around the eyelids as these need meticulous repair to prevent scarring.
4. Large areas of skin loss or devitalized tissue—refer to plastic surgeons.

Sutures (see p. 336 for practical details) Suturing small children's wounds is difficult as the child cannot understand what is happening to him. A brief demonstration on 'teddy' may dispel fear.

Wounds which can be easily sutured in the A & E department are those which involve skin only. Decide whether adhesive strips or tissue adhesive may be more appropriate than sutures.

When you have finished suturing it is important to give the parents instructions about the care of the wound, i.e. keep it clean and dry, and to check for signs of infection (redness, pain, swelling, and discharge). A printed instruction card may be helpful. Tell the parents when the sutures should be removed and refer the child to the general practitioner or district nurse for this to be done (see p. 338). Lacerations which have been difficult to suture, have had areas of skin loss, or are potentially infected should be reviewed in the A & E department. Advise the parents about signs of infection and tell them to return if concerned.

Adhesive strips These are a suitable alternative to suturing for small superficial wounds. They are not suitable for wounds over a moving part (e.g. a joint) or where they might easily get damp. The wound must be fresh and clean. The advantages of adhesive strips are that they are painless to apply, do not require any expertise for removal, and do not leave suture marks. However, it is essential that the basic principles of wound management are adhered to and the wound is cleaned and explored adequately. Gaps must be left between the strips to allow for any discharge to escape. Opposition of skin edges should be accurate, and wounds not suitable for suture are unlikely to be suitable for adhesive strips. Tincture of benzoin applied with cottonwool to the skin adjacent to the wound will help the strips to adhere. It may be helpful to use forceps to lift up the skin edges to ensure they do not roll under and, therefore, cause the wound to heal poorly. The parents should be instructed to keep the strips clean and dry. They are removed after a similar period of time as sutures, or can be left longer if necessary.

Tissue adhesive This is a modified 'superglue' which will hold together skin edges, provided there is no tension or movement. The wounds must be superficial. The wound is cleaned and dried and a thin layer of adhesive applied over the wound. The skin edges are held together for 1 minute while the glue sets. The reaction produces heat which may be uncomfortable for the patient, but otherwise the procedure is painfree. The wound can be left exposed and the glue, which is biodegradable, will hold for several days. The method is ideal for small scalp wounds and some facial lacerations.

Antibiotic prophylaxis Although all the wounds which are seen in the A & E department are contaminated with bacterial organisms, prophylactic antibiotics are rarely required. If the wound is only superficially dirty then adequate cleansing should suffice to prevent infection. The wound must be repaired so that no necrotic tissue is left to encourage infection, and the wound should not be under tension as this may compromise the vascular supply and hence healing. If the wound is clean and has a good blood supply then there is only a small risk of infection and this may be treated later if it occurs. However, prophylactic antibiotics should be considered in the following cases:

1. Wounds which have been very heavily contaminated with dirty material, for example mud from a field or garden.
2. Penetrating wounds where it is impracticable to clean the whole wound tract without extending the wound and causing more tissue damage (for example rusty nails).
3. Bites (see p. 90).
4. Wounds in which there has been a delay in presentation (of more than six hours) where bacterial multiplication may already have occurred.
5. Wounds in which there may be some dead space or areas of poor vascular supply.

Note: Prophylactic antibiotics are no substitute for meticulous wound cleaning and adequate debridement and repair of the wound.

Suitable antibiotics need to be chosen according to the most likely pathogen. Send a wound swab for bacteriological studies so that, on review, the pathogen may be identified and the appropriate antibiotic given.

1. Flucloxacillin—this is active against staphylococci which are found on normal skin and are a frequent cause of wound infection. It may also be used in conjunction with ampicillin or augmentin which is a broad-spectrum antibiotic.
2. Augmentin is ampicillin combined with clavulanic acid and is active against many bacteria, including some anaerobes and the penicillinase-producing organisms. It is especially suitable for animal bites.

3. Penicillin is used where streptococci may be the suspected organism, it will also kill *Clostridium tetani* (but tetanus prophylaxis is vital).

4. Erythromycin is a useful broad-spectrum antibiotic suitable for patients who are sensitive to the penicillins. The dose given should be appropriate for the child's age and is usually given orally for five days.

Tetanus toxoid Every child who attends the A & E department with a wound should have their tetanus immunization status checked. Even if the wound is not thought to be tetanus prone it is essential to maintain immunity in case infection occurs in future wounds.

Most children have their routine immunizations, including tetanus toxoid, at two, three, and four months of age (primary course—TTC) and a booster (TTB) at 5 years of age. These will provide immunity from tetanus until the child is 15-years-old, however, some children may not have received adequate immunizations, in which case Table 4.1 should be used for reference.

Contraindications to tetanus vaccine are:

• Acute febrile illness—except in the presence of a tetanus prone wound.
• Severe reaction to a previous dose.

The community health physician should be informed of children who have received tetanus immunization in

Table 4.1 • Tetanus chart

State of immunity	Wound tetanus prone	Requirements
TTC or TTB	Yes	nil*
within 10 years	No	nil
TTC or TTB	Yes	TTB and Human
more than 10 years ago		Tetanus
		Immunoglobulin
	No	TTB
Incomplete TTC	Yes	TTC and Human
or unimmunized		Tetanus
or unknown		Immunoglobulin
	No	TTC

* TTB may be given if risk high, for example stable manure.

hospital so that unnecessary further doses are not given in the community.

A tetanus prone wound has one or more of the following characteristics:

- Dirty (i.e. contact with soil or manure).
- Puncture wound.
- Devitalized tissue.
- More than six-hours-old.
- Clinical evidence of sepsis.

Stabbings If the history indicates a stab wound, be very careful. The innocuous looking skin defect may conceal serious underlying damage to vital structures. Always take a detailed history with a description of the sharp instrument involved, if possible. If the object is still *in situ* do not remove it as this may cause torrential bleeding. If the wound track lies near any major vessels then it should be removed in theatre with full resuscitation facilities immediately available. Probing wounds does not always give an adequate indication of the depth of the wound and can be dangerous.

Stab wounds to the chest, head, neck, and abdomen must be treated seriously. Even if the patient appears well, always insert an intravenous line and cross-match blood in case of sudden catastrophic bleeding. These wounds should always be referred for surgical investigation and exploration.

Stab wounds to the limbs should be thoroughly examined and checked for damage to deep structures. Patients may need to be referred to the orthopaedic department for exploration under general anaesthesia. Small shallow wounds with no underlying major structures may be explored and sutured in the A & E department.

Palatal penetration Children may fall while sucking a sharp object such as a pencil. In this case the object may penetrate the hard palate and may cause serious damage. There is also a risk of injury to the carotid artery. All penetrating wounds to the roof of the mouth should be referred to the appropriate surgical team for exploration under general anaesthesia.

Puncture wounds Puncture wounds to the feet are not uncommon. Unshod children may step on a sharp object, or the shoe may be penetrated by a nail. Ask and record what object caused the injury. Injuries caused by glass, needles, etc. must be X-rayed to exclude the possibility of a retained foreign body. If the causative object is unknown it is also wise to X-ray. Foreign bodies should be removed, usually under general anaesthesia. Occasionally, the wound becomes infected and this may lead to osteomyelitis or septic arthritis (sometimes due to a *Pseudomonas* infection). Prophylactic antibiotics are not necessary in every case of penetrating wound, but the parents should be carefully warned about the signs of infection and asked to return if they are worried.

Bites

Dog bites Dog bites vary in severity from the trivial to the life-threatening. The actual circumstances surrounding the injury are usually very frightening both for the child and the parent. The dog may cause damage with his teeth or claws. These wounds are always contaminated with bacterial organisms and often become infected. Because of the risk of infection, dog bites should not be sutured on the day of injury. The wound should be thoroughly cleaned and explored using local or general anaesthesia as necessary. The wound is left unsutured, an antiseptic dressing (for example chlorhexidine or povidone–iodine impregnated paraffin gauze) applied, and the patient given prophylactic antibiotics. After 3–4 days the wound is reviewed and assessed for infection. If the wound is clean then it can be repaired if necessary by delayed primary suture, or closed with steristrips. Before suturing or steristripping the wound, a millimetre or less of skin should be excised from each skin edge. The fresh skin edges can then be opposed and sutured as a fresh wound. It is essential that no tension is placed on the wound which may prevent it healing. Undermining the skin edges may help accurate apposition. The antibiotics are continued and the wound reviewed at regular intervals of about 2–3 days.

Facial wounds may leave ugly scars if left for delayed primary suture. As the face has a good blood supply, most dog bites of the face may be sutured early under antibiotic cover. These cases should be referred to the plastic surgeons unless they are very minor.

Cat bites Cat bites usually cause less tissue damage than dog bites, but create puncture wounds which are frequently infected with anaerobes such as *Pasteurella multocida*. Augmentin should be given for prophylaxis and review in two days is necessary.

Human bites The human mouth is very heavily colonized with bacteria, including anaerobes. Human bites should be treated in a similar fashion to dog bites, but they get infected even more frequently. Prophylactic antibiotics against anaerobic bacteria should be given (for example augmentin). The child may have been bitten by someone who is a Hepatitis B carrier or who carries the HIV virus. Hepatitis immunoglobulin and vaccine should be given. At present there are no recommendations for HIV prophylaxis. The wound should be thoroughly cleansed to reduce the amount of contamination.

Non-accidental injury should be considered (p. 181).

Insect bites These may cause a local allergic reaction with redness, swelling, and itch. If there is no evidence of infection then 1 per cent hydrocortisone cream applied topically will provide relief. Sometimes the child appears with a rash. Pointers that this might be due to a crop of insect bites are the linear nature of the line of red spots and the distribution, usually on the lower legs or around the lines made by elastic in clothing. Extensive numbers of bites may cause intense itching and an oral antihistamine can be given. Some bites become infected, and these may be an ascending lymphangitis or cellulitis around the bite. If this occurs then penicillin V or erythromycin should be given. A local abscess may need to be treated by incision and drainage.

Insect stings Wasp stings are usually a very minor problem, although they may occasionally cause an anaphylactic reaction. Symptomatic treatment is usually sufficient. If the child is stung in the mouth there may be some swelling but this usually rapidly subsides. However, a sting in the throat may cause enough swelling to obstruct the airway, the child should be observed in the A & E department for 2–3 hours after being stung. If the sting is on the hand then this should be elevated in a sling for 24 hours.

Bee stings are more likely to cause an anaphylactic reaction. if it is a simple sting then remove the embedded sting with a needle or forceps. Treat symptomatically, but the same caution with oral stings applies as above (for anaphylaxis see p. 44).

Soft tissue injuries

These are bruises, pulled muscles, etc. They are often trivial but some of the more serious injuries need to be treated with as much respect as a fracture (and may be difficult to differentiate from such). A sprain is an example of this type of injury (see p. 128).

Bruises A bruise is a bleed into the underlying skin or soft tissues. It may be classified as an ecchymosis which is a bleed into the skin, or a haematoma which is a more extensive bleed into the soft tissues.

1. Ecchymosis—this presents as a red/purple area on the skin. As the bruise ages it turns yellow/green with the altered blood pigment. It is important to determine the cause of the bruise, always bearing in mind the possibility of non-accidental injury. If assault is likely then document the size and appearance of the bruise carefully in the notes in case a police statement is required. An ecchymosis needs no treatment other than reassurance.

2. Haematoma—this usually presents as a swelling with an overlying bruise, and with pain on touching the affected part. Again it is important to take an adequate history to determine the cause. Check the distal circulation and sensation. The child will probably be more comfortable if the area is supported by firm bandaging and elevated. Very large haematomas may be aspirated. This must be done as soon as possible after the injury as clotted blood is difficult to remove. Use a large gauge needle (i.e. 16 g) and a strict aseptic technique. Choose the most dependent part of the haematoma to allow for drainage. Blood or occasionally yellow serous fluid

can be aspirated. Apply a firm bandage after aspiration to prevent re-accumulation of blood. The child should usually be reviewed in the Accident and Emergency department. If the haematoma is unusually large or increases markedly in size consider the possibility of a bleeding disorder such as haemophilia.

Fingertip injuries

- **History   Assessment   Management**

These are a common sight in any A & E department and cause distress to the parents and the child. Although the initial damage often looks alarming, most fingertip injuries heal very well, resulting in a normal finger. Amputated fingertips regrow spontaneously with remarkably good results.

History

The most common aetiology is for the child's finger to be trapped in a door or door hinge. It is important to determine the exact cause of the injury so as to assess the risk of infection. Injuries which happen in the garden or are caused by bites are particularly prone to infection.

Assessment

The child will be in pain and an early priority is to give analgesia. First look at the finger and examine the finger distal to the injury. Test for sensation and function of the tip. Once this has been documented, a digital nerve block can be inserted (see p. 335), before proceeding further. This will provide analgesia whilst further examination and treatment are carried out.

Examination Check for:

1. The site of the avulsion or injury—this will determine the management of the injury and the prognosis.

2. The degree of bony involvement—look to see if any bone is exposed or if there is any bone deformity. Occasionally there is an open dislocation of the finger when the articular surfaces of the bone are seen.
3. Nail damage—the nail may be completely or partially avulsed.
4. Sensation and function of the tip give an indication of the viability of the distal part.

Management

X-ray the finger—to check for bone damage and the length of bone remaining.

Crush injuries proximal to the distal phalanx—should be referred to the orthopaedic department for further treatment.

Reimplantation—this should be considered for any finger injury proximal to the distal interphalangeal joint, although a more distal injury in a thumb may be considered suitable, (see p. 78).

Injuries distal to the distal interphalangeal joint—these can usually be managed in the A & E department. Check that the initial ring block is still providing complete analgesia before proceeding. Some more complicated injuries and injuries in small children may need to be repaired under general anaesthesia. Cleanse the area thoroughly. Check the nail for damage. If the nail is almost completely avulsed then remove it. Occasionally the base of the nail is pulled away from the nail bed. This should be replaced by repositioning it under the nail fold. This helps prevent deformity of the new nail. The finger must be meticulously cleaned and any dead tissue debrided. If the tip is partially avulsed then any deformity should be corrected and the tip positioned in its correct state. This should be fixed in place by one or two absorbable sutures. It is not advisable to use many sutures for a fingertip as they tend to tear the skin. Adhesive strips are an excellent alternative. If the tip is completely avulsed then the distal end may be left without skin cover as the skin will eventually grow over and provide new cover. After completing the surgical repair a paraffin gauze dressing should be applied and this covered with a dry finger dressing. The dressing should not be removed until the child is reviewed after one week. (Removing the dressing, which often sticks, may cause damage by pulling off partially healing areas, it is also very painful. There is usually no need to see the wound earlier). The appearances at one week are often still poor, but the parents should be reassured about the eventual outcome. The child should be reviewed at weekly intervals until the tip is healed. If the bone is damaged, or exposed, then prophylactic antibiotics should be given, for example (ampicillin and/or flucloxacillin, or erythromycin if the child is penicillin sensitive.

Subungual haematoma—blood under the nail causes quite severe pain which can be relieved if the pressure is released. Using a flame-heated paperclip, puncture the nail in the centre over the haematoma. Blood will then drain through the hole. This is only effective if done within 24 hours of the injury, as old blood will have clotted.

Soft tissue infections

- **Abscess Cellulitis Lymphangitis Paronychia Ingrowing toe-nail**

Abscess

An abscess is a pus filled cavity, the usual contaminating organism being a staphylococcus. The organism enters through a breach in the skin which may have been caused by minor trauma or an insect bite. An abscess may present at any site. Perianal and axillary abscesses seen in adults are rare in children but may be seen in adolescents.

History
1. Possible cause of the abscess—this might indicate the type of infection, i.e. an insect bite may be infected with streptococci.
2. How long has it been present?—this may indicate the severity of the infection.

3. How painful is it and can the child sleep at night?—tense pus is extremely painful.
4. Any previous history of abscesses?—the child might need investigation for an underlying immune deficiency.
5. Ask about symptoms of thirst and polyuria—occasionally an abscess is a presenting sign of diabetes.
6. Previous medical history—diabetics and children on steroids are likely to have abscesses which are slower to heal.
7. Any treatment already given for this abscess, for example antibiotics—these will alter the symptoms and signs and might produce a walled-off abscess which does not heal but which is less invasive.

Examination
1. Size of the abscess—only small abscesses are suitable for incision and drainage in the A & E department. Large abscesses are too painful and need curetting adequately.
2. Is it fluctuant?—if the abscess is pointing or is fluctuant then it is ready for incision and drainage.
3. Site of the abscess—be wary of infected lumps in the neck as these may be infected branchial or thyroglossal cysts which need surgical referral.
4. Take the child's temperature and examine for lymphadenopathy—these indicate whether the child is toxic, i.e. has a systemic spread of the abscess infection which will require systemic antibiotic treatment.
5. Urine test—for sugar to exclude diabetes.

Management
1. Small fluctuant abscesses should be incised and drained using local anaesthesia (see p. 339).
2. Large abscesses need surgical referral.
3. Antibiotics should not be given unless the child is toxic or there is any cellulitis around the infected site. Antibiotics do not adequately penetrate pus and the end result is a partially treated abscess which is not fluctuant and is resistant to treatment.
4. A pus swab should be obtained in case further antibiotic treatment is necessary post-operatively.
5. The patient should be reviewed in 24–48 hours to check that the abscess is settling.

Cellulitis

Cellulitis is an infection of the subcutaneous tissues. The organism is usually a streptococcus or staphylococcus. The child usually presents with a painful, red, swollen area, usually on a limb. There is often a small cut or graze. The infected area will be inflamed, swollen, and tender. The regional lymph nodes may be enlarged. The child's temperature should be taken. If the child is toxic and unwell he should be admitted to hospital for parenteral antibiotics. If the infection is less severe then he can be managed at home. The affected part should be rested and elevated. A high arm sling is useful for an arm. If a leg is affected it should be elevated on a foot stool. An antipyretic/analgesic, for example paracetamol, should be given. Antibiotics should be prescribed, usually ampicillin plus flucloxacillin or penicillin V. Erythromycin can be used for penicillin-sensitive patients. Blood cultures should be done to identify the pathogen. The child should be reviewed daily to check the infection is subsiding. If vomiting occurs the oral antibiotics will not be effective, and admission and parenteral antibiotics may be needed.

Lymphangitis

This is an infection extending along the lymphatic channels to the local lymph glands and is almost always streptococcal in origin (occasionally staphylococcal). The patient will usually have a break in the skin (caused by minor trauma) which is the portal of entry for the infection. Ascending from this is a red line. The local glands will be palpable and the patient pyrexial. Oral penicillin plus an antipyretic, for example paracetamol, is usually sufficient for treatment. The limb should be elevated and rested. The patient should be reviewd 24 hours later. The lymphangitis should resolve within 24–48 hours.

Paronychia

Bacteria can enter through the base of the nail folds and cause inflammation of the surrounding tissues. A painful, red swelling forms on one side of the base of the nail, and develops into a pus-filled blister. It is easily treated by in-

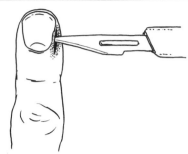

Fig. 4.1 • Incision of paronychia.

cision either through the area which is pointing or by a vertical incision just lateral to the base of the nail (see Figure 4.1). A digital nerve block should be used. The finger should be cleaned and dressed. Antibiotics are only required if there is marked cellulitis.

These infections must be distinguished from an herpetic whitlow, in which there are more discreet small papules or blisters and a longer history. Herpetic whitlows require no treatment but are very painful and often recurrent.

Ingrowing toe-nail

These are common in adolescent boys. The aim of treatment is to relieve the infection and prevent recurrence. The patient presents with a painful, red swelling adjacent to the medial distal edge of the toe-nail. Mild cases can be treated by elevating the edge of the nail involved and putting an iodine soaked wick underneath it. (This procedure is painful and may require digital nerve block.) This allows the pus to drain and enables the nail to grow long and away from the skin edge. More severe cases may need all or part of the nail removed. This allows free drainage and the skin to heal before the nail regrows. If the ingrowing toe-nail is recurrent, excision of the lateral part of the nail and phenolization of the nail bed produces good results. Nail avulsion can be done with a good digital nerve block, or it may need a general anaesthetic. To prevent recurrence the patient should be advised to wear broad-toed shoes and to cut the nail straight across. Good personal hygiene is also necessary.

Foreign bodies

- **Ears   Nose   Inhaled and ingested foreign bodies**

Ears

The parents might notice the child putting the object into the ear and come immediately to the A & E department. Sometimes, however, the incident is not seen and some days later the parents notice the object or the child admits to the incident. Examine the ear carefully using an auriscope. If the object is easily visible and the child cooperative then it may be possible to extract the material. It is preferable to use a hook to draw the object out (but be careful when going posteriorly to avoid damaging the drum). Forceps may push the object further down the canal. If the attempted removal is unsuccessful then the child should be referred to the next ENT clinic.

Nose

Foreign bodies in the nose are a more urgent problem as they may be inhaled and, therefore, should usually be removed the same day. Ask the child (if old enough) to blow his nose, occluding the unaffected nostril. This may dislodge the object. If it is possible to hook the object out then do so. A large syringe may be useful to suck out food debris. If unsuccessful then the child should be referred without delay to the ENT surgeons.

For inhaled and ingested foreign bodies see p. 218 and p. 171

Nasal problems

- **Trauma   Epistaxis**

Trauma

The nose is usually damaged by a fall on to the face or by a direct blow. The child may have an epistaxis. The bridge of the nose is usually swollen and tender. Important points to note in the examination are:

1. The presence or absence of a septal haematoma—in this case the nose is blocked and a cherry-red swelling is apparent inside the nose. This is an ENT emergency, as, untreated, the nasal septum may become necrotic and the nose will collapse. The treatment is drainage of the haematoma under general anaesthesia.
2. Nasal deformity—if the nose is bent, it will need straightening. This is usually done about one week after the injury when soft tissue swelling has subsided and it is easier to correct the alignment of the nose. This is done under general anaesthesia by the ENT or plastic surgeons.
3. Septal deformity—occasionally the septum is deviated to one side. Again this should be referred within a few days to the ENT surgeons.

Most nasal injuries do not require an X-ray (except when there is a skin break on the nose and one needs to determine whether there is a compound fracture present). In children under 5-years-old the nasal bones are mainly cartilaginous and do not show up on an X-ray, after this age the importance of the injury is based on clinical rather than X-ray findings.

Epistaxis

Children quite frequently have small nosebleeds. The aetiology may be trauma, allergy, infection, or foreign body. The bleeding is usually venous and unless the child has a bleeding disorder then simple measures such as pressure should cause it to stop. Ask the child to hold the soft part of the nose between his fingers for at least 15 minutes. He should breathe through the mouth and sit with the head forward.

Occasionally the bleeding is more persistent and further treatment will be necessary. A nasal pack may be inserted by someone experienced in the procedure. An anterior nasal pack has the disadvantage that there may be a persistent posterior nasal bleed. This can be seen by looking down the child's throat. The child should not be discharged whilst there is persistent bleeding. Assess the child for blood loss by checking the pulse and blood pressure, and looking for pallor and sweating (remember that more than 25 per cent of the blood volume must be lost before there are clinical signs of shock). The child may need to be admitted for observation and occasionally may need transfusion.

Dental problems

* **Mouth and tongue injuries**

Traumatic avulsion of a tooth is a common problem. It should be replaced as soon as possible. If this is done the tooth will usually reattach and remain viable. If the tooth is brought with the patient to the A & E department, then place it in normal saline. The dentist on call for the hospital should be informed immediately. Best results are obtained the earlier the tooth is reimplanted and this should be within 4–6 hours. Outside hospital it is recommended that the tooth is cleaned using tap water. It should then be placed in a container of milk. Older children may be able to keep the tooth in the mouth adjacent to the gum. Even milk teeth merit reimplanting as their presence ensures correct development of the underlying second tooth.

The child may also present with the teeth pushed forwards or backwards after a fall. These should be repositioned. This can often be done in the A & E department by standing behind the child and applying pressure. If unsuccessful, the child should be referred to the dental surgeons immediately. If the tooth is loose this can usually be treated by the child's own dentist. It is safe to wait overnight, unless the tooth is very loose and there is a danger of the tooth coming away completely and being aspirated. It may be possible to glue the loose tooth to adjacent teeth with tissue adhesive, until definitive dental treatment can be arranged.

Toothache is less common in children than in adults. It

may be due to a carious tooth which will be obvious on inspection. The child should be given some paracetamol and referred to his own dentist. The pain may be due to a dental abscess, in which case there may be swelling and tenderness around the tooth and swelling of the face. This should be treated with oral penicillin V and analgesia, for example paracetamol elixir. If something stronger is needed use combined paracetamol (120 mg) and codeine phosphate (12 mg/5 ml) elixir. The dose for 3–6-year-olds is 5 ml 3–4 times a day, and for 7–12-year-olds 10 ml 3–4 times a day. The child should then visit his own dentist the following day. Occasionally one can see the abscess pointing into the mouth. The child should be referred to the on-call dental surgeon for treatment.

Mouth and tongue injuries

Lacerations to the mouth and tongue occur after falls or direct blows to the face. Examine the mouth, tongue, and teeth carefully. Despite moderate bleeding the damage may only be slight. Most lacerations involving the oral mucosa can be left without suturing. The parents should be warned that a yellow slough may appear around the laceration. This is a local colonization from the mouth's common flora and does not need treatment. The child should be encouraged to eat normally. Cold foods, i.e. ice-lollies and ice-cream will help numb the pain and reduce swelling. If the laceration extends over the vermilion border this should be very carefully sutured as any slight irregularity will leave an ugly scar. Consider referring the child to the plastic surgeons. If there is a small laceration extending through from the oral mucosa to the skin, then the skin wound should be sutured as normal leaving the mucosal wound open. Large wounds should be referred to the plastic surgeons for suturing of the muscle layer. Lacerations to the tongue only need suturing if the laceration extends over more than one third of its surface, or if there is continued bleeding. The tongue is very difficult to suture and referral to the dental or plastic surgeons may be necessary.

Injuries to the palate may occur, especially if the child falls whilst running with a sharp object in the mouth (see p. 89).

Needlestick injuries

Children may find abandoned needles and suffer a puncture injury. The injury is usually trivial, but parents are usually concerned about the risk of HIV and hepatitis B infections.

The current recommendation is that children who suffer a needlestick injury receive an accelerated course of hepatitis B vaccine.

No prophylaxis is recommended for HIV infection, but serology can be undertaken at 3–6 months post-injury—an initial blood sample should be taken for comparison, after counselling.

It is important to stress to parents that the risk of being infected with either virus from a needlestick injury is extremely small. Both viruses, and especially HIV, are sensitive to extremes of heat and humidity and do not survive to infect in this circumstance.

Eye problems

- **Infections   Foreign bodies in the eye   Conjunctival abrasions   Eye injuries**

Infections

Eye infections are common and may present at any age:

1. Stye—this is a localized infection of the eyelash follicle, usually staphylococcal in origin. There is a small discrete swelling with erythema on the border of one eyelid. If possible, remove the offending eyelash to help the infection drain. Chloramphenicol eye ointment 1 per cent (or Gentamicin 0.3%) should be applied twice a day until the infection resolves. Systemic antibiotics are rarely necessary.

2. Blepharitis—a more generalized swelling of both eyelids may occur. This is often allergic in origin, associated with hay fever or asthma, or allergies to shampoo or soap. The symptoms are relieved by removing the allergen, for example using non-perfumed products, and an antihistamine if the

symptoms are severe. An infective blepharitis also occurs
with crusting of the eyelashes. This should be treated with
chloramphenicol eye ointment 1 per cent (or Gentamicin eye
ointment 0.3%).
3. Conjunctivitis—(see p. 279).
4. Orbital cellulitis—(see p. 279).

Foreign bodies in the eye

The child will say he feels something in his eye. This may be
very painful and there will be a reluctance to open the eye
for examination. It is important to make sure that the child
can keep still so that the eye can be examined under a bright
light. The eyelid should be everted to check for the presence
of a foreign body stuck under the tarsal plate. If there is a
history of a high velocity radio-opaque foreign body entering
the eye, for example hammering metal, then an X-ray should
be taken. If the child is cooperative, using amethocaine eye
drops for analgesia, attempt to remove the foreign body using
a damp cotton wool bud (do not attempt this unless you are
confident in your ability to do so). Small children will need a
general anaesthetic. After removal give the child chloramphenicol eye drops, or ointment, (or Gentamicin 0.3%) for a
few days to prevent infection.

Conjunctival abrasions

Again the child might feel as if there is something in the eye
or have pain in the eye. Stain the eye using fluorescein eye
drops. Any epithelial damage will stain and show up as a
fluorescent green area. Superficial abrasions may be treated
by giving chloramphenicol eye drops (or Gentamicin 0.3%)
and covering the eye with a pad. The lesion should be reviewed and restained after two days, by which time it will
probably have healed. Occasionally a herpetic dendritic
ulcer will be seen on staining. This has a branching appearance. The child should be referred to the ophthalmologists.

Eye injuries

Most eye injuries are potentially serious, especially if there
has been any possibility of a penetrating injury, and should

be referred to the ophthalmologists. An eye patch should be put over the eye to prevent eye movement and analgesics given if necessary.

Head injuries

- **History Examination Investigations Management**

This section describes injuries in the apparently well, conscious child (see also p. 69). Head injuries account for about 10 per cent of child attendances with trauma at an A & E department. Many of these injuries are trivial, but it is important to detect the case which may have a complication.

History

1. Degree of trauma—a useful guide to the potential seriousness of the injury is to assess the forces involved in the accident. Children who have been involved in road traffic accidents, fallen downstairs or fallen from a height are much more likely to have sustained significant brain injury, they may also have other injuries apart from those to the head.
2. Child's condition immediately after the accident—was there a period of unconsciousness? Did the child have a fit? Did he cry immediately? A few seconds loss of consciousness does not affect the child's prognosis. However, loss of consciousness of over a minute suggests a more serious head injury.
3. Vomiting—many children vomit once after almost any degree of head injury. More significant is persistent vomiting.
4. Drowsiness or irritability—ask whether the child has fallen asleep at an unexpected time or whether he has cried excessively or been fretful.
5. Visual symptoms—young children would not complain of double vision but might give some indication that their vision is blurred or different from usual. This is evidence of concussion with an inability of the brain to function normally.
6. Headache—a small child may only indicate the presence

of pain by excessive crying. An older child might complain of a pain in the head.

7. Length of time since the injury—children are sometimes brought days after an injury with a history of being unwell and vomiting. This may be due to a totally unrelated illness (for example otitis media), the symptoms of which the parents relate to the head injury. It is unusual to have a delay of more than a few hours before the symptoms of a head injury occur, hence symptoms occurring several hours or days after the injury may be related to something else. Children fall more frequently when they are ill, and it may be difficult to decide whether the head injury is causing the symptoms.

Examination

1. Assess the child's level of alertness. Bear in mind the time of day, since the child would be likely to be sleepy late at night, or a baby might often be asleep during the day. See how easily the child can be roused if sleepy.

2. Check the cervical spine for any tenderness or restricted movement.

3. Examine the scalp for evidence of injury. Look for lacerations or haematomas. Palpate the area around the injury for tenderness or evidence of bone deformity which might indicate a depressed fracture (this may be masked by haematoma).

4. Check the nose and ears for any evidence of bleeding or fluid leak. If fluid is present it may be CSF and would indicate a fracture of the base of the skull. Also look behind the ears for bruising (Battle's sign) which would also indicate a fracture of the base of the skull.

5. Orientation—an older child can be asked standard questions about time, person, and place.

6. Neurological examination—a full range of tests is not always necessary. Observe the child's limb movements, tone and power, and coordination. Test the limb reflexes. In a small child the parents may be the best guide of the child's behaviour.

7. Pupil reflexes and fundal examination—shine the torch in the child's eye to check for pupil size and reaction. Fundal examination should be performed. Look for papilloedema. This is unlikely to be present in the short-term, even with

raised intracranial pressure. Also examine for retinal haemorrhages which might suggest child abuse (see p. 182).
8. Take the child's temperature and look in the ears and down the throat. Evidence of an underlying upper respiratory tract infection might help explain symptoms which are out of keeping with the degree of trauma. If the child has a temperature or headache give him some paracetamol before sending him to X-ray. The child often looks better when seen later. Continue neurological observation whilst awaiting X-ray.

Investigations

Skull X-ray The following guidelines are suggested by the Royal College of Surgeons:

- Loss of consciousness or amnesia at any time.
- Neurological symptoms or signs.
- Cerebrospinal fluid or blood from nose or ear.
- Suspected penetrating injury or foreign body.
- Scalp bruising or swelling.
- Difficulty in assessing the patient, i.e. very young child.
- Alcoholic intoxication.

A minor scalp laceration is not an indication for X-ray, but a deeper laceration showing periosteum should be X-rayed. In addition, consider X-ray in the following:

- Following substantial trauma, RTA, fall from a height, heavy blow, for example golf club.
- Other findings suggesting basilar skull fracture (haemotypanum, Battle's sign, supraorbital haematoma).
- Depressed area on palpation (ask for tangential views).
- Non-mobile infants, as the likelihood of NAI is higher and accidental injury lower in these infants.
- Children in whom an adequate history is not available.

Brain injury and skull fracture are two separate and sometimes coexistent entities. There may be severe brain injury in an unconscious child with no skull fracture, and conversely most skull fractures will not cause any problems. The presence of a skull fracture is an indicator of possible complications following a head injury. However, children are more likely to suffer complications without a skull fracture than adults as their skulls are softer and may deform causing brain damage without a skull fracture. Babies may become shocked from bleeding into a scalp haematoma (sometimes without a fracture).

Cervical spine X-ray Always consider this with a significant head injury.

CT scan This should be considered in any child with neurological symptoms or signs, or decreasing conscious level (see p. 74).

Management

Criteria for admission following 'minor' head injury
1. Skull fracture.
2. History of loss of consciousness of a minute or more.
3. Drowsiness.
4. Persistent vomiting (many children vomit once or twice after a head injury and then stop; this is not an indication for admission).
5. Neurological symptoms or signs, e.g. severe headache, convulsions.
6. Lack of supervision at home.
7. Clinical evidence of basilar skull fracture.
8. Substantial trauma, e.g. fall from first-floor window.

If the child is alert, has no skull fracture and can be observed overnight by sensible adults then he can be discharged. Sometimes a further short period of observation in the A & E department may be sufficient to make the final decision easier.

If the child is discharged, the parents should be clearly informed about the symptoms and signs to look out for, and when to bring the child back to the A & E department for reassessment. It is useful to reinforce the information with written instructions. The parents should be told to wake the child once or twice in the night to make sure he is rousable. They should return if the child begins vomiting, complains of a headache unrelieved by paracetamol, visual disturbance, or if the child becomes unexpectedly drowsy, unusually irritable, ataxic, or has a convulsion.

CHAPTER 5

Fractures and orthopaedic problems

Key points in fractures and orthopaedic problems

1 Children's injuries differ from adults. They are less likely to sprain a ligament and more likely to sustain a greenstick or avulsion fracture. Radiographs should be taken more readily than in adults.

2 Injuries which involve the growth plate must be treated carefully as later growth disturbance may occur. On the other hand, a greater degree of fracture angulation can be tolerated in children compared to adults as growth will remodel the bone.

3 A limp should be thoroughly assessed as there are several possible underlying causes which may lead to problems if untreated.

Fractures

- **Types of fracture specific to children   Management of fractures**

Children have different types of fractures from adults as growing bones differ from the mature skeleton. Children's bones are less brittle than adult's and often deform to produce buckle or greenstick fractures. Comminuted fractures are unusual. A child's ligaments are relatively stronger but laxer than adults, and so sprains are unusual and growth plate fractures more common. Injuries which involve the growth plate must be treated carefully as they may lead to growth disturbances.

Types of fracture specific to children

Greenstick or buckle fracture This is an incomplete fracture of the bone. The cortex is disrupted on one side and intact on the other. Symptoms and signs are often minor. The fracture may only show as a small irregularity of the cortex on the radiograph. They heal very well, but immobilization in plaster of Paris is usually required for pain relief. Some greenstick fractures can be appreciably deformed and may need reduction.

Growth plate fractures The growth plate is a cartilaginous disc between the epiphysis and metaphysis. Fractures in this area are described according to the Salter–Harris classification (Figure 5.1).

Type I—epiphysis separates completely from the metaphysis.

Type II—the line of fracture travels through much of the plate before passing through the metaphysis and detaching a triangular metaphyseal fragment. This is the commonest injury.

Type III—the fracture line passes along the growth plate for a variable distance before entering the joint through a fracture of the epiphysis. This is very rare.

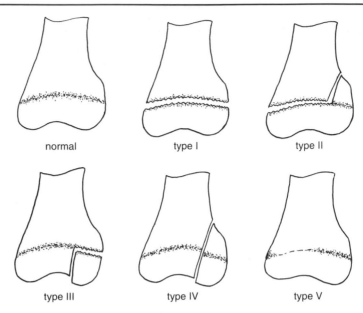

Fig. 5.1 • Salter—Harris classification of epiphyseal fractures in childhood.

Type IV—the fracture line passes from the joint surface across the epiphysis, growth plate, and into the metaphysis.

Type V—These are crush injuries of the growth plate. There is often very little to see on the X-ray at first, but deformity appears months or years later because bone growth has stopped. This type is rare.

Special attention should be paid to Types III and IV because of their intra-articular component.

Other fracture categories are as described in adults:

1. Closed—the skin is intact around the fracture site.
2. Compound—in this case the skin has been breached either from without, when the force causing the break has also broken the skin, or from within, when a sharp bone has pierced through the skin. These fractures are important because of the greater degree of blood loss and the risk of infection.
3. Pathological—the fracture has occurred through an

underlying bone abnormality, for example neoplasm or bone cyst. In these cases the history may suggest a force which would have been insufficient to break a normal bone, or the fracture may have occurred spontaneously.

4. Comminuted—the fracture has caused the bone to fragment into several parts. This may make reduction difficult, but the final healing process is often satisfactory.

Management of fractures

History
1. Assess the degree and nature of the trauma. The history may suggest the likelihood of a fracture, for example a fall from a height or a road traffic accident are likely to produce serious injuries, some of which may not initially be obvious. Knowledge of the actual mechanism of injury, for example whether a rotatory force was applied, may be helpful when reducing the fracture.
2. Pain—the amount of pain the child feels will vary from slight (for example in greenstick fractures) to severe (in many displaced fractures).
3. Function of the affected part—note whether the child can walk on the affected leg or use the damaged arm. Most fractures will lead to a significant loss of function.
4. If a fracture is compound ask about any bleeding apparent at the scene of the accident. There may be considerable blood loss from the broken bone and the surrounding muscles and soft tissues.
5. Ask about tetanus status and drug allergies, particularly in compound injuries where antibiotics and tetanus prophylaxis will be needed.
6. Previous trauma—frequent fractures might lead you to consider non-accidental injury or osteogenesis imperfecta.

Examination
1. Resuscitate the child if needed. Check the general condition, i.e. blood pressure, pulse, pallor, conscious level, especially if the injury is compound.
2. If indicated, i.e. road traffic accident, fall from a height, or possible non-accidental injury, examine the child for other injuries.

3. Tenderness—examine the area very gently, so as not to cause further pain. Palpate around the affected part.

4. Deformity—this may be immediately apparent, but children may have a significant fracture with minimal outward signs.

5. Swelling—the soft tissues surrounding a fracture are usually also damaged. This, with the deformity and bleeding from the fracture itself will cause swelling. With certain fractures, such as a greenstick fracture, there may be little or no swelling.

6. Crepitus and abnormal movement—these may be present at the site of a fracture. However, eliciting these signs is painful and should not be done intentionally.

7. Loss of function—ask the child to move the affected part in all directions. Do not do this if the fracture is obvious.

8. Examine for neurovascular damage distal to the injury. In particular, check and record the distal pulse. If the pulse is absent this indicates that there has been arterial damage and immediate treatment is required. Check and record sensation.

9. Assess soft tissue damage—sometimes the soft tissue element of the bony injury is as significant as the fracture itself. Check for ligamentous damage using a stress test. If a fracture is compound, assess the amount of skin damage and look for muscular tears.

10. Examine the limb and joint above and below the injury site as there may be damage to these areas as well.

X-ray The decision as to whether to X-ray the injured part, or not, can be difficult. There is a need to balance the fact that fractures can occur with minimal clinical signs against the risks and costs of unnecessary radiation. If the history of the degree of trauma is sufficient to cause a fracture in a symptomatic patient then the part should be X-rayed (i.e. RTA, falls downstairs, etc.). If the child shows any one of the clinical signs of a fracture (i.e. tenderness, swelling, loss of function, deformity, crepitus, or abnormal movement) then a radiograph should be taken. Radiographs should usually be taken in two planes. They should include the joint below and the joint above the injury.

Treatment The aims of treatment are to relieve pain and to restore the functional anatomy of the part. Initial splinting will prevent further deformity, provide some relief from pain, and help minimize further blood loss.

1. Resuscitate—some fractures especially those of the femur and compound fractures may bleed significantly and the child will need an intravenous infusion. Treat associated severe or potentially serious injuries first, for example chest, abdominal injuries (see Chapter 3).
2. If there is no distal pulse palpable—immediate action is required. If the limb is deformed then reduction of the fracture may restore the blood flow. This may be done in an emergency in A & E, using Entonox for analgesia. Restoration of circulation is a priority before X-ray. Call for urgent orthopaedic help. Always check the arterial pulses before and after splinting.
3. Immobilize the affected part—for example, a broad arm sling for the forearm, a padded splint for a leg.
4. Analgesia—if necessary this should be given prior to X-ray. In the case of finger injuries, digital nerve block may suffice. An opiate (for example morphine, pethidine) is required for displaced or compound fractures. Paracetamol is usually sufficient for children with greenstick fractures.
5. Reduction—if the fracture is displaced it will need reduction. In most departments this procedure is carried out by orthopaedic staff. Sometimes a minor degree of deformity is acceptable in a younger child who has a greater potential for bone remodelling. The reduction can be closed, usually by simple traction, or open when operative methods are used. Prolonged traction is sometimes needed, for example for fractures of the femoral shaft. Most reductions in children require a general anaesthetic.
6. Maintenance of reduction—the fracture must be held in position until it heals. In some cases, for example a single fracture of a middle metatarsal, there is adequate support from nearby structures without external fixation. Usually plaster of Paris is used. The fracture should be held by plastering the joint above and the joint below the fracture to prevent movement at the fracture site. If the limb is swollen,

a circumferential plaster should not be applied as further swelling may lead to distal ischaemia. In this case the child should be admitted overnight for elevation of the limb and delayed plastering. A half plaster (back slab) is used for temporary support until the swelling diminishes. Whenever a plaster has been applied the patient should be reviewed the following day for a plaster check.

7. If the injury is compound—check tetanus status and give intravenous antibiotics, for example ampicillin plus flucloxacillin, or a cephalosporin. Cover the open wound with a sterile dressing. These injuries should be referred to the orthopaedic department immediately.

8. Follow-up—most patients will be referred to the fracture clinic for follow-up. Local guidelines should be followed.

Management of specific fractures

- Clavicle   Humerus   Elbow: supracondular fracture Elbow: fracture of the lateral condylar epiphysis Elbow: separation of the medial epicondylar epiphysis Fracture of the head and neck of the radius   Elbow effusions   Pulled elbow   Proximal radius and ulna Greenstick fracture of the distal radius and/or ulna Distal radius   Carpal scaphoid   First metacarpal Other metacarpals   Phalangeal injuries   Phalangeal dislocations   Femur   Patella   Proximal tibial spine and tubercle   Tibia and Fibula   Ankle   Os calcis

Clavicle

History This fracture usually occurs after a fall on to the outstretched hand, or a direct blow to the shoulder. The child will have pain on moving his arm and usually holds the shoulder on the affected side forward.

Examination Palpate gently along the clavicle. There will be an area of tenderness, sometimes with a palpable deformity. Movement of the arm will be painful.

X-ray A single radiograph of the clavicle will usually show the fracture, which is often in the middle third of the shaft. There may be some angulation. An undisplaced fracture may not be visible until callus forms around the fracture.

Treatment Most fractures heal very well with symptomatic treatment in a broad arm sling (worn under clothes at first). This should be retained for approximately 2–3 weeks until the child can move the arm without pain. After this, active mobilization can be encouraged. It is helpful to warn the patient that a lump of callus will appear at the site of the fracture and may become prominent, but will gradually diminish.

Humerus

History A fracture to the humerus can be caused by a fall on to the outstretched hand or elbow, or a direct blow to the arm. The child will complain of pain on moving the arm.

Examination The arm will be tender at the fracture site and there may be bruising of the upper arm. Shoulder and elbow movements should be assessed. A spiral fracture of the humerus may damage the radial nerve, hence nerve function should be assessed by checking active extension of the fingers.

X-ray A fracture through the neck of the humerus may occur with fracture separation of the upper humeral epiphysis (a normal epiphysis may be mistaken for a fracture). A fracture of the shaft of the humerus may be spiral or transverse.

Treatment Unless the fracture is displaced (especially at the epiphysis) then immobilization is achieved by using the weight of the arm as traction. The arm should be placed in a collar and cuff type sling.

Occasionally a fractured shaft of humerus may be placed in a U-slab of plaster of Paris for support. The patient should be referred to the fracture clinic for follow-up, the fracture taking about six weeks to heal.

Elbow: supracondular fracture

History This is caused by a fall on to the hand with the elbow bent.

Examination The elbow is usually very swollen and tender with pain on any attempted movement. It is essential to feel the radial pulse and examine the hand for nerve injury.

X-ray The fracture through the distal humerus is usually displaced backwards and twisted inwards. Occasionally the fracture is undisplaced. The fracture line is usually visible and there will be a haemarthrosis as shown by a positive fat pad sign. The fat pad is a radiolucent area seen on the radiograph anterior to the humerus at the elbow. If there is an effusion in the elbow (of either blood or fluid) then the fat line is pushed forward. The lucent line stands out from the humerus. This is known as a positive fat pad sign.

Treatment The main complication of this fracture is Volkmann's ischaemia caused by damage to or kinking of the brachial artery at the elbow. The radial pulse must be checked before and after X-ray and after any manipulation. The child should always be referred to the orthopaedic department on the day of the injury. If the fracture is displaced it will need reduction. An undisplaced fracture can be held in a collar and cuff. The child should be reviewed early in the fracture clinic.

Elbow: fracture of the lateral condylar epiphysis

History This fracture is caused by a fall on to the hand. There may be a description of the elbow dislocating and spontaneously reducing.

Examination The elbow will be swollen. Tenderness will be mainly on the lateral side of the elbow. Movements of the elbow are painful and active wrist dorsiflexion will be limited.

X-ray The wrist dorsiflexors are attached to the lateral condyle. In a complete fracture these usually pull the fractured fragment away from the humerus and, therefore, this may be grossly displaced. Incomplete fractures are more difficult to see as there is little displacement. Comparison films with the other elbow may be useful.

Treatment The displaced fragment needs to be accurately reduced, and, therefore, the child should be referred immediately to the orthopaedic department as open reduction may be needed.

Elbow: separation of the medial epicondylar epiphysis

History Again this fracture is caused by a fall on to the hand. It occurs before the epiphysis is fused, usually in children under 16 years of age. It may be associated with a lateral dislocation of the elbow.

Examination There may be an obvious deformity and swelling. Tenderness will be felt on the medial side. The ulna nerve is likely to be damaged so check sensation in the lateral fingers.

X-ray The medial epicondylar epiphysis may be twisted or shifted downwards. If the elbow has dislocated the epiphyseal fragment may be in the joint. Comparison views with the other elbow are useful (X-ray in the same position as the injured elbow).

Treatment If it is displaced the epiphysis must be reduced and may require operative intervention. The patient should be referred to the orthopaedic surgeons.

Fracture of the head and neck of the radius

History A fall on to the outstreched hand but with the elbow in slight valgus position.

Examination Deformity and swelling are often slight or absent. There will be pain on rotation of the elbow and tenderness on the lateral side.

X-ray The fractured neck of the radius shows as a transverse line distal to the growth plate. The proximal fragment may be tilted. The radial head may show a vertical split, a lateral fragment displaced distally, or a comminuted fracture. There will usually be a positive fat pad sign.

Treatment If undisplaced, the elbow should be rested in a collar and cuff type sling and referred to the fracture clinic. If the head of the radius is tilted more than 15 degrees or if there is a large displaced fragment, the child should be referred for manipulation under general anaesthetic.

Elbow effusions

The child presents with a history of a fall on to the elbow or outstretched hand. The elbow may be swollen. There will be generalized or local tenderness. Movements will be restricted. X-rays show a positive fat pad sign, but no fracture can initially be detected. About a third of cases will eventually turn out to have a fracture not detectable on the original X-rays. Other causes are a haemarthrosis or traumatic effusion. Rarely, the trauma is a precipitating or exacerbating factor for another cause of joint swelling, for example septic arthritis. Any child with an elbow effusion should be treated with a collar and cuff and reviewed in an A & E department or fracture clinic to further assess the elbow and to check for recovery of movement.

Pulled elbow

This usually occurs in children under 5 years of age, (usually 1–3 years). The presenting symptom in this condition is that the child will not use his arm. He may complain of pain in the shoulder, elbow, or wrist. The parents may be worried that the arm is dislocated or broken.

The diagnosis is suggested by the history. There has usually been a pull or fall involving the arm. Often the child has nearly fallen and an adult has held the arm to help pull the child up. The child then stops using his arm and holds it to his side. The mechanism of the injury is that the radial head (being poorly formed at this age) has slipped through the annular liagment at the elbow. A pulled elbow is very easily reduced by flexing the elbow to 90 degrees and then supinating the forearm while extending the elbow. Usually a 'click' can be felt or heard and the child then starts using his arm normally. The arm need not be X-rayed unless there is any doubt that the child may have actually fallen or sustained direct trauma to the arm. A pulled elbow will look normal on a radiograph. The child may not always start using the arm immediately, especially if there has been some delay before reduction. Allow the child to play in the A & E department before reassessing. Most children will have recovered within half an hour. If the child is still not using the arm then put the arm in a collar and cuff sling and review the child the following day. Warn parents that a pulled elbow may recur (in either arm) but that the child will grow out of the problem. There will be no long-term sequelae. Ask them to avoid pulling on the child's arms.

Proximal radius and ulna

History These fractures are caused by a fall or a direct blow to the forearm.

Examination The fracture is usually obvious as there will be a deformity with swelling and tenderness of the forearm. Examine the hand for neurovascular damage.

X-ray The bones may break at the same or different levels either transversely or obliquely. There may be a degree of angulation. The fracture is often of the greenstick type with one side of the bone having an intact periosteum.

Treatment The fracture may need reduction. This will depend on the degree of angulation and the age of the child. The reduction will need to be done under general anaesthesia. Refer the child to the orthopaedic team for advice. In undisplaced fractures, or after reduction, an above elbow plaster will be applied. The child will often need to be admitted to hospital as the arm may become swollen and will need elevation.

NB Single fractures of the radius or ulna are unusual. In these cases always look for a possible dislocation at one or other radio–ulnar joints. Examples of these fractures are a Monteggia fracture, with a fracture of the upper third of the ulna and dislocation of the head of the radius, or a Galeazzi fracture, with a fracture of the lower third of the radius and a dislocation of the inferior radio–ulnar joint.

Greenstick fracture of the distal radius and/or ulna

History There will have been a fall on to the outstretched hand. Sometimes there may be a delay in presentation as the signs are often minimal.

Examination There may be some swelling of the wrist, but this is usually minimal. There will be some tenderness to palpation and wrist movements are reduced.

X-ray X-ray will show an angulation of the cortex of one or both bones. This may be detected in one plane only.

Treatment These fractures would probably heal well without any treatment. However, application of a plaster of Paris back slab will give pain relief and will protect the damaged bone from further trauma.

Distal radius

History A fall on to the dorsiflexed hand will have occurred.

Examination The wrist is often very swollen and there may be an obvious deformity. Check the neurovascular status of the hand.

X-rays This injury may be a fracture separation of the lower radial epiphysis. The epiphysis is shifted and tilted backwards and/or radially. There may also be a fracture of the radial metaphysis. The fracture may also occur without displacement, but there is a crushing element to the radial epiphysis. This is more difficult to detect but is important as it affects the growth of the arm.

Treatment Displaced fractures need to be reduced accurately under general anaesthesia. Some degree of displacement may be acceptable without reduction depending on the age of the child. Always seek advice about this.

Carpal scaphoid

History This fracture is caused by a fall on to the outstretched hand. It is an unusual fracture in small children, but may occur in adolescents.

Examination The wrist may look normal. Occasionally there is some swelling. Palpate carefully for tenderness in the anatomical snuff box. There may be pain on hyperextension of the wrist.

X-rays These should be taken in several planes as the fracture is usually undisplaced and difficult to detect (ask specifically for scaphoid views). The fracture is usually across the waist of the scaphoid, but the proximal pole or tubercle may also be damaged. The fracture line may be easier to detect on re-X-ray 10–14 days after the injury.

Treatment The main complication of a fractured waist of the scaphoid is avascular necrosis of the distal part as this receives its blood supply from the proximal segment which is disrupted by the fracture. The wrist needs to be adequately supported in a scaphoid cast to help the fracture heal. If a fracture is suspected clinically from the history and examination the wrist should be put in a full forearm cast even if the radiographic findings are inconclusive. Review in fracture clinic. Re-X-ray in 10–14 days time may show the healing fracture.

First metacarpal

History This fracture is often due to a punching injury.

Examination There is usually swelling and tenderness around the site. The thumb may look shortened and movement will be extremely limited.

X-ray Two main types of fracture occur:

1. Transverse fracture distal to the carpometacarpal joint. The distal portion may be displaced and/or impacted.
2. Fracture dislocation occurs with an oblique fracture extending into the joint. This fracture is unstable.

Treatment The fracture should be reduced under general anaesthesia and held in a Bennett's plaster. The child will be referred to the orthopaedic department for this treatment.

Other metacarpals

History A direct blow to the hand or a twisting or punching injury is described.

Examination The hand is often bruised and swollen. If the fracture involves the metacarpal necks there may be a visible lump. There will be a tenderness at the fracture site. Assess the movement of the fingers to check for any rotational deformity.

X-rays These may show a fracture of one or more of the metacarpals. The fractures may be spiral or transverse. A fractured neck of metacarpal is usually transverse, but the metacarpal head may be angulated.

Treatment Undisplaced or slightly displaced fractures need no treatment and active movements of the fingers should be encouraged. The patient may wear a simple support bandage for a few days. Displaced fractures may need reduction and should be referred. Fractures of several metacarpals may need firmer splintage with plaster, and advice should be sought.

Phalangeal injuries

History Finger injuries can be sustained in many different ways, i.e. direct blow, angulation force, or stubbing of the finger, often in ball sports.

Examination The finger is often swollen and tender. Look for any angulation or rotation of the finger. This is best assessed by asking the child to make a fist when rotation will become more apparent. Examine each joint affected by applying a lateral stress to the joint to check for ligamentous damage.

X-rays These will confirm the site of the fracture, any degree of angulation, and any joint involvement. Small chip fractures adjacent to a joint should not be ignored as they may indicate a significant injury.

Treatment If there is no angulation or rotation then most fractures can be simply treated by strapping the two adjacent fingers together (neighbour strapping). This provides lateral support but allows joint movement to prevent stiffness. A follow-up appointment at 7–10 days should be arranged to check for any development of rotational deformity. Spiral or angulated fractures should be referred to the orthopaedic department.

Phalangeal dislocations

History There will have been direct trauma to the finger.

Examination The dislocation is usually obvious. Check for circulation in the distal part of the finger.

X-ray This will show the dislocation and any associated fracture.

Treatment Reduce the dislocation as soon as possible by simple traction and manipulation using a digital nerve block for anaesthesia. Check for ligamentous stability after reduction. Strap the affected finger to its neighbour and arrange a follow-up appointment.

Femur

History The force required to fracture a femur is usually severe, for example during a road traffic accident. Infants may sustain a fracture with a lesser degree of force. A spiral fracture may be caused by a fall when the foot is stationary, whilst a twisting force is applied to the femur.

Examination There is usually mid-thigh swelling with some deformity. The child will be unable to walk on the leg. Check the peripheral pulses.

X-ray This will show the fracture site, type, and the degree of deformity.

Treatment Assess the child carefully for other injuries. Intravenous fluid replacement may be required as significant amounts of blood can be lost into the thigh. Insert an intravenous cannula and take blood for grouping in case transfusion is necessary. Give suitable analgesia, for example parenteral pethidine or morphine before X-ray or moving the limb. As soon as possible (before X-ray) the leg should be placed in a traction splint. The traditional treatment is using skin traction in a Thomas's splint. The distal pulses should be checked after application of the splint. The patient should always be admitted. The fracture is usually treated with skin traction, but occasionally an open reduction is considered.

Patella

History There is usually a significant fall, a direct blow, or crushing injury to the knee.

Examination The knee is swollen and will be held flexed. Movement will be painful. Ask the child to raise the leg to check whether the extensor muscles are functioning.

X-ray The patella may fracture without displacement.

Sometimes several comminuted fractures are present. Do not confuse a fracture with a bipartate patella in which a radiolucent line running obliquely across the upper outer corner of the patella is shown on X-ray. This is a normal finding.

Treatment Refer the child to the orthopaedic surgeons. The child will often need admission for treatment. If the fracture is displaced, open reduction and fixation may be necessary. A dislocated patella should be referred to the orthopaedic surgeons. A plaster cast is often applied after reduction.

Proximal tibial spine and tubercle

History Fractures of the tibial spine occur after a hyper-extension injury to the knee. In adults this is more likely to tear the anterior cruciate ligament. The extensor muscles of the knee are inserted into the tibial tubercle, and if resisted extension of the knee occurs the tubercle may be avulsed.

Examination The knee is held flexed and is swollen. There will be a haemarthrosis. The knee cannot be extended.

X-ray On a lateral view, the avulsed tibial spine will be seen elevated from its usual position. A fractured tibial epiphysis is often displaced forward. The patella will be high.

Treatment Some fractures may need reduction and the associated haemarthrosis aspirated. They should all be referred to the orthopaedic department.

Tibia and Fibula

History These bones can be fractured by a twisting force applied to the leg whilst the foot is stationary, as in a fall or by direct trauma.

Examination There may be obvious deformity after severe trauma. Palpate for tenderness down the shafts of both bones. Check the neurovascular status of the foot by testing sensation, palpating the distal pulse, and asking the patient to move his toes.

X-rays These must include the ankle and knee joint. The fracture can be spiral or transverse. Both bones or the tibia alone may be affected. Assess the degree of angulation, if any.

Treatment The fracture may need reduction. Injuries to the lower leg may cause a compartment syndrome in which the post-traumatic swelling compromises the vascular supply to the foot. Because of this risk these patients should be referred to the orthopaedic surgeons with a view to admission for elevation and observation of the limb. The fracture will usually be held by an above knee plaster of Paris unless the fracture has needed open fixation.

Ankle

History An inversion injury, similar to that which might cause a sprain, or a direct blow to the ankle are usually described. The child may have fallen from a height. Ask if the child can bear weight on the ankle.

Examination Look for any swelling of the ankle. Palpate gently for bony tenderness (if this is present a radiograph is necessary). Assess the stability of the ankle joint by putting a gentle inversion and eversion stress on the ankle (this may be too painful to confirm accurately). Pulling the foot forward on the ankle will also give an indication of stability. Check the peripheral pulses and ask the child to move his toes. Look for skin breaks.

X-rays These should be taken in two planes as an undisplaced fracture may show on one view only. Check the ankle mortise. If there is any degree of widening on one side this may indicate an unstable fracture and should be referred.

Treatment An undisplaced fracture can be put in a below knee plaster of Paris and reviewed the following day in fracture clinic. Any fracture with displacement should be referred to the orthopaedic surgeons.

Os calcis

History The child will have fallen from a height, for example jumped off a wall. He will be unable to bear weight on the foot.

Examination The heel may be bruised and swollen. There

will be tenderness to palpation and ankle movements may be painful. Always check the lumbar spine, as a fracture here may be caused by similar trauma to that which would cause an os calcis fracture.

X-rays Ask for os calcis views. The type of fractures seen are chip fractures, crush fractures, or a split fracture of the os calcis.

Treatment As the heel becomes very swollen initially and is painful to walk on, most cases are admitted for elevation and plaster of Paris applied when the swelling has diminished.

Sprains

- **Sprained ankle   Knee injuries**

A sprain is a stretch or tear of a ligament, commonly occurring around the ankle, although this term may be used to describe finger, wrist, or shoulder injuries. Sprains are less common in children than in adults because the young child's ligaments are extremely strong and the trauma instead causes damage to the bony attachment of the ligament around the epiphyseal plate. It is, therefore, more important in children when a sprain is suspected that the associated bone is X-rayed.

Sprained ankle

The usual mechanism is an inversion injury to the ankle (the child usually says he went over on his ankle) which may or may not have caused a fall. A stress is put on the lateral talo–fibular ligament and occasionally the anterior ligament. This results in the stretching or tearing of the ligament, and there may also be damage to the bony attachments to the fifth metatarsal or lateral malleolus.

History Ask about the exact details of the injury. This will help in assessing which ligaments may be involved and the type of injury which may be seen. Is the child able to bear weight? This will help indicate the severity of the injury.

Ask about the child's interest in sport. A sprained ankle in a child who is in a competitive sport may have significant implications for the child's training and achievements.

Examination

1. Swelling—the degree of swelling is not an indication of the severity of the sprain. It will depend on many factors, such as the length of time since the injury (most swelling occurs after 24–48 hours), the amount of walking done, and whether the ankle has been held dependent.
2. Bony tenderness—feel for the ligamentous insertions and the bones around the ankle. Bony tenderness is a definite indication for X-ray.
3. Stability—by putting a lateral stress on the ankle joint the amount of 'give' compared with the uninjured ankle can be assessed. However, this may be too painful to be performed adequately. A useful test is the anterior draw test, when holding the ankle with one hand the foot is held and pulled forward. This causes little pain and it is easier to compare the amount of forward 'give' with the normal ankle.

Management Most ankle injuries in children should be X-rayed as there may be an associated fracture. If the child cannot bear weight the ankle must be X-rayed (if there is a fracture see p. 127). Occasionally a small fragment of bone is seen on X-ray just distal to the lateral malleolus. This is an avulsion fracture and should be treated as a severe sprain rather than a more serious fracture. If the ankle appears unstable then orthopaedic referral is needed. The possibilities for treatment are operative repair (rarely needed), immobilization in a plaster case, or active mobilization. If the ankle is stable then the aim is to encourage the child back to full mobility as soon as possible. A firm support bandage, i.e a tubular elastic bandage is helpful initially as the child will feel more able to walk on the leg. If the ankle is very swollen then the leg should be elevated above hip height for periods during the day, for example 1 hour three times a day. A cold compress helps to relieve the swelling. Encourage the child to walk on the ankle as soon as possible. Sporting activities should be delayed until the child has no limp, then restarted gradually.

Knee injuries

Serious knee injuries are more often a problem for the adolescent than the smaller child. Sometimes an underlying abnormality, i.e. Osgood–Schlatter's disease, chondromalacia patellae, is precipitated or becomes apparent following an injury.

History It is important to gain an accurate description of the mechanism of injury as this indicates the most likely component of the knee to be damaged, i.e. a twisting injury on a fixed lower leg would indicate a meniscal injury.

1. Time elapsed since injury—the knee will often become swollen. If this occurs rapidly it would indicate bleeding into the knee. A slower rate of swelling is more suggestive of post-traumatic oedema.
2. Previous knee symptoms—might indicate an underlying knee problem.
3. Sporting history.
4. Previous medical history—haemophiliacs may present with a swollen knee due to haemathrosis.

Examination
1. Look at the knee for evidence of swelling, deformity, and note the position the knee is held in.
2. Palpate the knee. Feel for areas of tenderness which would indicate regions of damage, for example the joint line or ligamentous insertions.
3. Check for swelling. Is there an intra-articular effusion? Test this by feeling for an area of fluctuation around the patella or a patellar tap. There may be extra-articular swelling.
4. Put the knee through its usual range of movements both actively and passively, the knee should be able to be fully extended and should flex until the heel of the foot touches the thigh.
5. Test for any degree of adduction or abduction with the knee straight. Compare with the other knee. There is usually only a minimal degree of give. Any more than this indicates ligamentous laxity. Repeat with the knee flexed to 30 degrees, again testing the medial and lateral ligaments.

6. Flex the knee to approximately 90 degrees and pull the tibia forward from the femur to check for anterio–posterior glide. This would indicate damage to the anterior cruciates (again compare with the other knee).

7. Rotate the lower leg with knee flexed to different positions. If this is painful it may indicate meniscal damage. Ask the child to raise the leg with the knee in full extension. This assesses the quadriceps expansion and patellar tendon function.

Management Unless the injury is thought to be trivial an X-ray should be requested. Fractures are often difficult to detect clinically and other conditions, for example Osgood–Schlatter's disease may also be diagnosed. Indications for immediate orthopaedic referral:

- Avulsion of tibial tubercle.
- Moderate to large effusion.
- Any degree of instability of the knee.
- Bony abnormality.
- Inability to bear weight.
- Inability to fully extend the knee.

These may indicate serious intra-articular pathology which are best assessed soon after the injury.

If none of the above signs are present, then the knee should be supported in an elasticated tubular bandage (usually used double). Crutches may be used if the child has difficulty bearing weight. The child should be reviewed in about 5–7 days time in the A & E department or fracture clinic.

The limping child

- **Important points in the history**   **Examination**
  Investigations   Referral   Osteochondritis

A common problem in the Accident and Emergency department is a child who develops a limp or gait abnormality. In many of these cases no cause is found and normal gait recovers spontaneously. However, there are several conditions which need to be considered:

- Soft tissue or bony trauma.
- Irritable hip.
- Osteomylitis.
- Septic arthritis.
- Perthes' disease.
- Slipped femoral epiphysis.
- Neuromuscular disorder, for example Guillain–Barré disease (p. 264), cerebellar ataxia.

The history and examination should be directed at confirming or excluding the above conditions.

Important points in the history

1. The age of child—some conditions are more likely to occur in certain age groups, for example slipped femoral epiphysis usually occurs in adolescents. Irritable hip is more common in children under 7 years of age.

2. History of recent trauma—this will suggest soft tissue or bony damage as a cause of the limp. However, underlying conditions are sometimes unmasked by trauma or, since children often fall, the parents may recall a minor injury which they think is the cause of the problem.

3. History of recent illness (for example sore throat or viral infection). An irritable hip is thought to follow a viral infection two to three weeks previously. A superficial infection may suggest secondary osteomylitis or septic arthritis. Rubella often causes a mild transient arthritis which may present as a limp.

4. How long has the child been limping?—a history of several days duration might indicate a condition with slow onset, for example Perthes' disease, whereas septic arthritis is more acute.

5. Previous medical/surgical problems—a history of osteogenesis imperfecta would obviously lead to an examination for fractures. In a haemophiliac child one might expect to find a haemarthrosis.

Examination

Examine both legs completely. A limp may be caused by problems with any area from the foot to the hips. Observe the child lying down and the position in which the leg is held. Look for areas of swelling and redness. Palpate the whole leg for tenderness. Examine the knee, testing for an effusion. If an effusion is present, is the knee warm or cool? Put the knee through active and passive flexion and extension. Examine the hip for areas of warmth or redness. Carefully assess flexion, extension, internal and external rotation, and abduction and adduction of the leg. Note if the movements are painful or limited. Watch the gait if the child is able to walk. In addition note the following:

1. Child's temperature—if the child is systematically ill then this would suggest an infectious cause for the limp, such as osteomylitis or septic arthritis. (A normal temperature does not exclude these conditions.)
2. Child's general condition—look for evidence of other affected joints which may indicate an arthropathy.
3. Look for evidence of other injuries or bruising—bear in mind the possibility of non-accidental injury.
4. Examine the child neurologically—depressed lower limb reflexes will suggest Guillain–Barré syndrome.

Investigations

X-ray both hips and any other area of the limb in which bony damage is clinically suspected. The hip X-ray in irritable hip may show widening of the joint space, although this is better demonstrated on ultrasound. Look carefully at the femoral epiphysis for the ragged appearance of Perthe's disease and the appearance of a slipped femoral epiphysis. Also, take blood for:

- a white cell count and ESR (or equivalent), and
- blood cultures if the child is pyrexial.

Note These may all be normal in early osteomylitis or septic arthritis.

Referral

Most children should be referred to the orthopaedic department for further assessment and possible admission. The child may only be allowed home if no abnormality has been found on examination, the child is apyrexial and has a normal blood count, and the radiographs appear normal. However, he must be reviewed in 24 hours.

Irritable hip This occurs mainly in children under five years of age. There may be a history of a viral illness 2–3 weeks prior to the limp developing. The child is usually quite well, but has a definite limp. There is usually some limitation of hip rotation, but there may be very little else to find on examination. X-rays may show an effusion and blood tests should be normal. An ultrasound scan will show the effusion well. Treatment is to rest the limb and sometimes traction. The child may need admission.

Perthes' disease This is a form of osteochondritis of the femoral head which usually occurs in children 5–10 years of age. The onset may be gradual. There is no systemic upset. On examination there will often be limitation of movement, especially abduction and internal rotation. X-rays (include a 'frog' position) may show distinctive features, such as flattening, fragmentation, or increased density of the femoral head. Compare both femoral heads on X-ray. The child should be referred to the orthopaedic department.

Slipped upper femoral epiphysis This condition occurs in older children, usually from 10–15-years-old. The child may be overweight. There may be a history of trauma. On examination there is usually reduction in abduction and internal rotation. X-rays should be taken with a lateral or 'frog' view of the hip. (The A/P view may be normal). This will show the epiphyseal slip. Surgical intervention treatment may be needed and the child should be referred to the orthopaedic surgeons.

Osteomyelitis and infective arthritis Infection can occur in any age group and is potentially very serious. The child may be toxic and pyrexial with a raised white cell count and ESR (but these may also be normal). Examination will show the leg to be held externally rotated and abducted and the child will be reluctant to move it. Radiographs are initially normal. The child should always be admitted. In the early stages there may be few clinical signs. Later, local pain and tenderness develop.

Osteochondritis

The osteochondritides are a group of conditions in which there is abnormality of a growing area of bone. They present with pain around the region with some loss of function. The areas commonly involved are:

- Metatarsals   —Freiberg disease
- Navicular   —Kohlers disease
- Lunate   —Kienbock disease
- Capitulum   —Panner's disease
- Tibial tuberosity   —Osgood–Schlatter's disease
- Calcaneum   —Sever's disease

(Osgood–Schlatter's disease may also be due to a traction apophysitis.)

In these areas rapid growth is thought to occur with some resulting deficiency in the blood supply to the bone. Radiographs of the area may show deformity, fragmentation, or increased bone density. In most cases symptoms resolve with rest, but referral should be made for an out-patient orthopaedic opinion.

Osteochondritis dessicans is a particular form of osteochondritis when a fragment of bone actually separates from the main bone. This occurs particularly around the distal femur. In this case the bone may need to be fixed surgically and the patient should be referred.

Arthritis

- **History   Examination   Investigations   Treatment**

A child may present with one or more swollen joints. Commonly fingers, knees, or ankles are involved.

Common causes are trauma and infection, less frequently juvenile arthritis is found.

History

1. Age of child—most of these conditions can present at any age.
2. History of trauma—this would suggest an injury as the cause of the swelling. However, as children often fall, the swelling may incorrectly be ascribed to the injury. A history of trauma does not, therefore, exclude other diagnoses.
3. Time since onset–swelling following trauma usually occurs fairly rapidly. Swelling due to sepsis comes on more slowly but still has an acute time-span. In cases of arthropathy the swelling may have been present for several days or weeks.
4. Single or multiple joint involvement—arthritis is the likely diagnosis when more than one joint is involved. The pattern and type of joints affected also help diagnose the type of arthritis present.
5. Previous joint problems—again this might indicate an arthropathy.
6. Recent illnesses, for example exanthema, viral infection, sepsis. Rubella is frequently followed by an arthralgia in older children. This may also occur after rubella vaccination. Meningococcal infection may also be associated with an arthropathy.
7. Rash—this may be associated with some rheumatological conditions. A child with Henoch–Schonlein purpura usually has arthritis (p. 276).
8. Easy bruising or excessive bleeding—consider a bleeding disorder.
9. Diarrhoea—occasionally a reactive arthritis follows an episode of diarrhoea.
10. Eye symptoms—iritis and uveitis are associated with arthritis. The eye will be painful with some photophobia.

Examination

1. Examine the joint involved. In particular look for a joint effusion or generalized tissue swelling. Feel for warmth and

look for redness. Put the joint through a full range of movements to assess function.

2. Examine other joints for similar signs.

3. Assess the child's general condition. Take the temperature and feel the pulse rate. A child with osteomyelitis or septic arthritis may be pyrexial and toxic (although occasionally there are no systemic features). Children with rheumatoid arthritis may also be systemically ill.

4. Look for rashes.

Investigations

1. The joint involved may need an X-ray. Look for fractures. Sometimes a joint effusion may be apparent. In osteomyelitis there may be no initial X-ray changes, but later there is patchy rarefaction of the metaphysis and a periostitis which shows as a thin line parallel to the shaft. Later still, as healing occurs, there is sclerosis and new periosteal bone.

2. White cell count, ESR (or equivalent), and rheumatoid factors may be taken.

3. Other investigations as indicated, for example blood cultures.

Treatment

Trauma The commonest cause of swelling is trauma. If infection and arthritis have been excluded then the affected part needs to be rested and splinted. The patient should be reviewed in 48 hours, then active mobilization should be encouraged.

Osteomyelitis or septic arthritis usually the child is ill with a raised temperature, a rapid pulse, a leukocytosis, and a raised ESR. Occasionally, especially in the early stages, the child may look misleadingly well. If infective causes are suspected, the child must be admitted. The child holds the part very still. It will look more red and swollen as the disease progresses. Tenderness is felt over the bony metaphysis. In septic arthritis the child will not move the joint because of spasm. The child should be referred to the paediatric or orthopaedic department immediately for further investigation and treatment. Delay in treatment may lead to chronic osteomyelitis, altered bone length, suppurative arthritis, or metastatic infection.

Arthritis Juvenile arthritis can present in several forms and as it is unusual may be overlooked for some time. Early recognition is important as treatment may prevent later disability. The presentation may be with single or multiple joint involvement, or a series of joints over a period of time. The systemic form occurs in younger children. There is a rash and generalized toxic symptoms: joint involvement is not always initially apparent. Transient arthritis can also occur after a viral illness, in particular rubella. This may also occur 2–3 weeks after rubella immunization. Arthritis with a purpuric rash on the lower limbs is Henoch–Schonlein purpura (p. 276). The child with suspected arthritis should be referred to the paediatricians for investigation and treatment.

Sickle cell crises (see p. 284)

Further reading

1. MacRae, R. (1989). *Practical fracture treatment*, (2nd edn). Churchill Livingstone, Edinburgh.
2. Grech, P. (1981). *Casualty radiology*. Chapman and Hall, London.
3. Keats, T. E. (1988). *Atlas of normal roentgenographic variants that may simulate disease* (4th edn). Year Book Medical Publishers, Chicago.

Burns and scalds

Key points in burns and scalds

1 Thermal injuries may be extremely painful and analgesia should be a priority after resuscitation.

2 Children with injuries of over 10% of their body surface always require admission and intravenous fluids.

3 Inhalation injury is potentially fatal and its possibility should be actively considerd.

4 Even trivial burns should be followed up as they may develop complications.

5 Consider the possibility of non-accidental injury.

Epidemiology

- **First aid treatment**

Burns and scalds are the commonest cause of accidental death in children in England and Wales after road traffic accidents. Most deaths are the result of house fires, and many victims are under 5 years of age since they are incapable of making their own escape. The main causes of house fires are:

- matches found and used by children,
- cigarettes discarded by adults, and
- faulty room heaters.

The immediate cause of death in house fires is usually suffocation due to the reduction in ambient oxygen, carbon monoxide poisoning, and toxic smoke emitted from burning household furnishings.

Scalds are a common cause of admission to a burns unit or attendance at an A & E department. Scalds and contact burns are especially common in the under 5-year-olds.

Burns from playing with matches, fires, or flammable liquids are commoner in older children, especially boys.

First aid treatment

A parent who telephones the A & E department for advice on the emergency management of a minor burn or scald, should be advised to run cold water over the affected part for five minutes, cover the wound with a clean, non-fluffy dressing such as a tea-towel or pillowcase, and bring the child to the A & E department. No creams or ointments should be used.

Initial assessment of the patient

- **Cardiopulmonary status   Pain relief   Area of injury Thickness of burn   Note sites of burn   Site intravenous infusion   History   Other injuries**

- Assess cardiopulmonary status—especially the airway and breathing.

- Pain relief.
- Take history of the injury and patient's previous medical history.
- Note sites of burn.
- Assess area of burn.
- Site intravenous infusion (if a major burn or scald).
- Exclude other injuries.
- Weigh the patient.
- Insert urethral catheter (if a major burn or scald).

Cardiopulmonary status

If the patient is shocked or in respiratory failure, as shown by a weak, rapid pulse, low blood pressure, poor capillary return, depressed conscious level, respiratory difficulty, or cyanosis, then cardiopulmonary resuscitation as described in Chapter 2 should be instituted. Few patients, even with major burns, will be shocked on arrival but they can deteriorate quickly. At least hourly observations of pulse, respiration rate, blood pressure, and urine output should be made. Early intubation may be needed in victims of fires, inhalation of steam, or scalds or burns of the face and mouth (see inhalation injury p. 148).

Pain relief

Burns and scalds are extremely painful and pain relief is a priority. Patients with major burns (over 10 per cent body surface area) will need intravenous morphine (0.1 mg/kg) provided there is no contra-indication such as a history of head injury. This dose can be repeated if the child is still in pain. The injection should be given slowly, preferably into an infusion. Intramuscular morphine is poorly absorbed in the severely injured child but can be used after small burns if there is severe pain and distress. Patients with minor burns should be given oral analgesics, such as paracetamol 10 mg/kg, and cold compresses applied to the wound whilst the burn is being assessed.

History

A detailed history of the thermal injury and the patient's past medical history should be sought. Full details of the accident, including the time at which it occurred are important in assessing the severity of the injury and in assessing fluid requirements. Information may be gained from relatives, ambulancemen, and firemen.

The current tetanus immunization status should be noted. If the circumstances of the history are inconsistent with the extent or degree of the burn the possibility of child abuse should be considered (see Chapter 8).

Area of injury

The size of the burn should be assessed using Table 6.1 and Figure 6.1. It is important that this is done accurately, as it will determine the amount of intravenous fluid given, and whether or not the child is admitted to hospital or to a specialist burns unit. Table 6.1 gives the relative dimensions, at different ages, of the areas of skin shown in Figure 6.1. It will be noted that the relative proportion of head size diminishes as the child grows, while that of the leg assumes a higher percentage. One side of a child's palm and closed fingers cover approximately 1 per cent of his body surface area.

Table 6.1 • Assessment of burned/scalded area in per cent of total surface area

	0	1	5	10	15 years of age
A = ½ head	9½	8½	6½	5½	4½
B = ½ thigh	2¾	3¼	4	4½	4½
C = ½ lower leg	2½	2½	2¾	3	3¼

Burns covering greater than 10 per cent of the child's body surface are classed as major burns.

Thickness of burn

Treatment of the burned patient will depend not only on the extent of the injury but also on the depth of skin damaged. Thermal injuries are classified into superficial, partial thickness, full thickness, and deep dermal burns. Superficial

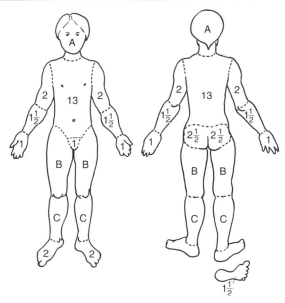

Fig. 6.1 • Lund–Brouder chart for assessment of burned or scalded area.

burns are those with erythema only. The skin is bright red and painful. The burn heals well within a few days without scarring (for example sunburn). Partial thickness burns are those in which the top layer of skin has been destroyed but the dermis remains intact. The skin looks red and blisters will appear. Some blisters may be apparent immediately, but further blisters may develop over the next 24 hours. These are painful. The wounds usually heal well in about two weeks. Full thickness burns are those in which the dermis has been destroyed. The dermis includes the layer of cells from which skin is formed, and contains hair follicles and nerve endings. As these are destroyed the wound will heal with scarring and will be painless. The burn usually looks white or black. The child may not appear to be in pain. These burns heal very slowly as they have to heal from the edges of the wound. Depending on the area involved and the size of the burn these burns need skin grafting. Deep dermal burns occur where part of the dermis has been destroyed leaving islands of skin cells. Burns which are deep dermal when initially seen may be converted to full thickness burns over a period time as the residual cells may not survive owing to a poor blood supply or infection. Deep dermal burns are usually red, but blisters do not form easily. They are difficult to diagnose and initially should be treated as partial thickness burns. Skin grafting is usually done after a few days when further assessment of the burn takes place.

Note sites of burn

The site of the burn will influence the management of the child. Facial burns are serious, firstly because they indicate potential airway burns, and secondly because they may result in distressing scarring. Burns to the hands may cause problems, as scarring over joints can lead to contractures, and damage to the skin of the fingers will lead to loss of sensation. Burns to the genitalia are difficult to manage and frequently get infected.

Site intravenous infusion

If the burn is greater than 10 per cent of the body surface area then fluid replacement will be required and an i.v. infusion should be set up. The cannula can be inserted through burnt skin if an alternative suitable site cannot be found. The line can be used to give analgesia as well as fluid replacement.

Other injuries

Especially in burns from house fires or electrical burns, there may be additional trauma caused by the patient jumping or being thrown from a height. If the history of the injury or the circumstances in which the child was found suggest this, then examination as described in Chapter 3 (major trauma) should be carried out. Special attention should be paid to head injury and cervical spine injury. The child's weight should be accurately measured, as this will be used to calculate infusion volumes and drug doses.

As urine output will be an important indicator of the child's fluid balance, urine must be collected. The child will not be mobile for toileting and it is necessary to avoid 'accidents' around the burn area.

Major burns and scalds

- **Monitoring   Investigations   Treatment of the wound Indication for referral of burns or scalds**

All children whose burned or scalded area is 10 per cent or more of their total body surface are considered to have a major burn however superficial the burn depth may appear. All these patients require intravenous colloid in addition to normal maintenance fluids. All burns, whatever their depth, are a cause of water, protein, and heat loss. *Senior help should be requested immediately.*

In the first four hours after the burn children with burns over 10 per cent body surface area should receive plasma, 5 per cent human albumin solution, or a colloid solution, for example haemaccel, according to the following formula:

$$\text{plasma amount (ml)} = \frac{\% \text{ burn} \times \text{weight (kg)}}{2}$$

i.e. for a 20 per cent burn in a 15 kg child 150 ml of plasma would be required.

This fluid should be infused over the first four hours after the accident. If there has been delay in bringing the patient to hospital the calculated amount should be given more rapidly so that the fluid is infused before the end of the first four hours following the injury.

In addition to this the patient's normal maintenance requirements should be given as 4 per cent dextrose with 0.18 per cent normal saline intravenously, or if the child is well enough, as oral drinks. Over the first four hours the maintenance fluid requirement will be 25 ml/kg.

Monitoring

1. Blood pressure, pulse, respiration rate, and mental status should be monitored at least hourly to observe for signs of circulatory collapse.
2. The urine output should be kept to at least 1 ml/kg/h and fluids adjusted accordingly. The placement of a urinary

catheter is almost always necessary. (Keep a urine sample to be tested for specific gravity.)
3. Core temperature should be monitored.

Investigations

The following investigations should be taken at presentation on all children with greater than 10 per cent burns:

1. Haemoglobin and haematocrit.
2. Blood group (cross-match for large burns).
3. Urea and electrolytes.
4. In patients who are shocked or who have respiratory problems from smoke inhalation (see p. 148), acid–base status and arterial oxygen concentration should be determined on an arterial sample.
5. Victims of smoke inhalation should have a baseline chest radiograph. This will usually be normal at first.

Treatment of the wound

The initial management of the greater than 10 per cent burn or scald prior to transfer to a burns unit is merely to clean with saline and cover in sterile sheets. If clothing is adherent to the wound it should be carefully removed.

Indication for referral of burns or scalds

The following patients may need referral to a specialist burns or plastic surgery unit depending on the wound severity and the patient's individual circumstances:

1. All children with injuries covering more than 10 per cent of body surface area should be referred to a burns unit even if the burn appears to be only superficial.
2. Children who have been the victims of an electric shock.
3. Children who have been in a smoking fire and who have evidence of inhalation of smoke or fumes.
4. Full or suspected full thickness burns even if the area is small. These patients may require skin grafting, so unless there are facilities in the receiving hospital for this procedure then plastic surgery referral will be necessary. Early referral

is important as modern treatment involves early grafting of burns.

5. Burns or scalds to the face, hands, perineum, or feet even if they are less than 10 per cent may have poor cosmetic or functional outcome and, unless trivial, should be referred.

6. Patients in whom burns or scalds are one of multiple injuries will require transfer to a specialist unit. This unit must be able to treat all the child's injuries. The individual patient's injuries and local facilities will determine the most appropriate place for the child's management.

Inhalation injury

• **Management of inhalation injury**

In the initial stages, evidence of inhalation injury must be actively sought if suspected on history and clinical findings. Any patient who has suffered a burn in an enclosed space is a candidate for severe inhalation injury. This of course includes all children who have been rescued from house fires. Signs which suggest inhalation injury include:

- Burnt face.
- Evidence of burns in the mouth.
- Singed facial or nasal hairs.
- Hoarseness, wheezing, dyspnoea, or cough.
- Sputum with soot particles.
- Decreased level of consciousness.

These signs progress rapidly and frequent repeat observations are necessary.

Management of inhalation injury

1. *The anaesthetist should be called urgently.*

2. The patient should be given 100 per cent oxygen by mask.

3. In the event of wheezing or breathlessness nebulized salbutamol driven by oxygen may be helpful.

4. Intubation must be considered urgently. If intubation is delayed then airway oedema may make the procedure impossible. A tracheostomy would then be necessary, and in patients with pulmonary damage and burn wounds a tracheostomy will predispose to severe pulmonary sepsis and a higher mortality.

5. Check arterial blood gases (NB pulse oximetry does not distinguish carboxyhaemoglobin from oxygenated haemoglobin).

Patients who are to be transferred to a specialist burns unit and are at risk from inhalation injury must be intubated before transfer. Patients with inhalation injury have fluid losses which exceed those of a simple skin burn. Fluid losses through the damaged tracheobronchial tree are difficult to estimate accurately and pulmonary oedema is easily caused by fluid overload. These patients are, therefore, difficult to manage and require careful circulatory monitoring in a burns intensive care unit.

Minor burns and scalds

- **Treatment of blisters   Dressings   Antiseptic and antibacterial burns dressings   Difficult areas Instructions to parents   Follow-up**

Burns that comprise less than 5 per cent of the child's surface area and are not full thickness can usually be managed as an out-patient. This will include the majority of children with burns and scalds attending an A & E department. Some children with burns of between 5 per cent and 10 per cent of surface area would benefit from overnight observation and re-assessment, but some can be treated as an out-patient.

When the patient with a minor thermal injury arrives, the first concern is analgesia. Cooling compresses and oral analgesics are usually sufficient, but some very distressed children may need intramuscular morphine.

The wound should be cleansed with normal saline (no antiseptic should be used). The burn should then be dressed. There are several different methods of dressing burns and you should become familiar with the accepted local practice.

Treatment of blisters

There are three alternative therapies. Leave them alone, drain the blisters using a sterile needle, or completely deroof them (i.e. cut away all the skin on top of the blister). Small blisters and those on the hands and fingers may be left alone or drained. Large blisters are uncomfortable and should be drained or deroofed. When draining a blister, asepsis is important as you may introduce infection and the warm moist environment under the blister skin is an ideal incubation area.

Dressings

Burns are painful when exposed to air. Paraffin gauze is an occlusive non-adhesive dressing which will help protect the burn. The dressing may be impregnated with chlorhexidine (Bactigras), or iodine, (Inadine), to help prevent infection. It is useful to put a few layers of dry gauze on top to help stop any exudate soaking through. The wound should then be covered with a dry bandage to keep the gauze in place.

Antiseptic and antibacterial burns dressings

The use of burns dressings which contain an antiseptic or antibacterial to discourage infection remains controversial. Local facilities and preference will determine what role these agents have in the A & E department. Silver sulphadiazine, (Flamazine), cream helps to prevent particular Gram-negative infections such as *Pseudomonas aeruginosa*, but alters the appearance of the wound and makes it more difficult to determine the depth of the burn. Mupirocin, (Bactroban), is effective against staphylococci (even those that are methicillin resistant), it, therefore, has a theoretical place in the management of burns to help prevent toxic shock syndrome (p. 153). However, there is, as yet, no evidence that it does so, and its widespread use may cause the development of resistant strains of staphylococci.

Difficult areas

Faces are difficult to dress and may be left exposed. Sometimes a colloid dressing is used. A layer of silver sulphadiazine or mupirocin can be applied to help prevent infection. Hands should not be put in tight dressings in which there is no finger movement or the fingers will become stiff. These burns may be dressed by putting on a thick layer of silver sulphadizine cream and then putting the whole hand in a plastic bag. The burn is then covered but free movement is allowed. The arm should be elevated in a sling.

Instructions to parents

The dressing must be kept clean and dry. There is often exudate through the dressing when the burn is fresh, and if this is enough to soak the bandage, the child should be brought back so the external dressing can be changed. You must make it clear to parents that if the child becomes unwell or pyrexial or there is anxiety about the wound, then he should be brought back immediately (see toxic shock syndrome p. 153).

Follow-up

The child should be reviewed after 1–2 days. The burn can be reassessed to check for areas of full thickness or deep dermal burn which may not have been apparent initially. Further blisters which have developed can be treated. The dressing is often soaked with exudate and can be changed. A new dressing should then be applied. The child can be reviewed again after a week. More frequent dressings are to be discouraged as removing the dressing is painful, and there is an increased risk of introducing infection.

Electrical burns

Electrical burns in the home are usually caused by children poking objects into electrical sockets or touching uninsulated wires. Older children can be injured through contact with high voltage wires, for example on railways.

Low voltage electrical injury causes arcing which produces discrete areas of full thickness burns (typically circular areas on the hand). There may be more than one area of burn (entry and exit points of current). Deeper structures may be damaged, and the area should be examined for blood vessel, nerve, and tendon damage. The injuries require surgical debridement and will often need grafting, especially in areas of major function such as the hand.

The most severe injury is caused by transmission of electrical energy through the body. This produces an entry and exit wound. In high voltage electrical injury, the electricity disperses from the point of injury through the lowest pathway of resistance. This means that electrical injuries are usually much more serious and extensive internally than may be expected from examination of the skin which may merely show a superficial burn. The electrical shock often throws the child some distance, or the child may fall, so also look for associated injuries.

On admission, a patient who has suffered an electrical injury should be generally assessed for cardiopulmonary status, and shock or respiratory depression treated as appropriate. An e.c.g. should be evaluated as there may be cardiac arrhythmias. The severity of the electrical injury is suggested by swelling and pain on passive extension of limbs, absence of pulse, or distal cyanosis and poor capillary refill.

These latter signs also suggest the development of compartment syndrome due to swelling from the electrical injury. Early decompression and even amputation is sometimes necessary. These patients must be urgently referred to a regional burns unit who will advise on immediate treatment and care during transfer.

More frequently however, high voltage injury may arc around the surface of the victim, setting his clothes on fire and causing a direct flame injury without an internal electrical injury.

Chemical burns

Chemical burns are much less common in children than in adults. The burned area should always be sluiced with *large* amounts of water. No specific chemical antidotes should be used as the possible resultant heat of reaction will cause further skin injury. The resulting burn should be treated as any other burn or scald. A poisons centre should be consulted for further specific therapy. Occasionally inhalation of toxic vapours can produce secondary pulmonary injury. The management of this problem is similar to that of smoke inhalation injury.

Toxic shock syndrome

This condition is caused by a phage group 1 staphylococcal infection. It is uncommon, but can occur in burned and scalded patients or those with skin abrasions, whatever the size and depth of their injury. The clinical picture includes a high fever, headache, confusion, conjunctival and mucosal hyperaemia, scarlatiniform rash with secondary desquamation, subcutaneous oedema, vomiting, watery diarrhoea, hepatic and renal damage, disseminated intravascular coagulation, and severe prolonged shock.

Parents should be warned that if their child develops a fever, a rash, diarrhoea, or becomes unwell, they should immediately bring him back to the A & E department.

Patients with toxic shock syndrome require intravenous colloid and anti-staphylococcal antibiotics, such as flucloxacillin. *Urgent burns unit and paediatric help should be sought for management* and the patient may require transfer to an intensive care unit.

Sunburn

During the summer, large numbers of children attend A & E departments with sunburn. Young children and especially infants can sustain serious burns to the skin after a relatively brief exposure to the sun.

Sunburn injuries should be assessed and treated as any other thermal injury.

Further reading

Muir, I. F. K., Barclay, T. L., and Settle, J. A. D. (1987). *Burns and their treatment*, (3rd edn). Butterworths, London.

CHAPTER 7

Poisoning

Key points in poisoning

1 Many children have ingested non-toxic substances. Neither gastric evacuation nor admission is necessary in these cases.

2 Gastric evacuation using ipecacuanha as an emetic has a good safety record and is at least as efficacious as other methods in the conscious child.

3 Activated charcoal is indicated for certain poisons.

4 In general, gastric evacuation is contraindicated for ingestion of household products.

5 Seek advice from a poisons centre if in any doubt about management.

6 Children who have poisoned themselves intentionally or those who are abusing drugs or solvents should be referred promptly to the psychiatric department.

7 Consider poisoning as the cause of obscure serious symptoms such as coma.

Poisoning

Suspected poisoning in children results in about 40 000 attendances at A & E departments per year in England and Wales. Less than half of these children are admitted to hospital for treatment or observation.

Deaths are uncommon; there are usually less than 10 per year in England and Wales. The most common fatal poisons in children are the tricyclic antidepressants.

The most frequently ingested drugs are analgesics (especially paracetamol), anxiolytics, cough medicines, oral contraceptives, and dietary drugs such as vitamins. The most frequently ingested household products are bleaches, detergents, disinfectants, and petroleum distillates.

There has been a fall in the incidence of admissions for analgesic poisonings since the introduction of child-resistant containers for these drugs in the mid 1970s.

Types of poisoning incidents

1. Accidental poisoning—this is the commonest form of poisoning incident in childhood, and usually occurs in the 1–3 years age-group. The products involved are most commonly drugs, followed by household products, with a few children ingesting plants. Accidental poisoning usually occurs when the child is unsupervised. An increased incidence in poisoning is seen in households where there has been a recent disruption such as a new baby, a change of address, or where the mother is depressed.
2. Intentional overdose—suicide or para-suicide attempts are usually made by girls in their teens.
3. Drug abuse—alcohol ingestion and solvent abuse are the commonest forms of drug abuse in children in the UK.
4. Iatrogenic—the commonest offender is diphenoxylate with atropine. This combination is toxic to some children at therapeutic doses. The most frequently fatal drug is digoxin.
5. Child abuse—rarely, symptoms are induced in children

by their parents or caretakers by means of the administration of drugs. These incidents do not usually present as a poisoning incident but as an unknown illness (see Chapter 8).

General management of the poisoned child

• History   Examination   General management

History

Poisoned children usually present with a history of ingestion, but poisoning should be considered in any ill child, and particularly in any unconscious child, in whom the diagnosis is obscure. The poison container and its contents should be brought to hospital along with the child. Always assume the worst, i.e. if ten tablets are missing assume the child has taken them all. Children will ingest substances which are abhorrent to adults, for example bitter substances. Parents may not know or may be reluctant to admit how much of the poison their child has taken.

Points to note in the history:

• which poisons have been taken?
• an estimate of how much has been taken (examine the container);
• at what time ingestion occurred;
• description of any subsequent symptoms;
• any acute or chronic illness and any current medication.

Examination

Frequently the child shows no immediate ill-effects from the poisoning. Sometimes evidence of the substance involved may be apparent, for example the smell of a domestic substance on the child's clothes, or coloured particles, or burns in the mouth. Many drugs produce characteristic signs (Table 7.1).

Table 7.1 • Specific signs of drug overdose

Pinpoint pupils	— opiates
Dilated pupils	— atropine (more commonly, atropine containing compounds, e.g. diphenoxylate/atropine), tricyclics
Drowsiness	— alcohol, sedatives, narcotics, hypnotics, diphenoxylate/atropine, aspirin, tricyclics
Confusion, ataxia, excitability	— alcohol, tricyclics, antihistamines, salbutamol, dexamphetamine, solvent abuse
Convulsions	— alcohol, dexamphetamine, tricyclics, theophylline, lithium
Extra-pyramidal dystonic reactions	— phenothiazines (e.g. prochlorperazine), metoclopramide
Cardiac arrhythmias	— tricyclics, amphetamines, potassium, theophylline, salbutamol, digoxin, beta blockers
Hyperventilation	— salicylates
Hypotension	— sedatives, narcotics, hypnotics, iron
Hypertension plus tachycardia	— amphetamines, sympathomimetics
Haematemesis	— iron, salicylates

> **Box 7.1 Points to note on examination of poisoned child**
> - Conscious level.
> - Blood pressure and pulse rate.
> - Respiratory rate and depth.
> - Pupil size and reactivity.
> - Skin and mouth for contact burns.

General management

1. Resuscitation—if necessary this should follow the usual procedures (see Chapter 2).
2. Airway care—if the conscious level is depressed then intubation should be considered, especially if gastric lavage is to be performed. The anaesthetist should use a cuffed ET tube in older, unconscious children when gastric lavage is performed.

3. Respiration—ventilate if respiration is inadequate. A pulse oximeter is helpful. If the patient is unconscious or there is any concern about respiratory adequacy, an arterial blood gas estimation should be done.

4. Hypotension—if there is hypotension insert an intravenous cannula and give aliquots of a plasma expander at 10 ml/kg in addition to elevating the foot of the trolley. Monitor e.c.g.

5. Keep the patient warm—some drugs may cause hypothermia.

6. Check blood glucose levels in any unconscious patient—and consider a trial of naloxone (10 µg/kg i.v. initially, see p. 167).

Elimination of the poison

- **Activated charcoal   Recommendations for management Admission**

Many children do not need stomach evacuation as they have not taken anything dangerous. There is continuing controversy about the best way to empty the stomach of ingested poisons. There are two main methods of doing this, gastric lavage or induced emesis using ipecacuanha. With either method, even under ideal conditions, less than half the poison is retrieved.

Problems with lavage include the unpleasantness of the procedure, a small risk of accidental perforation of the oesophagus and a risk of aspiration of gastric contents. Lavage may wash poisons into the duodenum and enhance absorption. The limitations of gastric lavage in children are largely because of the small diameter of tube which can be used. Many pills are too large to pass through a narrow tube. However, lavage may sometimes be useful through its mechanical action in breaking up concretions of pills, such as insoluble aspirin and iron, in the stomach. The fluid for gastric lavage should be one-fifth normal saline in 4 per cent dextrose (except in special circumstances, see individual poisons), and aliquots of 10 ml/kg should be used. In older children water can be used. The stomach should first be aspirated and then lavage should be carried out with the patient in the left Trendelenburg position. A sample of the stomach aspirate should be saved for chemical analysis if necessary.

Emesis induced by ipecacuanha is safer and more efficacious than gastric lavage in the vast majority of poisoning incidents, with the exception of patients with a depressed conscious level. The time from administration of ipecacuanha. to emesis is usually about 20 minutes, and during this time the child must not lie down. Occasionally vomiting may persist for several hours. The dose of ipecacuanha for children over one year is 15 ml. Over seven years of age 30 ml can be used. This should be followed by a drink of 100–200 ml of water or fruit juice (seek paediatric advice in infants—dose of ipecacuanha is 10 ml). A second dose may be given if vomiting has not occurred within 20 minutes.

Never evacuate the stomach, by any means, after the ingestion of corrosive substances. It is usual not to evacuate the stomach after ingestion of paraffin, petroleum products, turpentine, etc. because of the risk of inhalation pneumonitis. However, evacuation may occasionally be recommended after the ingestion of very large amounts of petroleum products. Seek advice from a poisons centre.

If saline has been given at home, as an emetic, by the parent, the patient may be hypernatraemic—check the serum sodium.

Activated charcoal

Activated charcoal absorbs some toxic substances, especially those that are weakly acidic. It is useful for the treatment of poisoning with tricyclic antidepressants, theophylline, digoxin, barbiturates, salicylate and carbamazepine and will increase the non-renal elimination of these drugs when given by repeated doses over 48 hours. This latter activity is thought to act by binding drug in the bowel thus allowing the drug to diffuse from the blood into the bowel lumen where it can in turn be bound to the charcoal.

Charcoal is at its most effective if given very soon after ingestion of the poison. Patient acceptability is low as a large volume of the black, gritty liquid needs to be taken. There is a particular problem in giving activated charcoal in a patient in whom emesis has been induced by the use of ipecacuanha. If the charcoal is given first, the emetic will not work as it will be bound to the charcoal. If the emetic is given first the charcoal is often vomited. There is, therefore, a case for stomach evacuation by gastric lavage if activated charcoal is to be used subsequently. A further advantage is that the charcoal may be introduced via the gastric tube. There is some evidence that charcoal alone, without gastric evacuation, may be effective treatment for poisonings.

Recommendations for management

1. Many household products (most cosmetics, paints, and inks) and some drugs (most antibiotics, vitamins, and the contraceptive pill) are not toxic and do not require gastric evacuation or patient observation. If in doubt ask for advice from a poisons centre.

2. Current practice in children is to induce emesis with ipecacuanha if the child is suspected of taking a substance with potentially toxic effects within the previous four hours. Emesis should also be considered for aspirin, opiates, and tricyclic antidepressants up to 12 hours following ingestion, as these drugs may cause gastric stasis. Advice should be sought on the necessity for emesis after four hours.

3. Gastric lavage is indicated:

- in association with endotracheal intubation in an unconscious patient (seek anaesthetic help);
- in patients who cannot be persuaded to take ipecacuanha or who have failed to vomit after two doses of ipecacuanha;
- in paraquat poisoning, after lavage a slurry of Fuller's earth can be passed down the tube to bind any unabsorbed paraquat, keep a sample of the gastric contents to test with dithionite for the presence of paraquat;
- in patients who have taken large doses of insoluble aspirin or iron tablets to attempt to break up the concretions in the stomach, and to give sodium bicarbonate or a specific antidote (see p. 166 and p. 168).

4. Activated charcoal is particularly indicated for the treat-

ment of poisoning with tricyclic antidepressants, theophylline, digoxin, and barbiturates. The dose is 1–2 g/kg. In patients where significant amounts of these drugs have been taken, gastric evacuation is best done by lavage so that activated charcoal can be left in the stomach.

Admission

Many children require 12–24 hour observation. Some children may be discharged after 4–6 hours observation if the drugs they have taken will have passed their peak serum levels by that time.

Box 7.2 **Criteria for admission of poisoned patient**
- Symptomatic patient.
- Potentially toxic ingestion.
- History unclear.

Prevention of poisoning incidents

1. When the child is discharged a discussion should be held with the parents about the need for prevention of further incidents. A lockable medicine cabinet should be recommended, and advice given on the safe disposal of old unwanted medicines.
2. Child-resistant containers have proved a great success in reducing the number of admissions to hospital of children with analgesic poisoning. These containers should be used for all drugs and household products wherever possible.
3. The parents should be warned against transferring drugs or household products to unlabelled bottles.
4. It is helpful if the health visitor visits the home after a poisoning incident for further discussion on prevention.

Poison information service

It is often difficult to assess the potential toxicity of the wide variety of substances that may be ingested. It is also useful to check the up-to-date treatment of common poisons. Poison information centres have been set up to collate information about poisons and can give details on identification and treatment. The two main centres are The National Poisons Information Service at New Cross Hospital, London, telephone number: 071-635-9191 and the Scottish Poisons Information Bureau at Edinburgh, telephone number: 031-229-2477. The Poisons Information Services provide a 24 hour service.

Specific drug poisoning

- **Paracetamol   Salicylates and aspirin   Narcotic analgesics   Tricyclic antidepressants (TCAs) Benzodiazepines   Iron poisoning   Phenothiazines Quinine   Digoxin**

Paracetamol

An excess of paracetamol is extremely toxic, but children are more resistant than adults to its effect. The toxic dose for adults is 150–250 mg/kg. The toddler who takes some extra paracetamol elixir is rarely severely poisoned, but the adolescent who takes over 20 tablets is at serious risk of liver damage without treatment with acetylcysteine. Initially there may be no clinical features of toxicity, but later the patient may develop nausea, vomiting, upper abdominal pain, and tenderness. Finally the patient may develop acute liver failure and a small percentage develop renal failure.

Management
1. Emesis should be induced by giving ipecacuanha up to four hours after ingestion.
2. Measure serum paracetamol level at four hours.
3. Assess toxicity risk on the basis of this level.
4. Administer acetylcysteine intravenously if the paracetamol levels are above 200 mg/l (1320 μmol/l) at four hours. If the patient presents later than four hours Figure 7.1 indicates the paracetamol level above which treatment is re-

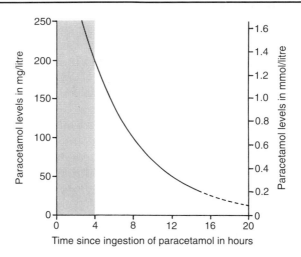

Figure 7.1 • Graph to estimate need for acetylcysteine treatment in paracetamol poisoning.

quired. A dose of 150 mg/kg acetylcysteine over 15 minutes initially followed by an infusion of 50 mg/kg over four hours should be given. Acetylcysteine occasionally causes a rash. Bronchospasm may occur in asthmatics and anaphylaxis has been reported.

Note: acetylcysteine is most effective if started within 8 hours of the overdose, but can be started at up to 15 hours.

If the patient presents at more than 15 hours, discuss the management with a poisons centre. If the result will not be known until more than eight hours after ingestion, oral methionine can be used in non-vomiting patients suspected of significant overdose prior to receipt of the paracetamol level result.

Admission This depends on the paracetamol level. If the level is clearly below the toxic level (see Fig. 7.1) the child may be sent home, otherwise admission and treatment are necessary. Patients who present with a history of a possible large overdose, however long after ingestion, should be admitted for monitoring and, if necessary, treatment of hepatic or renal failure.

Salicylates and aspirin

Aspirin poisoning is now less common than paracetamol poisoning. Children's preparations of aspirin are less readily available as they are discouraged in children under 12 years of age (due to the possible association with Reye's syndrome). It is important to remember the high salicylate content of Oil of Wintergreen. The threshold for salicylate toxicity is close to that of therapeutic levels, and children are very susceptible to toxicity.

Clinical features of aspirin poisoning in children are often different to those in adults. Children frequently develop a metabolic acidosis and hypoglycaemia. Loss of consciousness is rare but implies severe poisoning. Common features are nausea and vomiting, deafness or tinnitus, sweating, hyperventilation, vasodilatation, and tachycardia. Convulsions occasionally occur.

Management

1. If the overdose was small and/or of a soluble preparation emesis may be induced by ipecacuanha.
2. If the overdose was large and of an insoluble preparation gastric lavage with 1 per cent sodium bicarbonate solution or with water is indicated.
3. If the overdose was very recent, i.e. less than one hour, activated charcoal may be left in the stomach.
4. The serum salicylate level and blood sugar levels should be measured at two hours. Salicylate levels of less than 250 mg/l are unlikely to be associated with symptoms.
5. A symptomatic child, or one with a salicylate level of more than 500 mg/l, should be treated with an intravenous infusion of one-fifth normal saline and 4 per cent dextrose. Blood sugar levels should be measured at regular intervals, and the child should be referred immediately to the paediatricians as forced alkaline diuresis may be required in some instances.
6. Children with salicylate levels of 250 mg/l or more should be admitted for observation, as levels may rise.

Narcotic analgesics

The clinical features of poisoning are similar even with different types of opiates. The main cause for concern is respiratory depression which may occur quite late after the poisoning. The child may become comatose and have convulsions, hypotension, and arrhythmias.

Pinpoint pupils are an important diagnostic sign but are not always present.

Management
1. Ensure an adequate airway and prevent aspiration of vomit by lateral positioning.
2. Ventilate with bag and mask if necessary. Anaesthetic help should be sought urgently if there is respiratory depression.
3. Assess conscious level.
4. Administer intravenous naloxone (dose 0.2 mg for a child less than 1-year-old, 0.4 mg for a child 1–12-years-old, 0.8 mg for a child over 12 years of age) if the child is symptomatic. Naloxone has a short half-life and this dose may need to be repeated every 15–20 minutes. Sometimes larger doses or an infusion are needed.
5. Treat by emesis or lavage depending on conscious level.
6. Children should be admitted and observed carefully as depression of conscious level and respiration may occur suddenly.

Tricyclic antidepressants (TCAs)

These are extremely toxic compounds and the commonest cause of death in childhood poisonings. TCAs are prescribed for children with enuresis (but are ineffectual) and are widely prescribed for adults. TCAs block the uptake of monoamines in the brain and also have anticholinergic effects. They have a direct effect on cell membranes and this accounts for their cardiotoxicity.

Symptoms appear within four hours of overdose and include dry mouth, blurred vision, drowsiness, and tachycardia. This may progress to coma, convulsions, respiratory depression, hypotension, and cardiac arrhythmias.

Management
1. Institute continuous e.c.g. monitoring.
2. Evacuate stomach. Gastric lavage with airway protection

is necessary if the patient is drowsy or comatose. Gastric lavage is preferable to emesis with ipecacuanha if activated charcoal is to be left in the stomach after evacuation. Evacuation of the stomach may be useful up to 12 hours after ingestion as TCAs slow gastric emptying.

3. Give activated charcoal (1–2 g/kg).

4. All children must be admitted for e.c.g. monitoring and many will need intensive care monitoring. A wide QRS complex indicates serious toxicity. Adequate oxygenation and avoidance of acidosis are vital in order to decrease the risk of arrhythmias. An arterial blood gas estimation should be done. If bradycardia or arrhythmias develop, the child is probably hypoxic and needs ventilating. If arrhythmias persist, despite ventilation on oxygen, give sodium bicarbonate 1 mmol/kg i.v. This alters the protein binding of the tricyclic antidepressant and reduces the free drug concentration and the cardiotoxicity. Urgent specialist cardiology and poisons advice should be sought in the event of arrhythmias.

5. Treat convulsions with diazepam intravenously. Artificial ventilation will probably also be required in this instance.

Benzodiazepines

The ready availability of these drugs makes them a common cause of poisoning. They are relatively safe, the main effect being CNS depression. The child will appear drowsy and may be ataxic. In more serious overdoses coma and hypotension can occasionally occur.

Management
- Induce emesis with ipecacuanha unless drowsy and
- Admit the child for observation.

Iron poisoning

This commonly available substance is extremely poisonous, causing severe gastric haemorrhage and shock. The initial symptoms are nausea, vomiting, abdominal pain, and diarrhoea.

Management
1. If the patient is symptomatic on arrival then intramuscular desferrioxamine (30 mg/kg) should be given immediately

(take care that this does not enter a vein as rapid infusion of desferrioxamine may cause anaphylaxis).

2. Gastric lavage should be performed with airway protection if the child is drowsy. The lavage fluid should be 1 per cent sodium bicarbonate and 5–10 g of desferrioxamine should be left in the stomach.

3. The child should have an intravenous infusion sited, and depending on symptomatology may need the infusion of desferrioxamine over the next 24 hours. Advice from a poisons centre should be sought.

4. In cases of large overdose an abdominal radiograph after gastric evacuation will help in determining how much iron is left in the bowel.

5. All cases should be admitted to paediatric care and some will need intensive care.

Phenothiazines

The main side-effects of phenothiazine poisoning in children are drowsiness and extrapyramidal symptoms.

Management

1. Emesis should be induced or lavage performed with airway protection if the patient is drowsy.

2. In cases of a large overdose activated charcoal may be helpful.

3. Extrapyramidal side-effects should be treated with benztropine.

Quinine

Quinine poisoning should be treated with gastric lavage and activated charcoal. Hypokalaemia and metabolic acidosis can occur. Blindness is a particular complication. Stellate ganglion blockage has been used in the hope of preventing sight-loss but is probably ineffective. Advice should be urgently sought from the poisons centre.

Digoxin

Overdose is commoner in hospital than at home. Emesis or lavage should be followed by the use of activated charcoal.

Cardiac monitoring is essential. Digibind, digoxin-specific antibody fragments, can be infused as a specific antidote in severe poisoning. Poisons centre advice should be sought urgently.

Household products poisoning

- **Caustic soda   Methyl alcohol and ethylene glycol (antifreeze)   Ethyl alcohol**

These include bleaches, detergents, disinfectants, caustics, and compounds containing petroleum distillates. Most children swallow very small amounts of the product owing to its unpleasant taste, but often spill a lot. Morbidity is, therefore, low. However, it is important that each case is investigated thoroughly. More than one substance may have been ingested, and it is often surprising how toxic some apparently innocent substances are. Usually the advice of a poisons centre is needed in the case of proprietary products whose constituents are not clear.

In most cases emetics should not be given. Substances such as detergents and bleaches can cause chemical burns to the sensitive oesophageal mucosa which would be worsened by emesis. Petroleum distillates carry a high risk of pneumonitis and pulmonary oedema if aspirated, and, therefore, emesis is contra-indicated. Milk should be given to help dilute the poison and further treatment given as recommended by a poisons centre.

Caustic soda

Caustic soda is used as a cleaning agent and is found in dishwasher powders. Even a small amount can cause a stricture of the oesophagus. Milk should be given, and all children who have ingested alkalis should be admitted and referred to the surgeons in case oesophagoscopy is required.

Methyl alcohol and ethylene glycol (antifreeze)

Ingestion of these two substances is relatively uncommon in

children. The patient appears inebriated but there is no smell of alcohol. Rapid recognition of these poisons is important as there is a specific antidote, i.e. ethyl alcohol. The poisons centre should be contacted for detailed advice.

Ethyl alcohol

Children of all ages ingest alcohol. Younger children take it as an accidental ingestion either as an alcoholic beverage or by consuming cosmetics containing alcohol. Only small amounts of alcohol are necessary to produce symptoms in childhood, and children easily develop hypoglycaemia with alcohol poisoning.

The clinical features are similar to those in adults, and if the patient is unconscious, care must be taken to prevent the aspiration of vomit. The blood sugar level must be measured and an i.v. dextrose infusion set up if the patient is significantly intoxicated or is hypoglycaemic. Make sure there is no other cause for the patient's condition which may be associated with alcohol intake, such as drugs, trauma, or illness. Patients need observation until they are fully conscious and mobile. Treatment aimed at speeding up the elimination of the alcohol, i.e. lavage, intravenous fructose, and intravenous naloxone are ineffective and unnecessary. Frequent episodes of alcoholic intoxication in teenagers may indicate psychiatric or social problems and should lead to psychiatric referral.

Ingested foreign bodies

- **Button batteries**

Rounded non-penetrating foreign bodies are the most common objects swallowed. Of these, coins feature most frequently. Once past the pylorus, foreign bodies will pass through the bowel uneventfully. Removal is usually only indicated for those that stick in the oesophagus.

Children who have ingested a radio-opaque foreign body, such as a coin, should have a radiograph of the neck, chest, and upper abdomen with genital protection. If the object is in the pharynx or oesophagus the child should be referred for its removal at oesophagoscopy. Most of these children will be symptomatic with dysphagia, dyspnoea, dysphonia, or retrosternal pain, but some will be symptom-free.

If the object has passed into the stomach or bowel then the child may be allowed home and the parents told to search the stools until the object is found. If it has not been found after two weeks, then the child should return for re-X-ray, and surgical referral arranged for those in whom the foreign body is still visible. In the meantime the parents should be instructed to bring the child back to hospital if he should develop abdominal pain, vomiting, or pass blood per rectum.

Ingested sharp objects, such as an open safety-pin or pointed nail, should result in an immediate surgical referral as the child will require observation. Surprisingly, most of these objects do pass through the bowel leaving the mucosa unscathed. The necessity for surgical removal is low.

Button batteries

Small button batteries are easily swallowed by children. A few may disintegrate in the bowel causing secondary problems. The type of battery which has been ingested should be identified. The most dangerous are new, mercury batteries. The child should have a radiograph of the neck, chest, and upper abdomen with genital protection, and if the battery is in the oesophagus it should be removed at oesophagoscopy. The management of batteries in the stomach is debatable and specialist advice should be sought from a poisons centre as to whether the child should be observed or the batteries removed.

Suicide attempts

Toddlers take poisons accidentally. However, in the older child the overdose is most likely to be deliberate. The overdose is most commonly a 'cry for help'. Unfortunately, some of these children may succeed in killing themselves. The overdose may also be an indication of an underlying psychiatric illness.

In all cases the poisoning needs to be dealt with in the usual manner. It is then important that the child and parents be interviewed, usually by a psychiatrist experienced in adolescent problems. No child who has intentionally poisoned herself or himself should be discharged without psychiatric assessment and follow-up.

Substance abuse

- Management

Solvent and drug abuse is becoming more common in children—some even as young as seven years of age. Many solvents are readily available and include glue, chlorinated hydrocarbons (found in cleaning fluids, paints, varnishes, lacquers, and dyes), fluorocarbons (used as aerosol propellants and in fire extinguishers), petrol, acetones, butane, propane, etc. Abuse may lead to death caused directly by the toxicity of the substance or from trauma, anoxia, or aspiration of gastric contents during intoxication. Clinically, the patient may have similar symptoms to those caused by alcohol intoxication, including euphoria, blurred vision, tinnitus, slurred speech, ataxia, headache, abdominal pain, nausea, vomiting, chest pain, and bronchospasm. More serious effects include convulsions, respiratory depression, coma, and cardiac arrhythmias. Signs of a rash around the mouth and nose are suggestive of chronic solvent abuse.

Management

Stopping the inhalation will relieve the intoxication and there is no specific treatment needed, except for complications such as convulsions or respiratory depression. The patient should be referred to the psychiatric department for further management.

Ingestion of plants

Berries are the commonest plant parts to be ingested and the most likely to be poisonous.

For ingestion of unknown berries, emesis induced by ipecacuanha and observation for 6–12 hours is recommended.

Laburnum seeds are one of the commonest types of plant material ingested. Most children are asymptomatic. Vomiting, drowsiness, abdominal pain, mucosal irritation, and hypersalivation may occur, but serious poisoning is very rare. Emesis and observation are the treatment requirements if more than a few seeds have been ingested.

Yew berries cause gastrointestinal symptoms, tachycardia, then bradycardia and hypotension. Children should be treated with ipecacuanha and observation.

Holly and honeysuckle seeds produce gastrointestinal symptoms, and emesis should be produced for the ingestion of more than a few berries. Arum lily (cuckoopint, lords and ladies) and *Dieffenbachia* sp. (Leopard lily) seeds cause buccal and pharyngeal pain and swelling. Cold drinks should be offered and the child observed for several hours.

The following common berries are non-toxic—berberis, cotoneaster, mahonia, pyracanthus, rowan, but a mild gastrointestinal upset may occur.

Poisons centre advice should be sought for ingestions of unknown plants and in cases of doubt.

Further reading

1. Proudfoot, A. T. (1982). *Diagnosis and management of acute poisoning.* Blackwell Scientific, Oxford.
2. Vale, J. A. and Meredith, T. J. (ed.) (1981). *Poisoning: diagnosis and treatment.* Update Books, London.
3. Craft, A. W. (1988). Accidental poisoning. *Archives of Disease in Childhood,* **63,** 584–586.
4. Sibert, J. R. and Routledge, P. A. (1991). Accidental poisoning in children: can we admit fewer children with safety? *Archives of Disease in Children,* **66,** 263–266.

Child abuse

Key points in child abuse

1 If abuse is suspected, ask for a senior paediatric opinion.

2 Especially consider the possibility of abuse when examining injured babies of less than one year of age.

3 In a child with suspected sexual abuse, genital examination constitutes further abuse and should be undertaken by one experienced doctor only, unless life-threatening bleeding requires immediate aid.

Child abuse

Child abuse is an area in which professionals, both medical and non-medical, may feel confused, angry, or inadequate. The solution lies in consultation. Consultation will be amongst doctors and between doctors and members of other professions, such as social workers, the police, health visitors, and teachers.

The management of suspected child abuse should be directed to:

- supporting and protecting the child
- acting in the best long-term interests of all family members, and
- working within the framework of the Law.

The medical role is to:

- treat the child's injuries, including the psychological ones, and
- cooperate with others to ensure the child's safety.

Aetiology

1. Abuse is more common in a family where one or both parents suffered abuse themselves in childhood.
2. Abuse is more frequently identified in the children of younger parents living in stressful social conditions, but the problem can be found throughout society.
3. Abusing adults sometimes have unrealistic expectations of young children. They may expect a young child to be tidy, clean, quiet, and toilet-trained before the child has reached a state of development where these attainments are possible.
4. Abusing adults may have been disappointed by a child, for example the child is the 'wrong' sex or is handicapped.
5. Children under 5 years old are more usually victims of abuse than are older children, and those under 2 years of age are most at risk from permanent injury or death.
6. Abuse of older children is usually more to do with control

and over-harsh chastisement than stemming from an attachment problem as in abuse of younger children.

Recognition of abuse in the A & E department

- **Types of abuse   Physical abuse   Physical features of non-accidental injury (NAI)**

The experienced A & E doctor is in a good position to recognize abuse as he or she will have had the opportunity to see a large number of accidental injuries and, therefore, will be familiar with the types of injury children incur accidentally and the history that usually accompanies that injury.

Box 8.1

It is important to be clear that it is not the duty of the A & E SHO to diagnose child abuse. His or her duty is to recognize possible abuse and to refer these children for a senior paediatric opinion.

The A & E SHO must remember that in referring a patient with an injury about whose origin he is doubtful, he is not accusing a parent of abuse. He is merely asking a more experienced colleague for an opinion on a difficult case. A non-accusatory approach is vital—your worries about abuse may be unfounded and if the concerns are realized, antagonism is unprofitable.

Child abuse may be recognized by certain characteristics of the child, the history of the injury, and the injury itself. The suspicion of abuse is usually based on a combination of historical and physical features.

Types of abuse

In individual children, more than one form of abuse may co-exist, for example a sexually abused child may also be physically injured. A physically injured child may also suffer emotional deprivation, sometimes leading to failure to thrive.

Box 8.2 **Types of abuse**

1. Physical abuse
   (non-accidental injury):
   - superficial lesions—bruises, abrasions, lacerations;
   - bone injuries;
   - internal injuries—intracranial and visceral;
   - burns and scalds.
2. Sexual abuse.
3. Neglect (psychosocial deprivation).
4. Non-accidental poisoning.
5. Suffocation.
6. Munchausen syndrome by proxy.

Physical abuse (NAI)

Features in the history of the injury which should alert the doctor

1. Inappropriate delay in seeking advice after a significant injury, for example a bad fracture or burn. (*Note:* prompt A & E attendance for injury does not rule out abuse.)
2. Previous history of frequent accidents to the child.
3. The history of the injury is inconsistent with the findings on physical examination.
4. Absence of a reasonable explanation of the injury when one would normally expect one.
5. No history of accident given, but the child presented as 'crying' or 'not walking' with a significant injury present.
6. Significantly different explanations have been given for the same injuries.
7. The child is said to have contributed to his injury in a way which is inconsistent with his development.
8. Another child is said to have caused the injury in a way that is inconsistent with that child's development.

9. The adult may appear less concerned than most parents about the child's injury or may become hostile when the history is sought.

10. The child's explanation may differ from the adult's. If he is old enough, always ask the child what happened.

General examination of a child in whom there is concern about abuse

1. It is important to thoroughly examine any child in whom there is a concern about non-accidental injury in order to look for other signs of injury. All clothing should be removed, although this may be done in stages so as not to distress the child.

2. General demeanour—the child may be unusually quiet, although the classic 'frozen watchfulness' of the frequently injured child is rare and many children are very affectionate and clinging to their abusers. An indiscriminate friendliness to strangers is sometimes a feature of abused children, and, if noted, should be recorded.

3. Assessment of the growth status is important. The child should be weighed, measured, and the results plotted on growth charts. Non-organic failure to thrive is sometimes associated with physical abuse.

Physical features of non-accidental injury (NAI)

In injured children, some findings, such as retinal haemorrhage and fractured ribs, are highly suggestive of NAI. Others are sufficient to alert the doctor to the need for further consultation, such as bruising to a baby's face or a fracture in an under 1-year-old.

Soft-tissue injuries which are suggestive of NAI

1. Fingertip bruising—several small round bruises grouped together, perhaps on either side of cheeks or around a limb.

2. Slap marks—groups of linear bruises arising where a hard blow from a hand has forced blood out of adjoining skin capillaries, forming lines on either side of the hand or fingers impression. This bruising is often across the face, legs, or buttocks.

3. Bruising on both sides of, or inside, the pinna—this injury is not common accidentally.

4. Bruises showing the pattern of the artefact which caused them. This will be a line of bruising on either side of the object's impression, for example belt or stick marks.

5. Bruising of various ages, as shown by a change of colour from purplish red to yellow, suggests injuries at different times.

6. Any bruising in a non-mobile baby.

7. Torn frenulum—this may be caused by the thrusting of a bottle into a baby's mouth, but it does sometimes occur accidentally.

7. Bite marks—clearly human bite marks are intentional, but it is not always easy to determine whether they are of adult or child origin. A dentist's opinion is most helpful. If a dentist is not available, the injury may be photographed with a centimetre measure beside it.

Common patterns of accidental bruising

- Forehead in toddlers.
- Knees and shins in any ambulant child.
- Front of hips, outer thighs, and forearms in school-age children.
- Overlying spinous processes in school-age children.

Scratches on babies' faces are usually self-inflicted. In older children many other bruises, such as black eyes and buttock bruises, may be either accidental or non-accidental and need to be considered in the light of the history and complete examination. All mobile children have some accidental bruises, and some children have many of them.

Fractures Most accidental fractures occur in children of school age. Extra consideration of the possibility of abuse should be given to fractures in children who are under two years of age and especially in those under one year of age. A single fracture in an under 2-year-old child is usually an accidental injury, but if accompanied by signs such as multiple bruises, or failure to thrive, or accompanied by an inconsistent history, then referral for a senior opinion should be made.

Features of possible non-accidental fractures
1. Rib fractures are usually found incidentally on a chest radiograph and are identified by callus that forms at 7–10 days

after injury. Rib fractures rarely occur accidentally, except for example in a severe road traffic accident. Inflicted rib fractures are usually posterior.

2. Multiple metaphyseal and epiphyseal fractures can be caused when a child is pulled, twisted, or shaken by the limbs or trunk. The delicate growing areas of bone are damaged by pulling and shearing forces.

3. Multiple fractures in different stages of healing are highly suggestive of abuse in the absence of bone disease.

4. Spiral fractures of a long bone are more common in abuse than transverse fractures, but both may occur in either accidental or non-accidental injury.

5. Any fracture in a non-mobile baby.

6. Children may be presented as crying, limping, or refusing to walk with no history of injury given by the parent.

7. The injury may have been presented late, often again with no history of injury.

8. The finding of new periosteal bone on a radiograph indicates sub-periosteal damage, some 10–14 days previously. This may be associated with a fracture or may occur alone from a limb injury.

Head injuries Head injury is the commonest cause of death from trauma. In the school-age child the main cause of head injury is the road traffic accident. In the first year of life most serious intracranial injuries result from abuse. All non-mobile babies presenting with a head injury should have a skull X-ray. Although the history may be of a trivial injury, it may be false. Accidental head injury in a non-mobile baby usually occurs when the infant is dropped or falls, e.g. from a work surface onto a hard floor.

Severe intracranial haemorrhage, usually without skull fracture, may be caused in an infant who is violently shaken. The baby may be presented as generally unwell, drowsy, apnoeic, or convulsing. Retinal haemorrhage is characteristic of this injury.

Characteristics of accidental skull fracture in infants
- Single linear fracture or small depressed fracture.
- Commonly in parietal bone.

Characteristics of non-accidental skull fracture
- Multiple, wide branching fractures.

- More than one skull bone involved, fracture of the occiput is especially characteristic.
- Underlying brain damage more common.

Abdominal injuries A few children have serious intra-abdominal injuries which may be life-threatening. Presentation is usually as an ill or shocked child, or one with abdominal pain, distension, or rectal bleeding. Splenic or hepatic damage or rupture of the duodenum or small bowel may occur following severe blows to the abdomen. The management should be as indicated for severe abdominal trauma (see Chapter 3), but note should be taken of any associated bruising or other physical features.

Non-accidental burns and scalds Estimates of the incidence of non-accidental burns and scalds vary from 1 to 16 per cent of all children presenting at hospital with thermal injury.

Accidental scalding usually leaves splash marks, and the commonest injury is the scalded face and chest of the toddler who pulls a hot liquid down over herself. Accidental contact burns commonly affect the palms of the hands, the knuckles, and the forearms.

Characteristics of non accidental burns and scalds
1. Glove or stocking scalds which are caused by forced immersion in too hot water.
2. Some buttock and perineal burns.
3. Sometimes the imprint of a hot object may be seen on the skin at a site where the child could not have easily touched the object accidentally, for example the abdomen.
4. Cigarette burns, especially if more than one. Cigarette burns are circular, deep, and have a raised, indurated edge.

The differential diagnosis of physical abuse

- **Conditions in which pathological bruising may mimic non-accidental injury   Conditions in which skin lesions may mimic burns   Conditions in which bone disease may mimic non-accidental fractures**

Although physical abuse is probably under-diagnosed it is

also sometimes over-diagnosed. A clotting screen and full blood count should identify patients who have a clotting disorder accounting for their bruising. A skeletal survey which is performed to look for old fractures in a child suspected of being abused is also useful in identifying bone disease. These investigations would normally be ordered by the paediatrician after referral and assessment.

Conditions in which pathological bruising may mimic non-accidental injury

- Henoch–Schonlein purpura.
- Idiopathic thrombocytopenic purpura.
- Leukaemia.
- Clotting disorders such as haemophilia.
- Drug-induced thrombocytopenia, e.g. sulphonamides.
- Rare connective tissue disorders such as Ehlers–Danlos syndrome.

In addition, the commonly seen 'Mongolian blue spot' may be mistaken for bruising. This is a congenital skin lesion of no clinical significance. It is slatey-blue in colour and usually occurs on the lower back (although it may be found at any site), it is usually found in non-Caucasian children, although it can occasionally be seen in Caucasian children.

Conditions in which skin lesions may mimic burns

1. Impetigo is sometimes mistaken for cigarette burns. The cigarette burn is an ulcerated lesion with a raised rim.
2. Staphyloccocal skin infection in infants may resemble scalds, but in either case such an infant would require admission.

Conditions in which bone disease may mimic non-accidental fractures

- Osteogenesis imperfecta.
- Rickets.
- Pathological fracture through tumour or cyst.
- Copper deficiency.
- Caffey's disease.

All of these bone diseases are uncommon.

Management of suspected physical abuse

The suspicion of NAI usually arises from a combination of historical and physical features of an injury or of concern about a child, and rarely from one pathognomonic sign. The A & E SHO's duty is to refer, for senior opinion, any patient with an injury about whose origin he feels concerned. The decision whether to tell the parent that the referral is about the possibility of abuse is a difficult one. It is reasonable to merely say, 'I would like another opinion'. If the child is removed by the parent before the paediatrician arrives then the problem should be discussed with him and the social worker.

The suspicion that child abuse has occurred may be the first stage in a long process of investigation, protection, and rehabilitation that involves teamwork between several agencies, including the medical profession, social work departments, and the police. In most areas police departments have a specialist team of police officers, both male and female, who are trained and experienced in child protection work.

Social Workers have a statutory duty to protect children. In the United Kingdom they can seek legal orders from a magistrate, including an Emergency Protection Order, and may carry out a Supervision Order. The Social Worker will usually be responsible for convening a case-conference and it may be necessary for the A & E SHO to attend and contribute his findings verbally or in writing. He should first discuss the case with his consultant.

The social work department must be informed of all suspected cases of abuse. It will probably be the Social Worker who will check if the child is on the local 'at-risk' register. He or she will find out if there are other children at risk in the home and make appropriate arrangements for them.

Finally, it is imperative that all historical and physical findings in a case of suspected child abuse should be carefully documented in contemporaneously written notes. Bruises or other lesions should be described in words and also measured and drawn on a diagram. Where possible, a photograph of the injury is an invaluable record.

Sexual abuse

- **Management of child presenting with acute perineal injury (straddle injury)   Management of child presented as having been raped   Presentation of chronic child sexual abuse**

The incidence of child sexual abuse is unknown. It ranges from exposure of the child to pornographic information to penetrative rape. Boys and girls of all ages may be affected. The abuser is usually a male relative, cohabitant, or neighbour.

As far as the A & E department is concerned, sexual abuse may present in three broad ways.

1. As an acute event, usually presenting as perineal injury and occasionally as clear rape.
2. With parental anxiety on first suspicion of sexual abuse.
3. As a more chronic problem presenting with vaginal discharge, soreness, anal pain, or bleeding. Behavioural changes such as encopresis or academic failure are unlikely to present at an A & E department.

There are important points to remember in the management of children with suspected sexual abuse.

1. Genital examination constitutes further abuse and should be limited to one experienced doctor. Every hospital to which children may be brought should have access to a doctor experienced in child sexual abuse.
2. Important evidence may be lost or distorted by inexperienced doctors. The A & E SHO's role is to ensure the patient's general health and to contact more experienced colleagues.

Management of child presenting with acute perineal injury (straddle injury)

These children usually arrive with a history of having fallen astride a hard object. In most cases this history will be true, but in a few it is an attempt at concealment of recent sexual abuse. There are two important questions to ask about children who are brought in with acute perineal trauma.

1. Is there a need for surgical intervention to control bleeding or repair damage?
2. Has the injury been a result of sexual abuse?

The child's general well-being should first be assessed. Blood pressure and pulse should be noted and an assessment made of any blood lost. Other bruising or injury should be looked for. If there is blood loss, a brief visual inspection of the genital area is appropriate. This is to see if there is obvious severe trauma requiring emergency management. All children with any genital bleeding must be referred to the surgical department for consideration of examination under anaesthetic to exclude or treat vaginal or rectal tears. The examination will preferably be undertaken together with a forensic surgeon experienced in child sexual abuse. The child with perineal bruising only should be referred to the paediatric department for an opinion.

Management of child presented as having been raped

Occasionally a child, usually a girl, will be brought to the A & E department with a history of having been raped. These patients must be examined that day by a forensic surgeon experienced in child sexual abuse. After an overall assessment to ensure the child's well-being, no attempt at genital examination should be performed until the forensic surgeon has arrived. No evidence, such as clothing, should be removed or disposed of, and the child should not be cleansed. The forensic surgeon will examine the patient and take appropriate specimens. She/he will arrange investigation for genital infection and post-coital contraception if appropriate.

In the meantime, however, the child should be comforted and reassured.

Presentation of chronic child sexual abuse

Chronic child sexual abuse is not a situation best dealt with by emergency referral out of hours. Children who have been brought to A & E because they have disclosed sexual abuse or in whom an adult suspects sexual abuse should be referred to the Social Services Department. An arrangement will then be made for the child to be interviewed and examined by professionals expert in this difficult field.

The following symptoms usually have simple physical causes, but in a few children these symptoms will have arisen from repeated sexual abuse.

Presentation with local symptoms

1. Vulval soreness. This symptom is very common in pre-pubertal girls, and may be due to under- or over-hygiene or fungal infection. If the condition does not respond to simple measures (see p. 241) the child should be referred to paediatric out-patients.

2. Vaginal discharge. This may be caused by infection or occasionally by a foreign body. Swabs should be taken, including those for gonorrhoea and chlamydia. Antibiotics should not be given until the infection, if any, is identified. The child should be referred early to the paediatric out-patient department. The identification of a sexually transmitted disease in a child, although uncommon, is presumptive evidence of sexual abuse.

3. Anal bleeding and pain. This is usually caused by anal fissure related to constipation. Most will respond to laxatives but referral back to the child's general practitioner or to the paediatric out-patient department is necessary.

4. Perineal warts. These may be caused by self-inoculation from the fingers but may also be sexually transmitted. Children with perineal warts should be referred to the paediatric department.

Neglect (psychosocial deprivation)

In addition to failure to thrive (which should be assessed using standard percentile charts) neglected children may show certain well-recognized physical signs:

- Small size as well as poor weight.
- Sparse, dry hair.
- Protruberant abdomen.
- Cold, red, or blue extremities (acrocyanosis) even in a warm environment.

- Physically apathetic but wary ('frozen watchfulness').
- Unresponsive to mother/carer.

Such children should be referred to the paediatric team.

Less common types of abuse

Children will sometimes present to the A & E department with unexplained coma, drowsiness, or apnoeic spells. Clearly, these children will be admitted under paediatric care. A few of these children may have been intentionally poisoned or suffocated. It is wise to preserve samples of urine, vomit, and blood for further analysis from these children.

Munchausen syndrome by proxy is a condition in which factitious illness is induced in a child by an adult, for example spurious haematuria and induced rashes. The condition usually takes some while to diagnose and its recognition is often preceded by months of hospital admission and unnecessary investigation.

Further reading

1. Meadow, R. (ed.) (1989). *ABC of child abuse*. British Medical Journal, London.
2. MacCarthy, D. (1974). Effects of emotional disturbance and deprivation on somatic growth. In *Scientific foundations of paediatrics*, (ed. J. Davies and J. Dobbing). Heinemann, London.

CHAPTER 9

Respiratory and ENT problems

Key points in respiratory disease

1 The severity of acute respiratory disease is best assessed by observation of the child's work of breathing and his state of alertness.

2 The child with respiratory disease who is drowsy or agitated is probably hypoxic. Pulse oximetry is a useful tool to assess hypoxia.

3 Respiratory disease is more likely to be severe in infants under the age of one year

4 Inspiratory stridor is always a serious symptom.

Presentation of respiratory disease

• **Prevalence   Symptoms and signs**

Prevalence

Respiratory disease is the commonest cause of acute illness in childhood. Respiratory illness accounts for 50 per cent of consultations with general practitioners about children under 5 years of age and 30 per cent of consultations about 5–12-year-olds.

Most infections, (about 80 per cent) are limited to the upper respiratory tract (colds, pharyngitis, tonsillitis, otitis), but about 20 per cent affect the lower airway and respiratory tract (croup, epiglottitis, bronchitis, bronchiolitis, pneumonia) and are potentially more serious.

Asthma is the commonest chronic disease of childhood and the commonest single cause of admission of children to hospital.

Symptoms and signs of respiratory disease

Children with respiratory disease usually present with one or more of the following symptoms—cough, wheeze, stridor, breathlessness, or pyrexia. In addition, infants may present as generally unwell with poor feeding or occasionally with apnoeic spells. Older children with pneumonia may present with abdominal pain or chest pain on respiration. When taking the history it is important to be clear about what a parent is describing. For example, if a mother says 'his breathing is noisy' you need to ascertain whether she means wheeze, stridor, or the rattle of mucus in the airways.

The diagnosis of acute respiratory disease in childhood is largely a clinical one. It rests on history and examination with a chest radiograph in some cases.

When assessing a child with a respiratory illness, three questions should be addressed:

1. What respiratory illness does the child have?
2. How severely affected is he by this illness?
3. What is the likely progression of the illness?

In assessing the symptoms and physical signs of acute respiratory disease one should note:

1. *Nasal discharge*, which may be clear or mucopurulent with a cold.

2. The *characteristics of a cough*—is it barking, paroxysmal, or productive?

3. *Tachypnoea* indicates that increased ventilation is needed because of lung or airway disease (normal rate for infants is 40–50 per minute). Tachypnoea may also be a sign of metabolic acidosis, severe infection, shock, diabetes, aspirin poisoning, or of cardiovascular disease.

4. *Intercostal, subcostal, or sternal recession* shows increased work of breathing. This sign is more frequently seen in younger children who have a more plastic chest wall. Its presence in older children suggests moderate to severe lung disease. The degree of recession gives an indication of the severity of the respiratory difficulty.

5. The use of the sternomastoid muscle as an *accessory respiratory muscle* shows an increased work of breathing (in infants this may cause the head to bob up and down).

6. An inspiratory noise while breathing (*stridor*) is a sign of laryngeal or tracheal obstruction. In severely affected children stridor may occur also in expiration, but the inspiratory element is more prominent.

7. A *wheeze* indicates lower airways narrowing and is more prominent in expiration.

8. A *prolonged expiratory phase* indicates lower airways narrowing.

9. *Grunting* is caused by a child exhaling against a partially closed glottis in an attempt to generate a positive end expiratory pressure. It is a sign of severe respiratory distress and is usually seen only in infants.

10. *Flaring of the alae nasi* is seen especially in infants with respiratory distress.

11. *Tachycardia* will be produced by hypoxia, anxiety, and fever.

12. *Pulsus paradoxus* is an exaggerated fall in pulse pressure during inspiration and is a sign of severe air trapping. It is detected on palpating the pulse volume.

13. Auscultatory findings; *rhonchi* (wheezes) indicate partial obstruction of medium airways and *crepitations* (crackles) are usually thought to indicate opening of partially obstructed bronchioles.

Alarming signs requiring urgent treatment:

- restlessness, agitation, drowsiness, or hypotonia in association with respiratory distress indicate hypoxia;
- central cyanosis is a late sign of very severe hypoxia.

Note: In infancy the main respiratory effort is diaphragmatic so abdominal movement is more prominent than chest movement during breathing. Severe respiratory difficulty in a baby may produce a 'see-saw' pattern of breathing as the abdomen distends during inspiration and at the same time, the chest retracts.

Causes of respiratory infections

The peak incidence of respiratory tract infection comes between two and four years of age. Children of this age may have up to ten respiratory illnesses a year. Most of these illnesses are mild upper respiratory tract infections without constitutional disturbance. Infants under 1-year-old have fewer infections (probably because they are exposed to fewer sources of infection than the toddler), but a greater proportion of infants' respiratory illnesses involve the lower respiratory tract and are potentially more serious.

Parental smoking, overcrowded living conditions, and a history of prematurity significantly increase the frequency and severity of a child's respiratory infections.

Most respiratory infections are due to viruses, but it is often difficult to distinguish between viral and bacterial causes of infection either clinically or radiologically. Many respiratory pathogens can cause disease at several different sites in the respiratory tract. These differences are usually related to the child's age, for example respiratory syncytial virus (RSV) can cause a cold in an older child, otitis media in a toddler, and bronchiolitis or pneumonia in an infant.

RSV is the most widely found respiratory virus but other important respiratory viruses include parainfluenza viruses, influenza viruses, rhinoviruses, and adenoviruses. Important bacterial pathogens are haemolytic streptococci which cause some cases of tonsillitis and pharyngitis, *Streptococcus pneumoniae* which may cause otitis media or pneumonia, and *Mycoplasma pneumoniae* which causes pneumonia usually in older children. *Haemophilus influenzae* is important chiefly as the cause of epiglottitis, and is a less frequent pathogen in the respiratory tract in this country than in the United States, although it is a cause of otitis media in the United Kingdom. *Branhamella catarrhalis*, previously thought to be a harmless respiratory commensal, is now thought to cause some cases of otitis media. *Chlamydia trachomatis*, found in the female genital tract and which is a cause of conjunctivitis in the newborn, occasionally causes a severe pneumonia in young infants, but again this is not yet common in the United Kingdom. Staphyloccocal pneumonia, once not uncommon in small infants, is now very rare.

Upper respiratory infections

- **Coryzal illnesses (colds)   Otitis media   Otitis externa Sore throat**

Coryzal illnesses (colds)

Older children with colds rarely present to the A & E department as parents usually recognize these illnesses as self-limiting and benign. Most infections are mild with clear or mucopurulent nasal discharge, but some can be severe with fever, headache, and muscular pain in addition. Young babies with colds may have difficulty with feeding because of their blocked noses, and medical advice may be sought. Mechanical clearing of the nose is usually best and can be done with a cotton bud or by tickling inside the baby's nose with a fine twist of cotton wool. A sneeze will rid the baby of mucus. Ephedrine vasoconstrictor nasal drops are not recommended as their effect is short and there may be worsening of the nasal mucosal swelling as the effect of the drug wears off. Frequent use of these nose drops can cause chemical rhinitis. The parents of babies with colds should be advised to feed their baby smaller amounts more frequently so that the infant has an overall adequate fluid intake. Children with systemic symptoms may need an antipyretic and analgesic, such as paracetamol, regularly for the first day or so.

A patient with a cold may have redness of the throat, but this is not an indication for antibiotics. However, if the eardrums are also dull and red, it is wise to give an antibiotic, such as penicillin or amoxycillin, even though the infecting organism is likely to be viral. Up to 30 per cent of children with a cold will develop a cough which may last for up to two weeks. In the absence of respiratory distress or chest signs no treatment is needed. Expectorants, linctuses, cough suppressants, and other proprietary remedies for colds and coughs are of no benefit. Parents should be advised against their use in children.

Note: A runny nose is sometimes the first symptom of acute laryngotracheobronchitis, bronchiolitis, or pneumonia. In addition, viral upper respiratory tract infections are a common trigger of acute asthma. Parents of children who are discharged with a cold or sore throat should understand that they should seek further medical advice if their child develops new symptoms such as a barking cough, noisy breathing, or breathlessness. This is especially important in the case of infants under 1-year-old who are candidates for bronchiolitis and pneumonia. Children with a 'persistent cold' usually have allergic rhinitis and often have a personal or family history of atopic disease. They should be referred back to their GP for treatment.

Otitis media

Infants and young children are prone to middle ear infections. Improperly treated, these illnesses can cause partial deafness which may slow speech development in infants and cause poor concentration in the child at school.

Otitis media presents with a complaint of a painful ear in an older child. In a young child the presentation is less specific and may be of vomiting, pyrexia, irritability, or pulling of the ear. The diagnosis is made by examination of the tympanic membranes. The normal drum is smooth, flat, and shiny. The inflamed drum is reddened (this may be just peripherally in the early stages), dull, and may be bulging or perforated. A yellow or white appearance is due to pus in the middle ear. The eardrum can look pink in a crying child but if uninfected it will remain shiny. Wax in the external auditory canal may obscure an inflamed eardrum.

Treatment of otitis media In addition to respiratory viruses, the organisms usually found in otitis media are Streptococcus pneumoniae, Haemophilus influenzae, and possibly Branhamella catarrhalis. Amoxycillin, co-trimoxazole, or a cephalosporin are generally effective antibiotics for this condition, but a few strains of Haemophilus influenzae and Branhamella catarrhalis are beta-lactamase producers and will need augmentin (amoxycillin with clavulanic acid). All cases of otitis media should be treated with systemic antibiotics so that bacterial infections are not left untreated. In addition, an antipyretic and analgesic, such as paracetamol, should be used for symptomatic treatment in the first 48 hours. The antibiotic is given for seven days or until the infection has resolved. This can be assessed by a further examination of the eardrums. Parents should be advised to make an appointment, with the child's general practitioner, for review in 7–10 days.

Otitis externa

A painful discharging ear sometimes results from otitis externa, although the condition is less common in infants than otitis media. There is often profuse discharge from the ear in otitis externa making it difficult to see the eardrum and, therefore, to distinguish between otitis externa and otitis media (pain which stops when the ear starts to discharge is usually caused by a perforated eardrum). Pulling at the pinna, to straighten the external auditory canal during the examination sometimes produces pain in otitis externa but not in otitis media. A discharging ear should be cleaned with successive wisps of cotton wool wound on an aural probe and the canal and drum inspected. The pus should be cultured. If the drum cannot be seen ask the child to cough—if the pus pulsates then it is likely to originate from a perforated drum. In otitis externa, skin flora and *Pseudomonas aeruginosa* are the usual infecting organisms and treatment is with local antibiotic and steroid drops, such as Otosporin or Sofradex. If doubt remains as to whether there is a perforated eardrum, systemic antibiotics such as amoxycillin, co-trimoxazole, or a cephalosporin should be given as well as the local antibiotics. In some cases of otitis externa the external auditory canal is very swollen and systemic antibiotics may be required.

Sore throat

Throat infections may present with a specific complaint from the older child or may be discovered on examination as the cause of pyrexia or food refusal in the younger child. Accompanying symptoms may also include headache, enlarged and painful tonsillar nodes, and abdominal pain. In pharyngitis there is generalized pharyngeal erythema, and in tonsillitis the tonsils are red, swollen, and may have an exudate. Sixty per cent of sore throats are caused by viral infections. The majority of the remainder are caused by Group A beta haemolytic streptococci. Streptococcal infection is uncommon in children under three years of age.

Infectious mononucleosis can affect children of all ages. The condition should be considered when a sore throat with exudate is accompanied by a measles-like rash and lymphadenopathy. An enlarged spleen may be palpable. The diagnosis can be confirmed by a Monospot test and the appearance of characteristic mononuclear cells on a blood film.

Herpangina is caused by coxsackie viruses, and characterized by fever and sore throat with vesicles or ulcers on the fauces.

Pharyngoconjunctival fever is caused by adenoviruses.

The patient has fever, headache, conjunctivitis, and pharyngitis.

Scarlet fever caused by the erythrogenic beta haemolytic streptococcus will present with a rash accompanying a sore throat. In this case the rash is uniformly red and accompanied by a sore tongue with enlarged papillae. Occasionally pathognomonic striae may be seen on the flexor aspect of the elbows, and as the disease resolves there may be peeling of the palms.

Treatment of sore throats There is no simple way to differentiate viral from bacterial causes of sore throat clinically. An exudate can be present in both viral and bacterial tonsillitis. A petachial rash on the palate can be seen with both streptococcal infection and glandular fever. A differential white cell count is unhelpful. If the child also has a runny nose a viral infection is more likely. Antibiotics are usually given to children with marked tonsillar enlargement and to those who are systemically unwell. If a decision is made on clinical grounds to give an antibiotic, then oral penicillin is the drug of choice. Ampicillin or amoxycillin are less effective and can worsen the rash in glandular fever. For a patient who is sensitive to pencillin, erythromycin is the alternative choice. The antibiotic course should be given for ten days but most patients will be symptomatically better in two or three days time. Do not forget to advise an analgesic and antipyretic, such as paracetamol, for symptomatic relief, if necessary, over the first 48 hours. Unless the child worsens or improves only slowly there is no indication for follow-up after treatment for tonsillitis. Although it is unlikely to alter management, a swab of the patient's throat can allow the doctor to assess whether he has made the correct diagnosis clinically. Rheumatic fever following a streptococcal infection is now very rare in this country but occasional cases of poststreptoccocal glomerulonephritis are seen.

Acute laryngotracheal disease

• **Croup**   **Acute epiglottitis**

The hallmark of disease of the larynx and trachea is an

inspiratory stridor which may be accompanied by variable degrees of respiratory distress.

Croup

The term 'croup' is often used rather loosely to describe acute illnesses in which cough, inspiratory stridor, and respiratory distress occur. The different entities have different natural histories and require different management, therefore, they are described separately.

1. Acute laryngotracheobronchitis—is by far the commonest type of croup. It is caused by a virus, mainly parainfluenza but also respiratory syncytial virus, and occasionally measles or mumps. The disease usually begins as a coryza followed by the rather abrupt onset of stridor and barking cough, often commencing in the night. Most children with acute laryngotracheobronchitis are only mildly affected, and in them the most striking clinical feature is a frequent barking cough. A few children will have moderate to severe respiratory distress, and, of these, a small percentage will need intubation (see management p. 203). Most children will recover without treatment in 2–5 days.

2. Recurrent croup—some children, often with a personal or family history of atopy, have repeated episodes of croup without pyrexia or coryza. Hyper-reactivity of the upper airway may be the basis for their recurrent symptoms. In practice, it is difficult to distinguish an individual episode from the more common viral acute laryngotracheobronchitis.

3. Bacterial tracheitis—this is an unusual cause of croup but has a high mortality if untreated. The child will look toxic but has a croupy cough, unlike the child with epiglottitis. The usual infecting organisms are *Staphylococcus aureus* and *Haemophilus influenzae*. Intubation is usually required.

4. Tonsillitis—very rarely marked tonsillar enlargement, especially with glandular fever, or abscess formation with a streptococcal infection (quinsy) may cause an illness similar to mild epiglottitis. However, in these cases the obstruction is retropharyngeal rather than supraglottic. Intubation may be required.

5. Diphtheria—this is now a very uncommon cause of croup but should be considered in any un-immunized child.

6. Laryngeal foreign body—mechanical obstruction is less common than infection as a cause of acute stridor. However, the possibility of a foreign body should be considered in any case of stridor as the inhalation of the foreign body is often unwitnessed and, therefore, no inhalation history is given. For management see p. 33.

7. Angioneurotic oedema—laryngeal swelling occasionally occurs in acute anaphylactic reactions. For management see p. 44.

Acute epiglottitis

Acute epiglottitis is always a paediatric emergency. It needs immediate recognition and treatment, as untreated the disease carries a very high mortality. Acute epiglottitis is caused by *Haemophilus influenzae* Type B and results in rapid swelling of the epiglottis and obstruction of the larynx. It requires urgent, but experienced, airway control. *Certain clinical features of epiglottitis can alert the A & E SHO to summon senior anaesthetic, ENT, and paediatric help immediately:*

- Very painful throat, unable to talk or drink, with drooling of saliva.
- Pale, ill-looking child with a fever.
- Quiet 'snoring' stridor.
- No barking cough (unlike acute laryngotracheobronchitis).
- Marked respiratory distress with tachypnoea, tachycardia, and sternal retraction.
- The patient often sits with his chin slightly elevated to optimize airway opening.

Assessment of the child with stridor Two main questions need to be addressed:

1. How severe is the upper airways obstruction and is it worsening?

2. Does the child have epiglottitis? (See above for clinical features.)

Assessment of severity Note: Never examine the throat of a patient with stridor as this procedure may precipitate respiratory arrest.

1. The degree of tachypnoea, sternal, and subcostal recession shows how much respiratory effort is needed to ventilate across the airway obstruction. *Caution*, a slowing respiration rate and reduction in recession with the onset of drowsiness show that the child is tiring and respiratory arrest is imminent.
2. Tachycardia and agitation are signs of increasing hypoxia. Central cyanosis indicates profound hypoxia.
3. The loudness of the stridor gives no indication of the severity of the obstruction.
4. The initial assessment of a child with stridor is entirely clinical. Investigations such as full blood count, throat swab and lateral X-ray of the neck are unhelpful, and the procedures can precipitate complete obstruction by upsetting the child.

Management of acute airways obstruction If the child has marked respiratory distress the aims of A & E management are to:

- improve oxygenation by giving a high concentration of oxygen by face mask;
- prevent the child becoming agitated, which will worsen hypoxia and possibly laryngeal oedema; and
- involve senior experienced staff appropriately.

The parent's lap is a more reassuring place for the child than an A & E stretcher, and the parent is the best person to administer facial oxygen via a mask. A pulse oximeter will usefully monitor the patient's pulse rate and oxygen saturation if the child will tolerate the instrument on a digit.

Injections should not be given, and i.v. cannulae must not be inserted as they may precipitate acute obstruction by upsetting the child. Nebulized adrenalin (5 ml of 1:10 000 adrenalin nebulized with oxygen) can be helpful in children with severe obstruction to obtain transient improvement while awaiting senior help. There is no objective evidence that water vapor is helpful in acute upper airways obstruction and it should not be used in the A & E department. There is no clear evidence of the efficacy of steroids, except possibly in recurrent croup. Their use in A & E is not advised as they would need to be given parenterally in the very children in whom procedures such as cannulation would be contra-indicated.

Intubation All children with epiglottitis, and about 2 per cent of hospitalized children with acute laryngotracheobron-chitis, will require intubation. The decision to do this will be based on severely worsening respiratory distress or on the appearance of exhaustion, cyanosis, or confusion. Intubation of these children is very difficult and should not be under-taken by inexperienced doctors unless there has been a respiratory arrest.

Intubation should be performed by an experienced senior anaesthetist with an ENT surgeon at his elbow who is able to perform a tracheostomy if intubation fails. The anaesthetic induction should be with halothane and oxygen via a face mask. When the child is asleep observation of the throat and intubation can be performed together with intravenous can-nulation for culture of blood and the administration of fluids. Children with epiglottitis are septicaemic and should be given intravenous chloramphenicol (25 mg/kg).

Referral
1. Severely affected children (those with marked recession, exhaustion, confusion, or cyanosis)—*senior anaesthetic, paediatric, and ENT help should be obtained immediately* while ensuring good oxygenation, gentle handling, and administration of nebulized adrenalin.
2. Moderately affected children (those with stridor and re-cession at rest)—*paediatric referral should be made as soon as possible* so that the paediatrician may have an opportunity of assessing the child early.
3. Mildly affected children (barking cough, stridor on exertion only)—these should also be referred to the paediatrician. No child with stridor should be discharged by junior A & E staff. Stridor is usually a symptom of sudden onset and, therefore, the patient usually presents early in the evolu-tion of the disease. The condition may worsen before it improves. The younger the child the more caution should be observed.

Lower respiratory infections

- **Bronchiolitis Pneumonia Bronchitis Whooping cough**

Bronchiolitis

This is a viral infection of the small airways usually caused by the respiratory syncytial virus. It mainly affects infants under 1-year-old and occurs in epidemics in the winter. The disease starts with a coryza and mild fever and progresses to wheeze, dry cough, and respiratory distress. The sicker infants will have respiratory rates over 60 per minute, marked recession, flaring alae nasi, and difficulty in feeding because of tachypnoea. They will be mildly hypoxic. A very few infants become exhausted with slower respiration, severe hypoxia, and ventilatory failure. Apnoeic spells are a manifestation of the disease, especially in young babies and in those who have been born prematurely. These spells may be prolonged and frequent and are sometimes an indication for ventilation.

In bronchiolitis, on examination of the chest, there is hyperinflation which is also shown by an easily palpable liver. On auscultation there are widespread expiratory rhonchi and showers of fine inspiratory crepitations in the lungs.

Bronchiolitis: management and referral *Pale, tired, tachypnoeic babies should be given oxygen immediately and referred to the paediatricians.* Many babies, despite mild tachypnoea, are cheerful and well. However, most babies with bronchiolitis should be admitted. This is because the condition takes several days to resolve, usually worsens before it improves, and babies may become exhausted before the condition is better. The exception to this is the baby who has had the illness for several days, has not had much difficulty in feeding, and is clearly on the mend.

Bronchiolitis: investigations The respiratory syncytial virus can be rapidly identified using an immunofluorescent technique on a specimen of the infant's nasopharyngeal aspirate. A chest radiograph is sometimes ordered to exclude pneumonia, but the decision to admit the child is a clinical one. The radiographic appearances in bronchiolitis are those of hyperinflation, but one-third of children will have collapse or consolidation.

Bronchiolitis: treatment Antibiotics are not helpful in uncomplicated bronchiolitis, but are often given to babies who show pneumonic changes on the chest X-ray and to sicker babies in case there is additional undiagnosed bacterial infection. No drug except oxygen is useful in bronchiolitis. Bronchodilators, for example salbutamol, are unhelpful. Infants who have had bronchiolitis are often 'chesty' for the next year or so and some are later identified as asthmatics.

Pneumonia

Pneumonia can be a cause of death in very young or debilitated infants, or in children with underlying immunodeficiency, respiratory, cardiac, or neuromuscular disease. However, most children with pneumonia have a mild disease and can be treated at home. The causative organisms in the under 5-year-old child are usually the respiratory viruses. *Streptococcus pneumoniae* is the commonest bacterium identified and *Haemophilus influenzae* is an occasional pathogen. In over 5-year-old children a viral infection is rather less frequent, *Streptococcus pneumoniae* seems of greater importance, and *Mycoplasma pneumoniae* becomes more common. Pneumonia may present with some of the following symptoms:

- Cough, initially dry then often productive.
- Wheeze—especially in children with viral infections.
- Pyrexia.
- Respiratory difficulty with tachypnoea and recession.

More rarely:

- Abdominal pain—lower lobar pneumonia sometimes presents like this.
- Shoulder pain from diaphragmatic pleurisy.
- Pleuritic pain on inspiration.

Points to note in the history Enquiry should be made as to whether the child has an underlying chronic or congenital illness or was preterm. The history of the present illness and whether it is improving or worsening should be noted, together with what treatment has been received and specific enquiries about respiratory symptoms. Ask about the possibility of inhaled foreign body or food.

Points to note on examination
1. Is the child in respiratory distress as shown by tachypnoea, recession, and the use of accessory muscles?
2. Is he pyrexial?
3. Does he look 'ill'?
4. What are the auscultatory findings?

Investigation It is difficult to distinguish between bacterial and viral pneumonia clinically or radiologically, and a differential white cell count is not helpful. Bacterial and viral infections may co-exist in some cases. A chest X-ray should be performed if pneumonia is suspected clinically. A higher level of clinical suspicion for pneumonia should arise for children who have been preterm, have underlying cardio-respiratory disease, and in infants under the age of one year.

Referral Children in whom you suspect, or have shown, pneumonia should be referred to the paediatrician. Not all will require admission.

Treatment Most children with a diagnosis of pneumonia are treated with antibiotics. The choice of antibiotic is based on the knowledge of the likely pathogens in different age groups (see p. 206).

Penicillin or amoxycillin is usually prescribed unless the child has a typical history of *Mycoplasma pneumoniae* with headache and joint pains associated with the respiratory symptoms. In this case, or in a child failing to improve with penicillin, erythromycin should be used. A seven day course of antibiotics is usually prescribed, and a repeat chest radiograph and out-patient review is arranged for a few weeks time.

Bronchitis

There is no clear clinical definition of bronchitis. The illness usually labelled 'bronchitis' is a cough, often with sputum, which accompanies a coryzal illness. This may be treated with penicillin or erythromycin, although many children improve without this treatment as the majority of pathogens are viral. Children with so-called 'recurrent bronchitis' often have asthma, and a trial of asthma medication under their GP's supervision is warranted. There is no place for cough suppressants, linctuses, or expectorants for the treatment of 'bronchitis'.

Whooping cough

Despite the availability of pertussis immunization, whooping cough remains a common disease in children. There are several reasons for this. Firstly, pertussis immunization uptake remains at about 70 per cent, reflecting continuing parental anxiety and mis-information about vaccine-associated encephalopathy. Secondly, immunized children may have the disease mildly and pass it on to un-immunized children, and thirdly organisms other than *Bordetella pertussis* can cause a whooping cough-like illness. These organisms include *Bordetella parapertussis* and adenoviruses.

The disease usually starts uneventfully with a coryza and non-paroxysmal cough, but instead of resolving the cough worsens and becomes nocturnal, paroxysmal, and emetic. The characteristic whoop, (an indrawing of breath at the end of an exhausting coughing paroxysm) is not always heard and is rarely noted in infants. During paroxysms, children become red in the face and may become cyanosed for short spells. Clear or white mucus is often expectorated. After a severe coughing spell conjunctival haemorrhages may appear and petechiae may be noted on the face. Children with whooping cough are not 'ill' in between coughing and vomiting spells but they may be tired because of disturbed sleep. The diagnosis is made by a history of the characteristic cough persisting for several weeks, but may be supported in the early stages by a markedly raised lymphocyte count, and confirmed by the isolation of *Bordetella pertussis* from a pernasal swab.

No treatment has been shown to be effective for established whooping cough. In severely affected infants in hospital, steroids, bronchodilators, and sedatives have been used with little evidence of efficacy. There is no place for them in out-patient practice. Erythromycin, given orally for ten days in standard doses, is effective at clearing the naso-pharynx of organisms and, therefore, reducing infectivity. Erythromycin given to contacts who are still only in the coryzal phase may shorten the course of the illness but has no clinical effect in the established case. The antibiotic is worth giving to infant siblings of the index case. The GP should be asked to prescribe this.

Infants under six months of age who present to A & E with pertussis should be referred to the paediatric department for consideration of admission. These small babies may have apnoea and bradycardia with their coughing spells. It is in this age group that the majority of deaths occur (approximately 15 per year in the United Kingdom). In addition, children who have underlying chronic disease or who are severely socially disadvantaged are at risk from pertussis and should be referred to the paediatric department.

In general, however, otherwise healthy children over 6 months of age are as safe and less miserable when cared for at home and rarely need admission.

Asthma

- **Assessment of the asthmatic child presenting at the A & E department   Asthma: points to note in the history Asthma: points to note on examination   Investigations Treatment   Referral   Special problems of the under fives**

Asthma is the commonest chronic disorder of childhood. Wheeze affects more than 10 per cent of children at some time, although most have the symptom mildly. The prevalence of asthma seems to be increasing. Although new inhalation devices for treating asthma in children have become available, mortality has not decreased over the last ten years, and there has been a striking increase in the number of hospital admissions for asthma, especially in children under five years of age. As children with acute asthma frequently present to A & E departments it would be useful to have a clinical scoring system to aid in their assessment. Unfortunately no simple, reliable, and reproducible scoring system exists.

Assessment of the asthmatic child presenting at the A & E department

The clinical picture of the child's asthmatic attack will be built up from a history, examination, and some simple investigations. However, *a distressed asthmatic child should receive face mask oxyen and nebulized bronchodilators on arrival*, and not wait until all details have been assessed.

Asthma: points to note in the history

1. How long has this episode lasted?
2. How bad has the child been? Has he been able to talk?
3. What medication has already been taken in this attack, by what route and with what effect?
4. What asthma medication is the child regularly taking?
5. How frequent are the child's asthma symptoms usually?
6. Has the child had any previous severe attacks requiring steroid treatment, hospitalization, or intensive care?
7. Is there any identifiable trigger factor precipitating this episode?
8. Does the child have any other illnesses?

Asthma: points to note on examination

1. An increased respiration rate is a sign of respiratory embarrassment. The increase is usually directly related to the severity of the asthma.
2. Increased work of breathing is a reliable indicator of severity. Signs include the use of accessory muscles and nasal flaring.
3. Decreased respiratory compliance is shown by recession. The younger the child the more readily this will occur and may be seen in several sites—subcostal, intercostal, sternal, and suprasternal.
4. The degree of wheeze is an unreliable sign in the assess-

ment of asthma severity. Severely affected patients usually make little noise because their air flow is not high enough.

Note: Respiratory rate, work of breathing, and recession will all decrease in a fatigued child as well as in one who is improving with treatment. The two situations can be distinguished by the child's behaviour. The well child will be alert and orientated but the child who is becoming more hypoxic will be irritable and/or drowsy.

5. The child's skin colour must be assessed. Pallor may be a sign of hypoxia, and central cyanosis clearly indicates severe life-threatening asthma.
6. The restless, agitated child is hypoxic. Drowsiness is a sign of decreasing PO_2 and increasing PCO_2.
7. Inability to speak, or sentences broken by pauses for breath, are signs of severe respiratory distress.
8. A raised pulse rate 40 or more points above base level indicates moderate to severe asthma, probably with hypoxia. A rate of over 150 indicates severe hypoxia or possibly beta-agonist excess.
9. The presence of pulsus paradoxus (exaggerated fall in pulse pressure during inspiration) is a sign of severe air trapping. However, the absence of pulsus paradoxus should not be taken as indicating mild disease.
10. Percussion of the chest is rarely helpful. A resonant note is expected because of air trapping. Very occasionally a large pneumothorax may be spotted in this way but this complication is uncommon in childhood asthma.
11. Auscultation is more helpful and can give an idea of air flow in children too young or too breathless to use a peak flow meter.

Investigations

1. The peak flow rate is a very useful measurement in acute asthmatic attacks in patients old enough and well enough to use the equipment (usually over 5 or 6-years-old), especially if the patient is already familiar with the procedure.
2. The measurement of arterial oxygen saturation is easily achieved using the non-invasive pulse oximeter. It is useful

and informative in all but the mildest asthmatics and can demonstrate minor degrees of desaturation undetectable clinically. It is also extremely useful for monitoring patients undergoing treatment.

3. Estimations of arterial blood gases should be obtained in the most severely affected children, but the investigation must not delay treatment. Early in a severe asthma attack there is a fall in both PaO_2 and $PaCO_2$. As the obstruction increases the $PaCO_2$ rises towards normal and above, and the PaO_2 continues to decrease because of worsening ventilation/perfusion mis-matching and alveolar hypoventilation. A normal $PaCO_2$ in a distressed, hypoxic asthmatic is an ominous sign of impending respiratory failure. It is also worth noting that after bronchodilator therapy the PaO_2 may initially decrease rather than increase because there is better ventilation of poorly perfused lung areas.

4. A chest radiograph is not usually helpful and may delay treatment. It should only be performed if there is poor response to treatment or there are auscultatory findings suggestive of localized respiratory pathology. A chest radiograph should be taken to look for pneumothorax, if there is subcutaneous emphysema.

Treatment

Oxygen Oxygen must be administered via a face mask at 4 litres/min to all moderate or severely affected asthmatic patients. Asthmatic patients are often surprisingly hypoxic as ventilation–perfusion mis-match is added to airways obstruction.

β_2-**Agonists—salbutamol or terbutaline** Many patients presenting with acute asthma will already have failed to respond to their usual bronchodilator on arrival at hospital. This failure is due to poor airflow which, during a moderate to severe asthma attack, is insufficient to activate some inhaler devices and thus the dose inhaled is inadequate. A nebulized bronchodilator, such as salbutamol (2.5 mg for under 7-year-olds and 5 mg for over 7-year-olds), should be given in 5 ml of normal saline. The flow rate for air or oxygen should be 8 litres/min and the patient instructed to breath through his mouth. The nebulization should take 5–10 minutes. Nebulized terbutaline 2.5 mg or 5 mg is an alternative. A bad sign is a poor, or short-lived, response, in which case a further dose can be given in 15 minutes time but the paediatrician should be called urgently.

Aminophylline If the child fails to improve with nebulized salbutamol or relapses again within the next hour, then intravenous aminophylline, 6 mg/kg, should be given by the doctor over 20 minutes while monitoring the pulse rate. This should be followed by an infusion of aminophylline at 1 mg/kg/h. Aminophylline can cause ventricular arrhythmias if given quickly and may also cause nausea and vomiting. If the child has had a short-acting theophylline preparation in the previous 6 hours or a long-acting one in the previous 18 hours then the loading dose should be omitted and the infusion dose only used. If the child feels nauseous, the infusion should be slowed down, and it should be stopped if pulse irregularities occur. Patients on i.v. aminophylline must continue to have 2-hourly nebulized salbutamol or terbutaline, and oxygen continously.

Steroids Children who fail to respond or who relapse again quickly after nebulized salbutamol should also receive intravenous hydrocortisone, 4 mg/kg immediately, and then an infusion of 2 mg/kg/h. In addition, children who have a milder attack of asthma and do not require intravenous treatment but who are normally on regular inhaled steroids should have a short course of oral steroids during an acute attack. Children requiring more than two doses of nebulized bronchodilator will also usually receive oral steroids. The dose of oral prednisone is 1 mg/kg twice daily, usually for five days.

Antibiotics Antibiotics are rarely required in acute asthmatic episodes.

Referral

Patients in severe respiratory distress and those responding poorly, or not at all, to nebulized salbutamol and oxygen should be referred urgently to the paediatricians. An anaesthetist should also be called in case ventilation is required.

An experienced anaesthetist is needed to intubate and ventilate asthmatic children.

No child must be allowed home immediately after receiving nebulized salbutamol or terbutaline. Although marked clinical improvement may occur following this treatment it may be short-lived and the patient be just as bad again, or worse, in a few hours. It follows, therefore, that unless the A & E department or paediatric ward has appropriate child-orientated facilities for observation for a few hours, children who have had nebulized bronchodilators will require admission. If there are facilities for observation the child can be reassessed in approximately four hours. If the clinical response is maintained, the child is not wheezy, and the peak flow has not fallen again he may be allowed home with a suitable beta agonist for inhalation, using a large volume spacer device or a turbohaler 4–6 hourly over the next 48–72 hours. The parents should be instructed to bring the child back if he worsens, and review should be arranged for the next day. Children who are on inhaled steroids should receive a five day course of oral steroids in a dose of 1 mg/kg twice daily ('tailing off' of this course is not necessary). Other candidates for a short course of oral steroids are children whose asthma attack is not responding to treatment despite 24 hours of regular 4–6 hourly inhaled bronchodilator therapy at home.

It is important that the parent of a discharged asthmatic child understands that an apparent response to inhaled beta agonists does not mean the end of the asthma attack. Although the child may be apparently improved he will continue with significant small airways obstruction for several days. Treatment with inhaled beta agonists, and in many cases oral steroids, must, therefore, be continued over this time on a regular basis and the parents told to bring the child back if he deteriorates. If the patient is discharged from the A & E department his general practitioner or paediatrician should be informed as an acute attack may be a failure of prophylaxis and signals the need to reconsider the patient's regular asthma treatment.

Patients who have been observed over four hours and who are again wheezy or whose peak flow has fallen will require admission. Most children who are brought to hospital after failure of their usual asthma medication need admission. A few children who have not had previous asthma treatment or who have run out of their usual bronchodilators and who have only mild symptoms may not require nebulized bronchodilators. These children may be managed with a bronchodilator by inhaler 4–6 hourly at home if they are old enough to manage the device. Their GP should be informed.

Special problems of the under fives

There is evidence that wheezy illness in the under 5-year-olds is increasing even more rapidly than in any other age group. Children under 5 years of age have difficulty in using inhaled bronchodilators through a mechanical device. As oral bronchodilators are sometimes ineffective in acute asthma, many children in this age group need admitting to hospital when they have an acute attack. Although many under 5-year-olds are able to use a spacing device, such as a nebuhaler or volumatic, to take their inhaled asthma medication prophylactically, during an acute attack they may not be able to cope with drug inhalation through a spacing device due to distress and shortness of breath and will need nebulizers. There is almost no response to beta agonists, or theophylline, in the under 1-year-old wheezing infant, in whom in any case it is difficult to differentiate between asthma and wheeze associated with infection. However, it is worth trying severely affected infants thought to have asthma on nebulized beta agonists, or ipratropium bromide, as well as, of course, giving oxygen. If there is no clear immediate response the bronchodilator should be discontinued and the child in any case referred to the paediatric department for admission.

Chronic cough

• **Causes of chronic cough** **Examination** **Referral**

Occasionally a child with a chronic cough will attend an A & E department, especially if the symptoms have just worsened acutely. A careful history and examination should indicate those who require further investigation and referral.

Causes of chronic cough

1. The commonest cause is asthma which in some mildly affected children will be manifested only as a cough. Supporting features for this diagnosis are that the cough is dry, worsens at night and on exercise, and may be associated with episodes of wheeze. There may be a history of atopy in the family or eczema, urticaria or allergic rhinitis in the child.

2. Whooping cough is characterized by a paroxysmal, nocturnal, emetic cough sometimes accompanied by an inspiratory whoop (see p. 208).

3. Some children with apparent chronic cough will have frequent lower respiratory tract infections, perhaps associated with parental smoking, overcrowding in the home or preterm delivery.

4. Some children develop a habit cough after a respiratory illness. The habit cough is notable for its honking quality, absence in sleep, absence of sputum, and accentuation when the child is anxious.

5. An inhaled foreign body is a less common cause of a usually productive cough (see p. 218).

Rarer causes of chronic cough include:

6. Cystic fibrosis—this occurs in 1 in 2000 children, and is associated with poor weight gain and offensive stools.

7. Recurrent aspiration syndrome—causes repeated respiratory symptoms in infancy.

8. Immunodeficiency syndromes—recurrent serious infections should prompt a search for immune deficiency syndromes.

9. Tuberculosis—this infection produces wheezing and weight loss in childhood. However, some cases are discovered when a chest radiograph is ordered for a chronic cough or unrelated cause. The condition should be particularly remembered in children who live in immigrant communities.

Examination

The signs of chronic respiratory disease are:

- Poor growth.
- Abnormally shaped chest with a Harrison's sulcus or a barrel shape.
- Clubbing of the fingers.

All children with chronic cough should have a chest radiograph. In some a foreign body, tuberculosis, or radiological changes of chronic chest disease will be discovered. In asthma the chest radiograph will probably be normal. This investigation is not urgent and need not be done out of hours.

Referral

Referral to paediatric out-patients should be made for children with any physical signs of chest disease or abnormalities on their chest radiograph. Other children should be referred back to their general practitioner who should be sent a copy of the X-ray report.

Chest pain

Unlike adults, the complaint of chest pain in children and adolescents rarely points to cardiac disease.

Following trauma, bruising or rib or sternal fractures are causes of chest pain. In a child with respiratory distress or a history of respiratory illness, such as asthma or cystic fibrosis, a pneumothorax is a possibility. Worsening of pain on inspiration or a pleural rub or dullness indicates pleurisy or an effusion. An oesophageal or bronchial foreign body can give rise to chest pain.

Congenital aortic stenosis occasionally gives rise to chest pain. The disease can be diagnosed by the finding of a left ventricular impulse, a murmur in the aortic area at the right first intercostal space transmitted into the neck, and a thrill in the suprasternal notch. In addition to history and examination a chest radiograph should be useful in diagnosing any of these causes of chest pain.

Otherwise well patients with chest pain but no physical signs or chest radiograph abnormalities usually have viral myositis, oesophagitis, or psychosomatic chest pain. They should be referred back to their general practitioner. If clinically indicated, an antacid can be prescribed for a child who has chest pain from oesophagitis.

Foreign bodies

- **Laryngeal foreign body**   **Intrabronchial foreign body**

Laryngeal foreign body

Obstruction of the larynx is one of the commonest causes of accidental death in children under 1-year-old. Children with a partially obstructing foreign body in the larynx present with stridor, a distressing cough, and variable degrees of respiratory distress. A history of choking on food or a toy is usual, but not inevitable, and the possibility of a laryngeal foreign body should be remembered in any case of stridor.

Management as described on p. 33
A swallowed foreign body (for general management see p. 171) may lodge in the upper oesophagus and produce dysphagia, drooling, and difficulty in speaking. Urgent surgical or ENT help should be obtained and the foreign body removed by oesophagoscopy.

Intrabronchial foreign body

An intrabronchial foreign body is more common than a laryngeal one and is very unlikely to be initially fatal. There is considerable delay in diagnosis in a third of cases. Eighty per cent of patients with a bronchial foreign body are less than 4 years old; peanuts comprise half of the inhaled objects.

Prompt presentation Children who present acutely following a choking episode usually have a sudden onset of wheeze and cough. There may be diminished breath sounds over the affected area of the lung.

Delayed presentation If choking was not noticed or was

dismissed as unimportant, the patient may present days or weeks later with a cough, wheeze, and fever, unresolved pneumonia or recurrent cough with haemoptysis. Delay in diagnosis at this stage is usually due to the doctor not being aware that respiratory symptoms could be due to the inhalation of a foreign body.

Radiological investigation Most foreign bodies in the lung are not radio-opaque. However, the resulting collapse, hyperinflation, or consolidation is usually seen on a chest radiography. The actual radiographic changes will depend on whether the obstruction is complete or partial and whether there has been additional infection. Films taken in both full expiration and full inspiration are necessary in the assessment of the presence of a foreign body. In a young child, if these films cannot be obtained easily, the chest and diaphragm should be screened.

Management Most bronchial foreign bodies can be removed at bronchoscopy. However, especially after delayed removal, many children will have long-term pulmonary symptoms.

Further reading

Phelan, P. D., Landau, L. J., and Olinsky, A. (1990). *Respiratory illness in children*, (3rd edn). Blackwell Scientific Publications, Oxford.

CHAPTER 10

Gastrointestinal and genitourinary problems

Key points in gastrointestinal and genitourinary problems

1 Oral rehydration therapy is the mainstay of treatment in gastroenteritis.

2 Vomiting is a non-specific symptom of many illnesses, some of which are serious. A child should not be discharged with undiagnosed vomiting.

3 The concern in acute abdominal pain in childhood is whether appendicitis, or less frequently intussusception is present.

4 There should be a high index of suspicion for urinary tract infections in infants and young children. All children with urinary tract infection or haematuria must be followed up.

Gastrointestinal and genitourinary problems

Diarrhoea, vomiting, and abdominal pain are the commonest gastrointestinal symptoms with which children present to A & E departments.

Diarrhoea

• **Gastroenteritis   Chronic diarrhoea**

The normal range of stool frequency in children over six months old is from one stool on alternate days up to three stools daily. Very young infants, especially those who are breastfed, may normally have a motion with every feed. Parents may seek medical advice when their child's stools are more frequent than usual and/or when stool consistency is looser than usual.

Acute diarrhoea is the usual presenting symptom of gastroenteritis, but diarrhoea may occur during other infections such as otitis media. Diarrhoea may be caused by oral antibiotics or may be the presenting symptom of constipation when stool retention is followed by overflow.

Gastroenteritis

This is a major cause of death in children worldwide but in the United Kingdom gastroenteritis is usually a relatively mild condition, having become milder over the last 10 years. The decrease in severity is attributed to earlier use of Oral Rehydration Therapy (ORT), and fewer cases of hypernatraemic dehydration resulting from a decrease in the solute content of formula milks.

Clinical presentation Patients will present with diarrhoea, vomiting, or both. There may be abdominal pain, pyrexia, or blood in the stools. Points to clarify in the history are:

• Duration of symptoms.
• Number, volume, and description of stools and vomits.

- Number, volume, and type of feeds taken.
- Parent's assessment of child's well-being.
- Medication already received.
- History of underlying disease.
- Affected contacts.

Examination A full clinical examination is essential to:

- assess the degree of dehydration; and
- exclude other causes of diarrhoea or vomiting, e.g. acute abdomen, otitis media, meningitis, constipation with overflow.

The patient's weight must be recorded so that a baseline is available if he should return for follow-up.

Symptoms and signs of dehydration

1. Thirst—Note: a very ill baby may be too lethargic to suck.
2. Decreased urinary output—less than four wet nappies in the previous 24 hours suggests dehydration.
3. Dry mouth—a useful sign if the child is not a mouth breather.
4. Decreased skin turgor—this usually reliable sign may underestimate dehydration if hypernatraemia or obesity is present, or overestimate it in patients with hyponatraemia or malnutrition. Several sites, for example abdomen, inner arm, should be tested by pinching up the skin—any delay in return of the tested skin to normal indicates dehydration.
5. Sunken anterior fontanelle—this is a useful sign in infants, but some infants with a large anterior fontanelle always show some depression. Depression will be underestimated if the baby is crying or lying down.
6. Sunken eyes and decreased eyeball turgor—the latter is not an easy sign to elicit.
7. Tachypnoea—the metabolic acidosis of dehydration causes deep and rapid respiration.
8. Tachycardia—reduced circulatory volume will cause a rapid, poor volume pulse, but this sign is also present in ill children in general and is not specific for dehydration.
9. Child's demeanour—dehydrated children may be restless, lethargic, or irritable but these are general signs of ill health.

For assessment of degree of dehydration see Table 10.1.

Table 10.1 • Assessment of dehydration

	Mild	Moderate	Severe
	< 5%	5–10%	> 10%
Dry mouth	−	+	+
Reduced skin turgor	−	±	+
Sunken fontanelle	−	+	+
Sunken eyes	−	+	+
Tachypnoea	−	±	+
Tachycardia	−	±	+
Drowsiness	−	±	+

Stool specimens should be sent for bacteriology, parasites, and viral culture. Rapid tests are now available for the diagnosis of rotavirus infection. When results of these investigations become available the GP should be informed.

Indications for referral to paediatric care
1. Patients (usually infants) who are severely (more than 10 per cent) dehydrated with imminent circulatory collapse. These infants are pale, floppy, tachypnoeic, and have a rapid, weak pulse. They should have an immediate i.v. infusion of 10 ml/kg of plasma, a plasma substitute, or 0.9 per cent saline given over 5 minutes. The infusion should be repeated if there is little or no clinical improvement. Blood should be taken for electrolytes, a film (looking for evidence of DIC or haemolysed red cells), culture, acid–base status, urea, haemoglobin, and white cell count. *Meanwhile urgent paediatric assistance should be sought.*
2. Patients who have clinical signs of moderate dehydration (5 per cent plus). These patients will probably be managed with ORT but need hospital observation.
3. Infants under three months of age. Gastroenteritis is less common in very young infants. They are at greater risk of dehydration, and systemic illness and other causes for their symptoms are more difficult to exclude.
4. Children in whom you are not completely sure you have clinically excluded other causes of their symptoms. Particular

traps to look for include the infant with pyloric sternosis who may have small, loose 'starvation' stools as well as vomiting; superficially he or she may appear to have gastroenteritis. Also consider intussusception, the classical 'redcurrant jelly' stool is a late symptom.

5. Children with profuse vomiting and/or diarrhoea whom you think might become more poorly.

6. Children whose parents are in your, or the GP's, view very anxious or unable to manage at home.

7. Children with a high fever.

8. Children with underlying chronic disease, for example sickle cell disease, immune deficiency.

Patients who do not require admission The majority of patients will be older infants and toddlers with no clinical evidence of dehydration and who are not 'ill'. The mainstays of treatment for these children are:

- Oral Rehydration Therapy (ORT).
- Early re-introduction of normal feeds and diet.

For a period of not more than 24 hours normal feeds and diet are replaced by a water-based solution of electrolytes and glucose. The exception is for babies who are being breastfed. Breast feeding should continue and ORT should be offered in addition after the breast feed. Intestinal absorption of sodium and water occurs by active transport utilizing glucose. Replacement of fluid and electrolytes lost through diarrhoea can be achieved by giving a solution of sodium, potassium, and glucose with bicarbonate or citrate to counter acidosis. It seems clear from a number of studies that a range of solute concentrations can be tolerated by children with gastroenteritis. The World Health Organization formulation contains 90 mmol sodium/litre, but this is probably more appropriate to clinically dehydrated children. Commercially available preparations such as Dextrolyte, Dioralyte, Gluco-Lyte, and Electrosol (all 35 mmol sodium/litre), Electrolade and Rehidrat (50 mmol sodium/litre) are all satisfactory for out-patient use. Parents should be advised to give their child at least his normal daily fluid requirements as ORT (see Table 10.2). Extra ORT should be offered if he

Table 10.2 • Daily oral fluid requirements for well children

Age (yr)	0–1	1–3	4–6	7–14
Volume	150 ml/kg	100 ml/kg	90 ml/kg	70 ml/kg

appears thirsty and following the passage of a watery stool. If the child is vomiting, small frequent feeds should be given. If vomiting continues despite this, admission will be necessary. It is important that the parent understands that ORT is not a medicine to 'cure' the diarrhoea (although a reduction in stool number is usual), but it is to prevent dehydration and electrolyte imbalance. Normal baby milk feeds and then diet, if appropriate, are re-introduced after 24 hours (or earlier if the diarrhoea has settled or the child appears hungry). The re-introduction of feeds may cause an increase in the number or volume of stools, but further starvation is contraindicated. It is preferable that the child's bowel absorbs some nutrients than none at all. Further ORT or watery drinks should be offered in addition to feeds and diet if diarrhoea continues. Highly sugary, carbonated, or very cold drinks should be avoided as these will affect gut motility and absorption.

Follow-up Children should be reviewed at 24 hours. This should usually be arranged with the child's general practitioner. Parents should be asked to return with their child before this appointment if:

- he seems more ill, especially if drowsy or pyrexial;
- vomiting does not stop; and/or
- diarrhoea worsens.

At the review appointment the child should be reweighed and reassessed. Any anxieties at this stage should lead to a paediatric referral.

Rotavirus causes more than 50 per cent of cases of childhood gastroenteritis in the United Kingdom (Table 10.3). Respiratory symptoms are often associated with viral or *Cryptosporidium* gastroenteritis. In recent arrivals to this country, illnesses endemic abroad such as cholera and amoebiasis must be considered. Shigella and campylobacter infections may cause bloody diarrhoea while shigella infection may provoke convulsions. Remember that salmonella and shigella infections are notifiable diseases.

Antibiotics and antidiarrhoeals There is no place for antibiotics in the home management of gastroenteritis. In the vast majority of cases gastroenteritis is a self-limiting disease in which antibiotics appear to prolong the illness. Antidiarrhoeals (for example kaolin, Lomotil) of all types are always contra-indicated as they mask symptoms, prolong disease, and cause side-effects in children.

Complications of gastroenteritis Diarrhoea persisting beyond two weeks indicates reinfection, prolonged infection (for example E. *coli*, cryptosporidium), secondary lactose intolerance, or cows' milk protein intolerance. Fresh stools should be sent for culture, pH, and sugar chromatography, and the child referred to the paediatric department.

Table 10.3 • Organisms which cause gastroenteritis in the UK

Viral	Bacteria	Protozoal
Rotavirus	*Campylobacter* sp.	Cryptosporidium
	Shigella sp.	*Giardia lamblia*
Adenoviruses	*Salmonella* sp.	
	E. *Coli* (pathogenic)	
	Yersinia enterocolitica	

Chronic diarrhoea

Some children present to A & E departments with long-standing diarrhoea. These children should be referred to the paediatric out-patient clinic.

If the child is symptom-free apart from the diarrhoea, has no abnormality on physical examination, and is thriving then he may have 'toddler's diarrhoea' which is a disorder of bowel motility. The appearance of undigested vegetables in the stools is a feature of this condition. A non-urgent paediatric out-patient referral is appropriate. If, however, he has additional symptoms or abnormal physical signs, or is failing to put on weight, then urgent paediatric out-patient referral or admission would be appropriate. Conditions presenting like this with chronic diarrhoea are constipation with overflow, cystic fibrosis, coeliac disease, or sugar intolerances. In the older child, diarrhoea with blood or mucus in the stool suggests inflammatory bowel disease.

Acute abdominal pain

- **Common causes of acute abdominal pain in childhood**
  Appendicitis   Constipation   Rectal bleeding

Common causes of acute abdominal pain in childhood

- Acute non-specific abdominal pain (ANSAP). This is a diagnosis of exclusion but is still the commonest diagnosis in children admitted to hospital with abdominal pain. The term really means that we cannot find a cause for the pain, and it ceases spontaneously.
- Acute appendicitis (see below)
- Constipation (see p. 232)
- Gastroenteritis (see p. 223)
- Intussusception (see p. 236)
- Urinary tract infection (see p. 237)
- Pneumonia (see p. 206)
- Diabetes (see p. 40)
- Henoch–Schönlein purpura (see p. 276)
- Sickle cell disease (see p. 283)

Appendicitis

The most usual concern in a child with acute abdominal pain is 'is this acute appendicitis or not?'

The suspicion that abdominal pain is due to appendicitis is based on a good history and examination. Investigations do not clarify an uncertain picture.

History—points to note

1. Previous similar bouts of pain make this one less likely to be appendicitis.
2. Appendicitis pain usually begins at low intensity either initially in the right lower quadrant or moving there from

centrally. It becomes gradually more intense but is rarely agonizing. It is usually constant and less often colicky. It may improve a little with rest.

3. The child with appendicitis is usually not hungry but will drink.

4. A few vomits are usual but profuse vomiting is uncommon in uncomplicated appendicitis.

5. Although a history of constipation or diarrhoea may suggest an alternative cause for the abdominal pain, both bowel symptoms may coexist with appendicitis.

6. The duration of symptoms in appendicitis before you see the patient may be from a few hours to several days depending on the state the disease has reached, and any modifying treatment, such as antibiotics or analgesics, that may have altered the natural history of the condition.

7. Remember to ask for the presence of symptoms that might indicate a different diagnosis, for example polyuria (diabetes) or a cough (pneumonia).

The physical examination Before embarking on the physical examination the patient should be made comfortable and reassured by a parent close at hand. Analgesics should not be given as they will mask clinical signs.

1. Start by assessing the patient in general—uncomplicated appendicitis produces a moderately ill child. A desperately ill child may have widespread peritonitis or a completely different diagnosis.

2. A normal temperature and pulse rate may be present in appendicitis and both will be raised in an acute infectious disease so these measurements do not help in the differential diagnosis. However, they should be recorded as changes may be useful. A rapid respiration rate is a useful sign as this suggests pneumonia or diabetes as a cause of the abdominal pain and should lead to a chest X-ray and blood sugar estimation.

3. Examination of the abdomen should start with inspection. The child should be asked to point to the area of pain—a vague indication of all over the abdomen is a pointer away from appendicitis.

4. Palpation should start well away from the area the child says is painful. You are assessing tenderness and guarding. An area of tenderness and guarding at McBurney's point (two-thirds of the way from the umbilicus to the anterior superior iliac spine) is the classical sign of uncomplicated appendicitis. More widespread tenderness suggests peritonitis. Generalized guarding in a well child is more often a sign of anxiety than of peritonitis.

5. Halitosis is often absent in the younger child with appendicitis.

6. A rectal examination is not necessary if you have clearly decided to refer the child to the surgeons. They will want to repeat what is an unpleasant procedure for the child. However in any case of doubt, a rectal examination should be performed to identify pelvic tenderness caused by a retro-caecal appendix or pelvic peritonitis.

7. Pain apparently arising in the right hip may be caused by a retrocaecal appendicitis causing psoas muscle spasm.

8. In doubtful cases it is helpful to ask the child to sit up, get off the examination couch, and jump up and down on the floor. A child who can quickly and happily perform these activities is unlikely to have serious abdominal pathology.

9. If your department has the facility, observation for 3–4 hours and then re-examination may be useful in doubtful cases.

Investigations Full blood count, abdominal X-ray, and urinalysis are not useful in distinguishing appendicitis from other causes of acute abdominal pain and except for urinalysis they should not be done routinely.

Referral At this stage children in whom you have made a firm diagnosis of appendicitis and children in whom doubt remains should be referred to the surgical team. Children with abdominal pain who are allowed home should be given a review appointment in 24 hours, but should be asked to return earlier if the pain worsens or new symptoms develop. Most cases of non-specific abdominal pain will settle in 24 hours.

Pitfalls in the diagnosis of acute appendicitis

1. The patient has been given antibiotics for a supposed infection. This may mask clinical signs—have a higher degree of suspicion in these patients.

2. The patient is receiving analgesics. Again, a higher degree of suspicion is needed.

3. Appendicitis in the toddler is unusual but usually presents late with complications because the child cannot complain of abdominal pain so clearly as the older child.

4. It is easy to underestimate the pain experienced by a stoical child and overestimate that experienced by an upset child. You need to spend a little time forming an impression of the child's response to pain.

5. There is sometimes a 'window' of absent clinical signs when an appendix has just burst and before peritonitis has set in.

Constipation

This is a common condition in childhood and presents acutely in A & E departments as:

1. Acute abdominal pain.
2. Anal bleeding.

A history of infrequent evacuation of small, hard stools may be obtained, but the diagnosis is made on palpating a loaded descending colon and finding the rectum full of hard faeces. Especially in babies and young children an anal tear may initiate fear of evacuation and hence constipation occurs. Fresh blood on the stool is usually caused by an anal fissure. Children very rarely have haemorrhoids. An abdominal X-ray will show the extent of the loaded colon but is not necessary for the diagnosis of constipation. It is worth remembering that constipation is so common that it may co-exist with other illnesses such as appendicitis. Hirsch-sprung's disease is uncommon, but should be considered in constipated children with a history of late passage of meconium when newborn, poor growth, or constipation unresponsive to treatment.

Treatment If the child is in acute discomfort a micro-enema or a phosphate enema may be necessary to relieve him if he will tolerate the procedure. A few children with unresponsive constipation will need hospital admission, although where there is a paediatric District Nurse service home supervision is as effective. In most cases an oral stool softener such as lactulose is sufficient. Where lactulose has not been effective a laxative such as Senokot should be given. Patients with anal fissure will only need an oral stool softener. Advice on the usefulness of a high fibre diet should be given. The majority of patients should be followed up by their GP, but more severe cases should be referred to the paediatric out-patient department. Treatment for constipation is usually needed for at least several months to allow the stretched rectum to resume its normal size and elasticity.

Rectal bleeding

Although rectal bleeding is most commonly associated with constipation in childhood, other causes need to be considered and paediatric referral made.

1. Swallowed maternal blood or vitamin K deficiency in the newborn.
2. Shigella gastroenteritis—accompanied by diarrhoea.
3. Inflammatory bowel disease—usually in an older child. The history is of chronic diarrhoea with blood and/or mucus. There may be weight loss. Urgent paediatric out-patient referral is needed.
4. Intussusception—in the under 2-year-old rectal bleeding with abdominal pain is a potential surgical emergency (see p. 236).
5. Rarely, rectal bleeding may be the presenting feature of a clotting disorder. Ask for family history and look for abnormal bruising.
6. Again, rarely, more profuse rectal bleeding may originate from an intestinal polyp or Meckel's diverticulum.
7. Very occasionally rectal bleeding may be the initial presentation of sexual abuse (see p. 186).

Vomiting

- **Gastro-oesophageal reflux   Pyloric stenosis
  Intussusception**

Vomiting should be differentiated from possetting which is the regurgitation of mouthfuls of curdled milk in a young infant. Vomiting associated with winding of a baby suggests excessive swallowed air. A larger hole in the feeding bottle's teat will reduce the amount of air swallowed.

Vomiting is often a non-specific sign of illness in childhood; it may be a presenting symptom of:

- Gastroenteritis (see p. 223).
- Gastro-oesophageal reflux (see below).
- Otitis media and tonsillitis (see p. 197).
- Urinary tract infection (see p. 237).
- Associated with a cough, for example whooping cough (see p. 208).

However some causes of vomiting, although less common, are serious and should be actively considered:

- Appendicitis (see p. 229).
- Pyloric stenosis (see p. 235).
- Intussusception (see p. 236).
- Bowel obstruction, for example volvulus, adhesions from previous surgery, strangulated hernia (see p. 243).
- Meningitis (see p. 257).
- Raised intracranial pressure from any cause.
- Reyes syndrome (see p. 40).

No child should be allowed home with undiagnosed vomiting. Bile-stained vomiting should always lead to admission.

Gastro-oesophageal reflux

Gastro-oesophageal reflux is so common in infants that in its mildest form, of occasional regurgitation, it can be considered normal. Some infants, however, vomit many times daily and treatment may be necessary until the condition spontaneously resolves with increasing maturity and the use of solid food. Most infants improve in the second six months of life.

Complications in more severe cases include recurrent pulmonary aspiration, apnoeic spells, anaemia from gastrointestinal blood loss, failure to thrive, and oesophageal stricture.

Occasionally gastrointestinal malrotation may mimic reflux—a short or intermittent history of vomiting should raise suspicion of this.

History There is often a long history of frequent vomiting, usually after feeds and on handling the baby. Babies with reflux vomit less when asleep than awake and most gain weight normally.

Examination The diagnosis of gastro-oesophageal reflux in A & E is from the history. In an uncomplicated case there are no abnormal physical signs.

Management An explanation of the cause of symptoms should be given to parents. A carob-seed feed thickener (Carobel or Nestargel) should be prescribed.

Referral The baby's own GP should be informed and should continue management. In more severe cases refer to the paediatric out-patient department. Babies who are failing to gain weight require immediate paediatric referral.

Pyloric stenosis

Pyloric stenosis is commoner in boys than in girls. There is a family history of the complaint in about 10% of patients.

History Pyloric stenosis characteristically presents with a short history of forceful vomiting in a baby of 2–8 weeks of age. The vomit may contain altered blood subsequent to gastritis.

The baby may have had no stool for a day or so or may be passing small loose 'starvation' stools.

Examination Depending on the length of history the baby may be dehydrated or show evidence of recent weight loss. The upper abdomen may be distended and visible gastric peristalsis may be seen with patient observation. The diagnosis is made by the palpation of an evanescent olive-sized mass at the pylorus. This is most easily palpable while the baby is taking a milk feed. A hypochloraemic, hypokalaemic metabolic alkalosis may be present. Pyloric stenosis should be considered in any vomiting baby of less than two months of age.

Management Babies with pyloric stenosis require intravenous fluids, their composition depending on the results of serum sodium, potassium, chloride, and bicarbonate levels. They will also require aspiration of stomach contents. Biochemical abnormalities must be corrected before surgery. However, most babies will not require intravenous treatment in the A & E department.

Referral The baby should be referred to the paediatric team for confirmation of the diagnosis and biochemical correction before surgery.

Intussusception

This condition is commoner in children under 2-years-old. It presents as an acute onset of colicky abdominal pain, in some cases with vomiting. In late cases, findings are bloody stools and a palpable abdominal mass. Intussusception should be considered in any young child with acute abdominal pain often seen as episodes of screaming with or without pallor. An abdominal X-ray may be helpful in showing fluid levels indicating obstruction, but a normal X-ray does not exclude the condition. Referral to the surgical team is indicated if the condition is suspected. The diagnosis is confirmed on barium enema and the enema may be used to reduce the intussusception.

Recurrent abdominal pain

Children with recurrent abdominal pain may present to the A & E department with an acute episode of pain. It may be that the pain is especially bad and the parents are concerned that this time there may be something seriously wrong. This may be the case and the patient should be assessed as for acute abdominal pain (see p. 229).

Recurrent abdominal pain is a common symptom in childhood, and in an otherwise well and thriving child with no other symptoms or signs than occasional vomits or a headache it is unusual for there to be any demonstrable physical pathology. The symptom may be stress-related and there may be a family history of similar illness or of migraine.

Management Once acute abdominal pathology is excluded an MSU should be taken and the parents and child reassured that no acute illness has been found. The child may be discharged from A & E. The GP should be informed and the parents advised to consult further with their child's GP.

Threadworms

Although not an emergency, children with threadworms may present at the A & E department in the night when parents observe the alarming sight of worms emerging from their child's anus. Threadworms are an innocuous infestation which causes perineal itching, especially at night, and the diagnosis is made by observing the small thread-like white worms on perianal skin or in the stool. Piperazine is the standard treatment—one sachet stirred into a drink for children over 5 years of age and half this dose for younger children. The treatment may be repeated after 14 days. It is usual to also treat siblings and this should be done by the family's GP.

Urinary tract infections

- **Background**   When to suspect a UTI

Background

Bacterial urinary tract infections vary from asymptomatic bactiuria to pyelonephritis in an obviously sick child. Urinary tract infections occur in children with normal urinary tracts as well as those who have vesicoureteric reflux, neurogenic, or obstructive lesions. An infection may be the first evidence of a treatable urinary tract abnormality. It is thought that renal damage in sufferers from chronic renal failure associated with reflux nephropathy is initiated with the first urine infection in early childhood. It is, therefore, important that those caring for young children should recognize, treat, and investigate urinary tract infections appropriately. In early childhood, urinary tract infections do not present as dysuria and frequency but as pyrexia, vomiting, or malaise. Therefore, examination of the urine is part of the examination of every ill child except those in whom a clear alternative diagnosis has been established.

When to suspect a UTI

Urine should be taken for culture in the following circumstances:

- In children who complain of dysuria, frequency, or suprapubic pain.
- In any febrile child in whom the cause of the pyrexia is not found on examination.
- In any child with poor weight gain, vomiting, poor feeding, lethargy, or irritability (as part of full investigations).
- In children with haematuria.
- In febrile children with pain and tenderness in the renal area.
- In a sick neonate as part of a bacteriological work-up.
- In children with abdominal pain.
- In children whose parents have observed abnormalities of colour or smell in their urine.
- In children with enuresis.

The urine specimen To be correctly interpreted the urine specimen must be properly collected and examined within an hour by the laboratory. Specimens taken at night may be refrigerated or taken into a specimen pot containing the preservative boric acid.

Methods of urine collection.

1. Mid-stream clean voided urine (MSU)—this is the method of choice for collection from the continent child. Collecting

the middle of the stream allows the urethral organisms to be flushed out before the specimen is taken. The perineum should be first cleansed with sterile water.

2. Bag specimens—this method is suitable only for the exclusion of urinary tract infection. A positive bag specimen should lead to a clean catch or suprapubic aspirate. The perineum must be cleansed before the bag is affixed and the patient must be kept upright, the bag must be removed as soon as urine has been passed.

3. Clean catch urine in infants—this requires patience on the part of nursing staff or parents. An adult must sit with the semi-naked baby until urine is passed, catching the middle of the stream in a sterile container. It is worth remembering that babies micturate at mealtimes, when handled, and usually about every two hours.

4. Suprapubic aspiration—this is needed in the sick neonate or young infant (see p. 343).

5. Catheter sample—this is sometimes necessary in handicapped older children who cannot produce a clean midstream specimen.

The diagnosis of a urinary tract infection is made when a culture shows greater than 10^5 pure growth of a urinary pathogen in a correctly collected and handled urine specimen. A single catheter or suprapubic specimen is adequate to diagnose a urinary tract infection, but other methods of collection require at least two samples.

The presence of large numbers of pus cells or red cells in the urine may be suggestive of a urinary tract infection, but is not diagnostic and their absence certainly does not exclude UTI. The presence or absence of protein is unhelpful. Bacteria visible on microscopy are strongly suggestive of UTI.

Treatment When a urinary tract infection has been diagnosed a seven day course of an antibiotic to which the organism is sensitive should be given. If the child is clearly unwell or in discomfort then treatment can be started on clinical suspicion as long as two correctly collected specimens have been taken. In this instance either trimethoprim or nitrofurantoin can be chosen until the results of culture are known.

Follow-up At the end of treatment, a further urine sample should be cultured to ensure bacterial eradication. The under 5-year-olds will probably need urinary prophylaxis (see below).

Referral Patients with urinary tract infections should be referred to the paediatric department for consideration of further investigation. All under 5-year-olds will require a micturating cystogram and renal imaging. Local preference and expertise will determine whether this is ultrasound, intravenous pyelography, or DMSA scan. Until investigations are completed the patient should remain on a prophylactic urinary antibiotic, such as trimethoprim once daily.

Haematuria

Haematuria may present as macroscopic bleeding, which is noted by parents, or as red cells seen on microscopy. All children with haematuria must be referred to the paediatric or surgical departments.

Urinary tract infection, abdominal or pelvic trauma, and glomerulonephritis are the most likely causes of haematuria. Red urine may sometimes be caused by eating beetroot and pink stains on an infant's nappy may be urates, but in both instances an MSU should be examined.

A history of trauma preceding the bleeding should lead to immediate referral to the surgical department and renal imaging. A concurrent history of abdominal or loin pain may indicate calculus (rare in childhood). These children should have a plain abdominal X-ray, MSU, and referral to the paediatric department.

It is important to look for oedema and to measure the blood pressure in children with haematuria. Children with oedema or hypertension must be admitted under paediatric care immediately.

If a child with haematuria is otherwise well and has no abnormal physical signs it would be appropriate to arrange for a urea and creatinine estimation, a urine culture, and urgent referral to the next paediatric out-patients clinic.

Genital problems

- **Torsion of the testis Balanitis Paraphimosis Vulvovaginitis Vaginal discharge Pregnancy Acute retention of urine Hernia**

Torsion of the testis

This urgent surgical problem is most frequent in the neonatal period and around puberty. In the older child the onset of symptoms is sometimes gradual rather than acute, with abdominal pain radiating to the groin and over the testicle. The testis is swollen, tender, and sometimes retracted. Differentiation is from epididymo-orchitis or mumps orchitis. Any boy with a painful, swollen, or discoloured testis must be referred immediately to the surgical team as early surgery may save the organ. It is usual at operation to fix the contralateral testis to the scrotal septum as the condition may become bilateral.

Balanitis

Inflammation of the prepuce is quite common in male infants and toddlers. The foreskin may become infected causing redness and swelling. Sometimes pus is seen at the urinary meatus. Treatment is with an oral antibiotic, such as amoxycillin or co-trimoxazole, after a swab has been taken and a urine cultured. The child should be reviewed in a few days time to see if the balanitis has settled down. Recurrent episodes of balanitis is an indication for surgical referral for circumcision.

Paraphimosis

Swelling of the glans penis may occur if the foreskin is irreversibly retracted. Cold compresses and lubrication may overcome the obstruction, but if not the child should be referred to the surgical department.

Vulvovaginitis

The symptoms of dysuria and frequency in little girls is often an indication not of a urinary tract infection but of perineal soreness. This is often associated with under- or over-hygiene of the area. The use of bubble baths may cause vulvovaginitis. A urine specimen should always be examined for infection, and remember that threadworms are a common cause of perineal irritation (see p. 237). Inspection of the vulva shows no discharge but reddened labia and introitus. The treatment is to avoid over- or under-cleansing, and to apply an emollient cream such as zinc and castor oil cream when the patient complains of discomfort. Occasionally a sore vulva may be the presentation of sexual abuse (see p. 188), but it must be remembered that a sore vulva is a common symptom in normal healthy little girls. The child's GP should be informed about the attendance.

Vaginal discharge

Causes
- Normal secretions.
- Bacterial infection for example *Strep. pneumoniae* and haemolytic streptococci.
- Foreign body.
- Sexual abuse (see p. 188).

The majority of pre-pubertal girls with a vaginal discharge have excessive normal secretions or a streptococcal infection. Swabs should be taken (including those for gonorrhoea and chlamydia) and the child treated with oral penicillin if streptococci are identified.

The child should be referred to the paediatric out-patient department for follow-up and further management. Identification of venereal disease warrants immediate paediatric referral.

Pregnancy

With the advent of over-the-counter pregnancy tests the incidence of girls presenting to the A & E department with pregnancy has fallen. However, it is a condition worth remembering when adolescent girls present with vomiting or abdominal pain. Only abdominal examination must be performed. It is reasonable to ask pubertal girls with abdominal pain when their last menstrual period occurred and to sympathetically enquire whether there is a possibility of pregnancy, when appropriate. If pregnancy is confirmed, social work support should be offered and the patient's GP contacted.

Acute retention of urine

Acute retention of urine is more common in boys than girls, and is almost always associated with the discomfort arising from a urinary tract infection or balanitis. Sometimes a child can be induced to pass urine while sitting in a warm bath but it is important to ensure that a specimen of urine is obtained. If the retention is unrelieved then referral to the paediatric department is indicated.

Hernia

Umbilical hernias are fairly common in small babies. No treatment is indicated and the condition will usually resolve spontaneously.

Inguinal hernias are found more frequently in male babies who were born prematurely. If they are irreducible they require immediate paediatric surgical referral. The baby's legs will usually be elevated to encourage the hernia to reduce before surgery. If the hernia is reducible then urgent out-patient referral is needed.

Transilluminating scrotal swellings in infants or children are usually hydroceles and also require out-patient surgical referral. In young infants some hydroceles will disappear spontaneously.

Further reading

1. Postlethwaite, R. J. (ed.) (1986). *Clinical paediatric nephrology.* Wright, Bristol.
2. O'Donnell, B. (1985). *Abdominal pain in children.* Blackwell Scientific Publications, Oxford.

Neurology

Key points in neurology

1 Convulsions must be controlled as soon as possible as brain damage may occur after 30 minutes convulsing.

2 Convulsions in infants may present as apnoeic spells or loss of awareness.

3 Remember the importance of hypoglycaemia in both convulsions and coma in infancy and childhood.

4 Most convulsions with a fever in children aged from $^6/_{12}$ to 5 years are 'febrile convulsions' but meningitis should be actively considered.

5 A high clinical awareness for the possibility of meningitis should be maintained when assessing any infant or young child who is unwell, lethargic, irritable, feverish, or vomiting.

Convulsions

- Management of convulsing child   Pharmacological control of convulsions   Further management   Causes of status epilepticus   Febrile convulsions   Convulsions in a patient known to have epilepsy   New non-febrile fits Salaam attacks

At all ages, convulsions may be caused by hypoglycaemia, head injuries, poisoning and infections, especially meningitis. Other causes vary with age:

1. *Birth to six months of age*—meningitis and hypoglycaemia are the commonest causes of convulsions in young infants in the community (see also p. 299).
2. *Six months to five years of age*—a febrile convulsion is the commonest cause in this age group but meningitis should always be considered.
3. *Over five years of age*—epilepsy is the commonest cause.

Prolonged convulsions, from any cause, may result in permanent brain damage or even death as a result of hypoxia. During a prolonged convulsion cerebral blood flow and oxygen consumption increase about 5-fold. Oxygen delivery to the brain may be reduced by inadequate ventilation in the tonic phase of the fit and by airway obstruction from secretions or vomit.

A continuous convulsion lasting more than 30 minutes or repeated convulsions without recovery of consciousness constitute status epilepticus. In the first or 'compensated' stage of status epilepticus there is tachycardia, hypertension, hyperglycaemia (unless the convulsion was due to low blood sugar), decreased pCO_2, and a rise in blood lactate levels. In the second or 'decompensated' stage of status epilepticus, oxygen consumption exceeds demand and the patient develops hyperpyrexia, hypotension, raised serum potassium levels, hypoglycaemia, severe metabolic acidosis, a fall in cerebral blood flow, raised CSF lactate levels, and cerebral oedema. If this stage is untreated cardiac arrest and death supervene.

Management of convulsing child

The convulsing child should be taken immediately into the resuscitation room. It is essential to clear the airway, maintain oxygenation, and stop the fit as soon as possible. While this is being done another doctor or a nurse should obtain a rapid history from the accompanying adult. The history should especially clarify the following points:

1. How long has the child been convulsing?
2. Has the child had a recent accident, especially involving a head injury?
3. Is he a known epileptic?
4. Has he a neurological handicap or other disease, such as diabetes?
5. He has been unwell over the last few days—a history of increasing illness would suggest meningitis or other serious infection.
6. Could he have had access to a poisonous substance?
7. Is he on any medication? If on anticonvulsants has he actually been taking them or has the dose been changed recently?

Immediate and supportive care As soon as the patient is on the emergency trolley in a lateral position the airway should be cleared, an oral airway inserted, and a high concentration of oxygen administered through a face mask. If the child is cyanosed or breathing inadequately he should be ventilated with a bag and mask and 100 per cent oxygen. *Anaesthetic help should be requested if there is no rapid improvement.*

The patient's blood sugar should be rapidly checked with a reagent strip, such as BM stix. If this reads less than 4 mmol/l take blood for blood sugar and insulin levels if the patient is not a diabetic. Infuse 2 ml/kg 50 per cent dextrose intravenously. A hypoglycaemic fit will then usually cease.

The priority is to stop the convulsion, but while the anticonvulsant drug is being prepared the doctor should quickly note:

- The patient's cardiorespiratory status. (Airway, colour, respiratory adequacy, and peripheral pulse volume and rate).

- Any evidence of trauma, especially to the head.
- The characteristics of the convulsion, for example laterality.
- Any obvious physical signs, for example a petechial rash suggesting meningococcal septicaemia.

Pharmacological control of convulsions

Diazepam is the drug of first choice in most circumstances, and may be given intravenously or rectally. Diazemuls is the best preparation for intravenous use. It is an emulsion and less irritant to veins than the aqueous solution. The dose for intravenous use is 0.25 mg/kg up to a maximum of 10 mg. The injection must be given slowly at a rate of not more than 2 mg/min. The injection should be stopped when the convulsion ceases (the patient often sighs) even if the full calculated dose has not been used. Peak brain levels occur about 1 minute after injection but fall to subtherapeutic levels by 15 minutes, so fits may then recur requiring further treatment. Diazepam controls status epilepticus in nearly 90 per cent of cases. A second dose should be given after five minutes if the convulsion has not ceased with the first dose of diazepam.

Problems with diazepam

1. Accidental intra-arterial injection must be avoided as this causes severe arterial spasm.
2. Too rapid injection may lead to apnoea, but this is usually brief and managed with bag and mask ventilation.
3. Patients who are already on a barbiturate for control of their convulsions are more likely to be apnoeic with diazepam.
4. Intramuscular injection of diazepam is ineffective and causes local tissue damage.

If intravenous access is difficult, rectal diazepam (Stesolid rectal liquid) can be given. The dose is 2.5 mg for children less than one-year-old, 5 mg for children 1–3 years old and 10 mg for children over 3 years old. The 2.5 mg dose should be decanted from the opaque tube in which the liquid is presented into a syringe so that the dose can be clearly seen. When giving Stesolid keep the tube squeezed flat when removing it from the rectum and hold the child's buttocks together afterwards to prevent leakage of the liquid.

Do not delay in using rectal diazepam in the event of difficult i.v. access. Rectal diazepam is extremely effective in stopping convulsions and if the convulsion continues after a further 5 minutes a second dose may be given by the same route.

Note: urgent paediatric help should be requested if the convulsion does not cease with the first dose of diazepam.

Use of paraldehyde If fits continue after the second dose of diazepam, paraldehyde should be used. Paraldehyde is a safe and effective drug for status epilepticus. It should be given as a deep intramuscular injection in the lateral thigh. The dose is 1 ml per year of age up to the age of five, following this an additional 0.5 ml for each year of life up to a maximum of 10 ml. If the volume to be injected is large it should be given as two separate injections, one in each leg. The same dose can also be given rectally as a 10 per cent solution made up with normal saline. Paraldehyde can be given from a plastic syringe but should be given within 10 minutes of drawing up from the vial. Paraldehyde is excreted in the breath 15 minutes after intramuscular injection, but its half life is six hours. It is usually effective in stopping the convulsion within five minutes.

Inadvertent intravenous injection of undiluted paraldehyde can cause pulmonary haemorrhage and hepatic necrosis. Paraldehyde can be given as a 10 per cent solution intravenously, although this is not usual practice in the UK.

If a child is still convulsing five minutes after the injection of paraldehyde, preparation should be made for a phenytoin infusion if the patient is not already on this drug. Senior anaesthetic help should be requested at this stage. While the preparation is taking place, the patient's BM stix should again be checked along with his blood pressure, pulse, and temperature. If the blood pressure has fallen, 10 ml/kg of a colloid should be infused. Active cooling measures with tepid sponging and rectal paracetamol, 20 mg/kg, should be undertaken if the patient's temperature is rising. Blood should be taken for blood sugar level, acid–base status, and electrolyte levels, as metabolic abnormalities may be contributing to the resistance of the convulsions to pharmacological treatment. Raised intracranial pressure will also

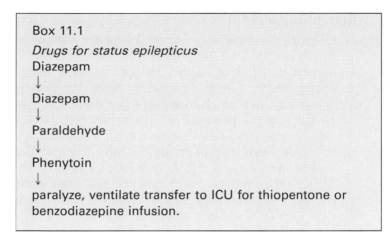

Box 11.1
Drugs for status epilepticus
Diazepam
↓
Diazepam
↓
Paraldehyde
↓
Phenytoin
↓
paralyze, ventilate transfer to ICU for thiopentone or benzodiazepine infusion.

cause resistance of convulsions to treatment. If there are signs of raised intracranial pressure, consideration should be given to the use of intravenous mannitol. This should be done in consultation with senior paediatric staff.

Administration of phenytoin E.c.g. and blood pressure monitoring should continue while intravenous phenytoin is being given. If arrhythmias or hypotension occur the infusion should be stopped for a few minutes and started again at a slower rate. The cardiovascular side-effects of intravenous phenytoin are a result of the rate of infusion and not of the total dose infused. The initial dose of phenytoin is 15 mg/kg, and this should be given over 15 minutes. If the patient does not respond to this regime, he should be paralysed, ventilated, and transferred to an intensive care unit where thiopentone or benzodiazepine infusion may be used.

Box 11.2 **When to call for help**
If the *initial anticonvulsant drug* is not successful then *urgent paediatric help* should be sought immediately, although you should progress to the next stage of treatment while awaiting the paediatrician's arrival. *Failure of the second anticonvulsant drug* indicates a refractory status and *senior anaesthetic help* should be urgently sought while continuing treatment.

Further management

Once the convulsion is under control and the patient's condition is stabilized, the underlying cause must be sought. A more detailed history can be obtained and the child re-examined. Usually the paediatric team will have taken responsibility for the child at this stage. Particular note should be taken of the presence of a petechial rash (which would suggest meningococcal septicaemia), a pyrexia (suggesting infection), evidence of injury, or hypertension. The neurological examination will be partially masked by the effects of the anticonvulsant drug and the post-ictal status of the patient. However, neurological signs should be sought since they may indicate an underlying focal lesion. Differences in tone and reflexes on each side of the patient, inequality of the pupils, fixed deviation of the eyes, or an abnormal doll's eye reflex will suggest an underlying focal lesion. There may be a Todd's paralysis which should resolve within 24 hours. Evidence of meningitis should be sought, although neck stiffness may be masked by the effects of the anticonvulsant.

Causes of status epilepticus

1. An atypical prolonged febrile convulsion.
2. A prolonged convulsion in a child known to have epilepsy.
3. Meningitis.
4. Trauma (head injury or hypoxia).
5. Metabolic causes, for example hypoglycaemia associated with inborn errors of metabolism and diabetes, Reye's syndrome, hypernatraemia, hyponatraemia, poisoning.
6. Encephalitis.

Note: Sometimes patients who are in a tonic decerebrate state (usually following a severe head injury) are mistakenly thought to be in a status epilepticus. Dystonic reactions to an overdose of drugs, such as phenothiazines or metaclopramide, can also be mistaken for convulsions, but in both of these conditions the rhythmic jerking characteristic of status epilepticus is absent.

Febrile convulsions

Febrile convulsions occur in two per cent of otherwise

normal children. The majority are benign, short (less than 15 minutes) grand mal convulsions triggered off by a fever in children between the ages of six months and five years.

Management In most cases the convulsion will have ceased by the time the child has arrived at the A & E department. The parents will often be very distressed. Many parents think their child is dying when they witness a convulsion.

The child should be given paracetamol orally, or if this is not possible, rectally. Even though the convulsion has ceased and the child recovered consciousness, the cause of the fever must be ascertained. The history and examination may provide the necessary clues. Common infections are usually the cause of febrile convulsions. These will include measles, tonsillitis, otitis media, pneumonia, and urinary tract infections. Sometimes a convulsion will occur with a diarrhoeal illness and the organism involved is often a member of the *Shigella* sp.

Serious consideration must be given to the possibility of meningitis in every patient with a febrile convulsion. A combination of fever and a convulsion is a common presentation for meningitis.

Referral All children presenting to an A & E department with febrile convulsions should be referred to the paediatric department. Many of these children will be admitted to hospital. This will usually include those below two years of age, those with their first febrile convulsion, those in whom meningitis is suspected or cannot be excluded clinically, and those in whom the underlying infection is not identified. Sometimes a child over two years of age who has had a previous simple febrile convulsion, in whom a clear benign source of infection has been identified, whose parents are sensible and keen to take him home may be discharged with antipyretics, by the paediatric team.

Convulsions in a patient known to have epilepsy

If the convulsion has stopped before the patient arrives at the A & E department, the patient has recovered consciousness, and examination reveals no new abnormality, admission may not be necessary. If possible, discuss the case with the patient's paediatrician or neurologist. It is advisable to take a blood sample for anticonvulsant levels and to re-arrange the patient's next out-patient appointment for an earlier date.

New non-febrile fits

If a child presents with a non-febrile convulsion which has ceased before arrival at the A & E department and the child has recovered consciousness, referral should be made to the paediatric team, but admission may not be necessary. A full physical examination should be carried out, including the blood pressure and CNS. If the convulsion has been an iso-lated one, the child has no abnormal physical signs, and the parents are happy to take him home, he may be discharged with an e.e.g. appointment and an urgent paediatric out-patient appointment. Before discharge, the parents should be instructed about what to do should their child have a further fit. He should be placed in the recovery position and the parents should telephone for an ambulance if the fit does not stop spontaneously within a few minutes. In the short term, bicycle riding, high gymnastic apparatus, and unsuper-vized swimming should be advised against.

Salaam attacks

This condition is a type of epilepsy of sudden onset in infancy. It is relatively more common in children with Down syndrome. The episodes, which may occur many times a day, consist of sudden falling or truncal flexion, but it should be considered in any child who has serial abnormal movements of the head, trunk, or limbs. A loss of social awareness is often a feature, i.e. the baby does not seem to 'be himself'. Salaam attacks are sometimes mistaken for episodes of colic. A characteristic e.e.g. pattern (hypsar-rhythmia) is diagnostic. These infants must be admitted im-mediately to hospital as early treatment with ACTH will improve the prognosis for some.

Funny turns

- Infants Toddlers Older children

Children are sometimes brought to the A & E department after a parent or teacher has witnessed an alarming, but self-correcting, episode. The causes vary in differing age groups.

Infants

There are many causes for self-limiting apnoeic, cyanotic, or choking spells in babies under one year of age.

- Normal shallow irregular breathing of small infant when asleep.
- Convulsions.
- Reflex laryngeal spasm with gastro-oesophageal reflux.
- Associated with pertussis or bronchiolitis.
- Perioral blueness associated with wind.
- Inhaled foreign body.
- 'Near-miss cot death' (see p. 320).
- Rarely, intentional suffocation.

A good history of exactly how the episode appeared to the observer and any associated symptoms is usually very helpful. All infants with alarming episodes must be admitted for observation, some will need further investigation.

Toddlers

1. Breath holding attacks—these episodes only occur after a toddler has been injured or thwarted. He holds his breath, rapidly turns blue, usually loses consciousness, and falls to the ground. Some children will briefly convulse. After consciousness is lost, breathing starts again and the child recovers. On examination after recovery the child is well with no abnormal physical signs. No treatment is required, but an explanation of the mechanism should be given to the child's parents.

2. Reflex anoxic episodes (pallid syncope)—are episodes of

vagal stimulation often occurring in the course of an illness or after an injury. The child's heart rate drops, he becomes pale, loses consciousness, and may convulse. They are self-limiting episodes and are often mistaken for febrile convulsions. No treatment is needed, but an explanation of the mechanism should be given to the parent.

In both of these attacks a good history is vital for diagnosis. Children who have had breath-holding attacks or pallid syncope do not require admission but their GP should be informed.

Older children

1. Faints—faints or vasovagal episodes often occur in school assembly. The child is described as being very pale, sweaty, and falls to the ground. Brief limb jerking is occasionally noted. On arrival at the A & E department the child has usually recovered, and on examination has no abnormal physical signs. Again, a good history is vital for the diagnosis of a vasovagal episode. If there is a poor history or the episode is unwitnessed, it may be difficult to distinguish the attack from a convulsion. If this is the case then the child should be referred to the paediatricians.

Note: Episodes of syncope arising on exertion may be symptomatic of underlying obstructive congenital heart disease, such as aortic stenosis or coarctation of the aorta, or of cardiac arrythmias. In children whose syncope arises on exertion a chest X-ray and e.c.g. should be performed and the child should be referred to the paediatric department.

2. Hyperventilation—these episodes are common in teenagers. Some upset usually triggers an episode of hyperventilation and during the attack the patient may lose consciousness. The classical physical sign of carpopedal spasm is caused by an increased arterial pH decreasing available calcium. If the patient is still hyperventilating on arrival at the A & E department, a calm environment and gentle, but firm, reassurance usually calms the patient down. Re-breathing into a paper bag is sometimes recommended but is usually unnecessary.

Bacterial meningitis

- **Diagnosis of bacterial meningitis   Meningitis treatment
Meningitis: prophylaxis of contacts**

After the neonatal period, the organisms which cause bacterial meningitis are in order of frequency—*Haemophilus influenzae, Neisseria meningitidis* (Meningococcus) and *Streptococcus pneumoniae*. The overall incidence of bacterial meningitis has remained unchanged for several years, at a rate of about 18 per 100 000 children per year. There is still a mortality rate of more than 5 per cent and a similar rate of permanent serious neurological sequelae.

Diagnosis of bacterial meningitis

In the under 3-year-old child—bacterial meningitis is most common and yet most difficult to diagnose in its early stages in this age group. The classical signs of neck rigidity, photophobia, headache, and vomiting are often absent. A bulging fontanelle is a sign of advanced meningitis in an infant, but even this serious and late sign will be masked if the baby is dehydrated from fever and vomiting. Almost all children with meningitis have some degree of raised intracranial pressure, so that, in fact, the signs and symptoms of meningitis are primarily those of raised intracranial pressure. The following are signs of possible meningitis in infants and young children:

- Drowsiness (often shown by lack of eye contact with parents or doctor).
- Irritability that cannot be easily soothed by parent.
- Poor feeding.
- Unexplained pyrexia.
- Convulsions with fever.
- Apnoeic or cyanotic attacks.
- Purpuric rash.

Older children of four years of age and over—are more likely to have the classical signs of headache, vomiting, pyrexia, neck stiffness, and photophobia. In all unwell children, and children with an unexplained pyrexia, a careful search should be made for neck stiffness and for a purpuric rash. The finding of such a rash in an ill child is almost pathognomic of meningococcal infection for which immediate treatment is required (see p. 39).

Meningitis: neck stiffness Neck stiffness is often a difficult sign to be sure about in an irritable child. Its absence in no way excludes meningitis in a young child. The sign is not an inability to completely flex the neck but evidence of pain, seen by watching the child's face, on neck flexion. In toddlers and older children it can be difficult to decide whether apparent neck stiffness is due to meningeal irritation or childhood resistance. Neck flexion can be made into a game by asking the child to kiss his knee, perhaps after drawing a face on it. A child who is well enough to join in a game and can kiss his knee is very unlikely to have meningitis. Kernig's and Brudzincki's signs are less helpful in childhood than neck stiffness, although they may be positive in a child who has neck rigidity.

Meningitis: referral *Any child in whom you diagnose or suspect meningitis must be referred urgently to the paediatricians.*

Meningitis: lumbar puncture The purpose of a lumbar puncture is to confirm the diagnosis of meningitis and to identify the organism and its antibiotic sensitivity. Lumbar punctures should not usually be done by the A & E SHO. There is a risk of coning and death if a lumbar puncture is performed in a child with significantly raised intracranial pressure. Normal fundi are quite consistent with acutely, severely raised intracranial pressure. The following are possible contra-indications to a lumbar puncture without discussion with a senior paediatrician.

1. Focal seizures.
2. Focal neurological signs, for example asymmetry of limb movement and reflexes, ocular palsies.
3. A widespread purpuric rash in an ill child—in this case intravenous penicillin and chloramphenicol should be given immediately after a blood culture.

4. Impaired conscious level—this can be rapidly assessed by judging the child's response to a peripheral, painful stimulus. The normal reaction is a purposive removal of the painful stimulus. Mere withdrawal of the limb indicates a depressed conscious level.
5. Sluggish, relatively dilated pupils.
6. Impaired oculocephalic reflexes (doll's eye reflexes).
7. Abnormal posture or movement—decerebrate or decorticate posturing or cycling movements of the limbs.
8. Inappropriately low pulse and elevated blood pressure.
9. Coagulation disorder.

Meningitis: treatment

If the paediatrician is unavailable and the child is very seriously ill with a purpuric rash, or focal neurological signs, or a decreased conscious level, then antibiotic and supportive treatment should be started after blood for culture and throat swab have been taken. A lumbar puncture should not be done as it may precipitate coning. A dose of intravenous penicillin 50 mg/kg (up to a maximum of 2 g) and chloramphenicol 25 mg/kg should be given. In a case of penicillin allergy see p. 40. Subsequent doses of chloramphenicol should be 12.5 mg/kg in babies less than a year old. The antibiotics should be given slowly over 10–15 minutes. If the child is deteriorating neurologically then mannitol 0.5 g/kg can be given and the child nursed in the 30° head-up position. Consideration should be given to ventilation and the child should be transferred to intensive care.

Meningitis: prophylaxis of contacts

Prophylaxis is properly the responsibility of the paediatric department and the community health team. However, following a 'meningitis scare' anxious contacts of a meningitis patient may seek advice from the A & E department. Prophylaxis with rifampicin is necessary for household contacts of a case of meningococcal meningitis. This includes everyone living in the same house as the index case. If the child was at a baby minder's, the same recommendation also applies at that home. Casual or school contacts are not at risk from a sporadic case of meningococcal meningitis. Health service personnel are only at risk if they have performed mouth-to-mouth resuscitation on the patient. Prophylaxis with rifampicin is also offered to household contacts of a *Haemophilus influenzae* type B case where there is an under 4-year-old child in the house besides the index case. It is worth remembering that meningococcus can be isolated in the throat swabs of up to 10 per cent of the normal population. When prescribing rifampicin it is important to inform patients that it makes the contraceptive pill less effective and may turn soft contact lenses pink.

Viral meningitis

Viral meningitis is caused by mumps and enteric organisms, such as coxsackie and echoviruses. It usually occurs in children over the age of two years. The usual signs of photophobia, headache, neck stiffness, and vomiting are present, but the child is less ill than a patient with bacterial meningitis. All such children require admission and lumbar puncture to establish the diagnosis. The virus is best isolated from faeces.

Coma

- **Causes of coma   Management**

The initial management of the child in coma can be divided into three main areas. *Immediate paediatric and, if necessary, anaesthetic aid should be requested.*

1. Maintain airway, breathing, and circulation.
2. Attempt to prevent cerebral damage, for example from hypoxia, hypotension, hypothermia, acidosis, and convulsions.
3. Diagnose and treat the treatable, for example i.v. dextrose for hypoglycaemia and i.v. antibiotics if any suspicion of meningitis.

Causes of coma

(commoner causes are indicated by *italic type*)

1. Infections with a direct cerebral effect:
- *bacterial meningitis;*
- viral encephalitis; and
- cerebral abscess.

2. Ischaemic–anoxic conditions:
- *from fluid loss in severe gastroenteritis;*
- *from shock in overwhelming infection, for example meningococcaemia;*
- *from prolonged status epilepticus;*
- from 'near miss cot death';
- from near drowning or hypothermia; and
- from heat stroke.

3. Trauma:
- *accidental head injury with or without skull fracture;*
- *non-accidental head injury, especially in infants;* and
- *shock from blood loss.*

4. Non-traumatic cerebral haemorrhage.

5. Poisoning:
- *accidental or intentional poisoning,* for example tricyclic antidepressants, barbiturates, iron, alcohol, antifreeze, etc;
- *drug abuse* for example alcohol, narcotics; and
- *solvent abuse.*

6. Metabolic:
- *hypoglycaemia,* for example diabetes, severe infection, Reye's syndrome, some inborn errors of metabolism, hyperinsulinaemic states;
- *hyperglycaemia and acidosis* in diabetes;
- hyperammonaemia, for example Reye's syndrome, some inborn errors of metabolism;
- uraemia and hypertension, for example haemolytic uraemic syndrome; and
- hepatic failure.

Management

The patient should be admitted to the resuscitation room. Assess the airway, adequacy of respiration, and circulation clinically, treating as appropriate as described in Chapter 2.

Check the patient's blood sugar by means of a dextrostix or BM stix test. If this is less than 4 mmol/l then take blood for an accurate sugar level and an insulin level if the patient is not a diabetic. Then infuse 2 ml/kg of 50 per cent dextrose. In young infants with small veins 25 per cent dextrose causes less vein damage. A further BM stix test should be done to ensure that the hypoglycaemia is corrected. In all cases set up an i.v. infusion of 4 per cent dextrose and one-fifth normal saline or other appropriate fluid.

Monitor continuing adequacy of respiration and circulation both clinically and with a pulse oximeter, e.c.g., and sphygmomanometer (both manual and automatic).

If there is any possibility of opiate poisoning the patient should have a trial of naloxone (p. 167).

A history should be taken from the accompanying adult or ambulanceman, including whether the patient is known to have a chronic disease, such as diabetes or epilepsy, whether there has been any recent injury or access to poisons, and the history of the patient's health in the last 24 hours.

Examine the patient looking for external signs of trauma (especially to the head), a rash, (especially a purpuric one), focal neurological signs, jaundice, hypertension, or enlarged liver or spleen. The fundi should be carefully examined for papilloedema or retinal haemorrhages.

An assessment of the depth of coma should be performed using a Coma Scale (see p. 71).

It is important to keep the patient normothermic, normotensive, normoglycaemic, well-oxygenated, and in normal acid–base balance to prevent secondary brain damage. Initial investigations should include a blood sugar and arterial blood gas estimations, haemoglobin and blood smear, electrolyte levels, and blood culture.

Further investigations will be ordered by the paediatrician, depending on the history and clinical findings. Lumbar puncture should not be performed, because of the risk of coning, until raised intracranial pressure has been excluded, usually by a CT scan.

If there is any suggestion of bacterial meningitis or the condition cannot be excluded, then intravenous penicillin and chloramphenicol should be given (see p. 259). If viral encephalitis is thought likely, intravenous Acylovir should be given.

Arrangements may be needed for the patient to undergo a CT scan and to be transferred to a paediatric intensive care unit.

Occasionally, a patient, usually a teenager, will be 'shamming' unconsciousness. The absence of any genuine physical signs usually makes this obvious. Counselling for an underlying behaviour problem may be required.

Headache

Headache is often a feature of acute upper respiratory infections, and a worried parent may bring a child to the A & E department because of concern about meningitis. It is usually not difficult to differentiate meningitis from other infectious illnesses in the child old enough to complain of a headache. If in doubt, of course, referral to the paediatrician would be appropriate.

Headache can be caused by referred pain from dental disease or sinusitis. The latter is uncommon in young children as the frontal sinuses are not sufficiently developed until about 10 years of age. Headache may be associated with systemic hypertension, and all children presenting with headache must have their blood pressure measured. Bleeding from an arteriovenous malformation is a rare event in childhood. It may present as the sudden onset of a very severe headache. Loss of consciousness and stiff neck are less common than in adults. Children will usually show, in addition to the headache, a seizure, focal neurological deficit, or general increased irritability.

A child with recurrent headache may also present to the A & E department when parents are distressed with the child's symptom and worried about possible underlying causes. A full history and careful examination is necessary, including the blood pressure.

Migraine and recurrent stress headaches are common in middle childhood. Migraine typically is associated with nausea and vomiting and relieved by sleep. A few children with migraine have temporary neurological abnormalities, such as hemiplegia. These children must be admitted for investigation. A child with a headache present on waking or one whose headache wakens him from sleep should be referred to the paediatric department as this may be a sign of raised intracranial pressure.

A child with an uncomplicated recurrent headache should be referred back to his GP after reassurance to the parents that there is nothing acutely wrong.

Acute motor weakness

- Guillain–Barré syndrome   Bell's palsy

Guillain–Barré syndrome

Guillain–Barré syndrome is now the commonest form of acute motor weakness in childhood. This illness usually occurs after a mild viral infection. Patients are sometimes thought to be hysterical when they first present. The development of peripheral nerve weakness usually starts in the legs and the patient often complains of a painful back. The reflexes are depressed and there may be painful paraesthesiae. Later on, bulbar signs, dysphonia, and dysphasia may develop. All patients with Guillain–Barré syndrome must be admitted under paediatric care. Some will progress to ventilatory failure as the intercostal muscles are involved.

Bell's palsy

The sudden onset of unilateral facial weakness involving all three branches of the facial nerve is not uncommon in children. Parents are often very alarmed by this and may bring the child straight to an A & E department thinking that the child has had a stroke. Children with facial weakness should be referred to the paediatrician for assessment although they may be managed as an out-patient.

Bell's palsy is a diagnosis of exclusion, so a careful examination for other neurological signs should be made. Additional signs would indicate a possible underlying tumour as the cause of the abnormality. The blood pressure should be measured as hypertension in childhood occasionally presents as isolated nerve palsies. The presence of a vesicular rash suggests the Ramsey–Hunt syndrome, and an erythematous or indurated rash suggests Lyme disease (for which penicillin or erythromycin would be beneficial). Evidence of local inflammation in the ear or mastoids should be sought.

In Bell's palsy, complete recovery is usual in over 90 per cent of children in 6–8 weeks. If the child is seen in the first two or three days a 5-day course of prednisone, 2 mg/kg/d in two daily doses, is often prescribed, although there is no proof of efficacy. An eye patch and chloramphenicol eye ointment should be used in patients who cannot close the eye properly, in order to prevent conjunctival infection and damage. Occasionally there is poor recovery and later cosmetic surgery may be required.

Further reading

1. Gordon, N. and McKinley, I. (ed.) (1986). *Neurologically sick children: treatment and management.* Blackwell Scientific Publications, Oxford.
2. Levin, N. and Heyderman, R. S. (1991). Bacterial meningitis. In *Recent advances in paediatrics* Vol. 9, (ed. T. J. David), pp. 1 19. Churchill Livingstone, Edinburgh.

CHAPTER 12

Skin and infectious diseases

Presentation of skin diseases

Children may be brought to the A & E department because of the sudden appearance, or worsening, of a rash, or its poor response to treatment.

The diagnosis of a rash is based on its history, appearance, distribution, and associated physical signs. An ophthalmoscope set at about 8 dioptres is often helpful for close inspection of skin lesions.

1. Erythematous, maculopapular rashes are usually due to an infectious disease or an allergic reaction.
2. Itchy skin lesions suggest eczema, scabies or insect bites.
3. Vesicobullous eruptions are characteristic of chickenpox, herpes simplex, and hand, foot and mouth disease. Staphyloccocal infection, bullous erythema multiforme, and drug reactions are less common but potentially more serious causes of a vesicobullous rash.
4. A sore mouth may be due to primary herpes simplex, candida infection, scarlet fever, or rarer, more serious diseases, such as Stevens–Johnson syndrome or Kawasaki's disease.
5. A non-itchy, scaly lesion suggests psoriasis or a fungal infection.
6. Purpuric (non-blanching) lesions are caused by vasculitis, trauma, or clotting disorders and always require paediatric referral.

Note: a purpuric rash in an ill child is almost certainly meningococcal septicaemia. Urgent treatment is needed (p. 39).

Eczema

Sudden deterioration in eczema is usually due to infection. Bacterial infection causes pustules, discharge, and crusting. The causative organisms are usually Staphylococcus aureus and beta haemolytic streptococci. For one or two small infected areas a topical antiseptic, such as 10 per cent povidone–iodine cream, or an antiseptic hydrocortisone cream, such as Vioform HC, may be sufficient. Topical antibiotics are best avoided as they can cause sensitization. Any more widespread infection requires oral penicillin and flucloxacillin for 7–14 days.

Ill or pyrexial children with widespread infection should be admitted to hospital, but others can be treated as outpatients. A skin swab is important to ensure that the organism is sensitive to the antibiotics prescribed. Most children with infected eczema will noticeably improve within 48 hours and they should be reviewed then. If they have not improved by then, the usual explanations are non-compliance with treatment, bacterial resistance, or else the infection is due to herpes virus. The child should be referred to the paediatric department.

Primary herpes simplex infection may cause serious systemic illness in eczematous children. Vesicles can appear over the face, trunk, and limbs and they soon turn to umbilicated pustules. Scratching and secondary infection may make herpes infection difficult to distinguish from simple bacterial infection. The virus can be identified by culture of skin exudate or, more rapidly, by examination of vesicular fluid under the electron microscope. Mild cases are self-limiting, but severe cases with systemic illness and fever require treatment with antibiotics and intravenous acyclovir.

If the eczema is not infected but help is sought because of itching, an emollient, such as emulsifying ointment or white soft paraffin, can be used whenever the skin is dry. If night time itching is disturbing the child, the sedative effect of Vallergan (trimeprazine) tablets may reduce the damaging effect of scratching. These children should be referred back to their GP for continued management.

Seborrhoeic dermatitis

Seborrhoeic dermatitis is most easily recognized by the thick scalp scale known as 'cradle cap'. On the face, neck, and in the nappy area the rash is greasy, red, and scaly, but not apparently itchy. The application of a mild keratolytic agent, such as 1 per cent salicylic acid in white soft paraffin twice a week, followed 12 hours later by shampooing, will treat the cradle cap, and 1 per cent hydrocortisone ointment is suitable for other areas. The child should be referred back to his GP.

Psoriasis

A guttate psoriasis with round, red, scaly lesions over the trunk may follow a streptococcal throat infection. Less frequently, children present with typical red and scaly psoriatic lesions on the extensor aspects of elbows, knees, and in the scalp. Skin and scalp should be treated with coal tar ointment or shampoo. Failing improvement with coal tar, 0.1 per cent dithranol ointment can be prescribed. Steroid creams should be avoided as their use is associated with early relapse of the skin condition. Refer the patient back to his GP.

Infestations and infections

- Scabies   Fungal infection—tinea   Warts   *Molluscum contagiosum*   Impetigo

Scabies

The cause of scabies is infestation with the mite *Sarcopes scabiei*. There is a widespread papular urticarial rash on the trunk and limbs. It is often most noticeable on the feet and ankles in toddlers. Scratch marks are often seen, but burrows can be difficult to find. Scabies is characterized by severe itching of the skin, especially at night. If other family members are also itching then the diagnosis is very clear. There is a one month latent period from infestation to the allergic urticarial rash.

Treatment is with 1 per cent lindane lotion which should be applied to all skin from the neck downwards and left for 24 hours before bathing off. For under five year olds, very thin individuals and epileptics, aqueous malathion should be used. If using malathion, the treatment should be repeated 3 days later. All bed clothes and clothing should be washed. The rest of the family should be advised to seek advice from their general practitioner as other family members may also be affected.

Fungal infection—tinea

Tinea corporis produces round, red, scaly, non-itchy lesions which are sometimes mistaken for psoriasis. The classical paler centre which gives the lesion its name of ringworm appears later in the disease. The lesions should be treated with clotrimazole, 1 per cent, or miconazole, 2 per cent, cream twice daily. Treatment is usually required for two or three weeks and should be continued for several days after the lesions have disappeared.

Tinea unguum appears as a thickened and yellow nail not caused by trauma, or as a persistent or relapsing paronychia. A nail paring can be examined by the microbiology laboratory for hyphae.

Tinea capitum presents as bald patches from which broken hairs protrude. The hair is fluorescent under Wood's light. Both nail and scalp infections are difficult to treat and require systemic griseofulvin. These patients should be referred back to their general practitioner or to a dermatologist for treatment since long-term follow-up is required.

Warts

Warts and plantar warts (verrucae) are virus-induced hyperkeratotic skin tumours. Verrucae are sometimes presented as foreign bodies in the foot. Warts are self-limiting but disfiguring, and in the case of verrucae often painful. Treatment is either time-consuming (keratolytic) or painful (destructive methods, such as freezing and curettage). Children should be advised to await resolution or be referred back to the general practitioner.

Molluscum contagiosum

Molluscum contagiosum is another virus-induced skin infection. The rash consists of pearly papules with a central umbilication in crops often around the face, axillae, neck, and knees. The papules will disappear spontaneously but may take several months. Their disappearance can be speeded up by breaking the skin with a needle and extruding the caseous contents. The child should be referred back to his GP.

Impetigo

Impetigo is a staphylococcal or streptococcal infection of the skin which develops on skin damaged by abrasion, insect bites, scabies, or other preceding skin injury. The initial pustules soon rupture and leave a yellow crust over a weeping, red area. Small lesions can be treated by cleansing and an antiseptic cream, such as 10 per cent povidone–iodine. Widespread lesions warrant systemic flucloxacillin for a week. A swab should be first taken to make sure that the organism is sensitive to the antibiotic prescribed.

Allergic rashes

• **Urticaria   Angioneurotic oedema   Insect bites**

Urticaria

The sudden onset of urticaria, ('nettle rash'), is common. Sometimes a precipitating factor is identified in a child known to be allergic to foodstuffs such as egg, nuts, or fish. More frequently, no allergen is identified. Treatment with oral antihistamines is usually effective.

Angioneurotic oedema

A few children with an allergic reaction will have swelling of the face, including the lips and sometimes the tongue and buccal mucosa. These children should be referred to the paediatrician as there is a small risk of laryngeal oedema.

Insect bites

Insect bites present as multiple itching papules with urticaria.

Usually they are in crops on the trunk and limbs. There may be no history of exposure to insect bites, especially in young children. Topical antihistamines are not effective. Calamine lotion or crotamiton, 10 per cent cream or lotion, are mildly antipruritic and may help symptomatically. Any pets at home should be treated with an insecticide.

Nappy rash

A rash in the nappy area is usually ammoniacal dermatitis with red, ulcerated areas but with sparing of the inside of skin folds. It is best treated by leaving the nappy off until the rash has healed. (This may take two or three days.) Its return can be prevented by frequent nappy changes, cleansing, and a barrier cream. A rash which causes red, macerated skin inside the groin folds and satellite areas on the abdomen is caused by candida and requires topical nystatin cream. The skin of babies with eczema or seborrhoeic dermatitis who have nappy area involvement may improve with an anti-fungal and hydrocortisone cream such as Nystaform or Canesten HC.

Painful mouths

1. Candida infection of the buccal mucosa is common in babies up to a few weeks old. The baby may cry on sucking or refuse feeds, although he is otherwise well. White patches with a red base are seen in the mouth. Treatment is with oral nystatin after feeds.
2. The commonest cause of stomatitis in young children is *primary* herpes simplex. This unpleasant disease starts abruptly with a painful ulcerated mouth, fever, and refusal to eat. Treatment is symptomatic with analgesics. Solid foods cannot be attempted for several days, but most children can be managed at home with drinks of milk through a straw. A few children may need admitting for nursing care if the parents cannot be relied upon to prevent dehydration of

the child. Recurrent herpes is usually found around the mouth (cold sores), but some children have recurrent, vesicular outbreaks in other areas, such as on a finger as a herpetic whitlow or on the pinna. The frequency and severity of these outbreaks gradually decreases with age.

3. Coxsackie virus A16 is the usual cause of hand, foot, and mouth disease. The mouth lesions are ulcers, but vesicles are seen on the palms and dorsal surfaces of the hands and sometimes on the feet. No treatment is needed.

4. Stevens–Johnson syndrome is a potentially fatal disorder which presents with mouth ulcers in conjunction with a vesicular or bullous erythema multiforme which may be present on the perineum. The condition is sometimes precipitated by drugs (especially sulphonamides) or may occur following an upper respiratory tract infection. Special hazards are a severe conjunctivitis, which may lead to blindness, and septicaemia from secondary infection of affected skin with Gram-negative organisms. Any child suspected of having Stevens–Johnson syndrome must be admitted to hospital under paediatric and ophthalmic care.

Purpura

Purpura is a red or purple skin rash that does not blanch on pressure, brought about by blood in the skin. Causes include vasculitis, thrombocytopenia, a clotting disorder, or trauma. All children with purpura should be referred to the paediatrician.

1. *A purpuric rash in an ill child is usually meningococcal septicaemia and is a medical emergency* (see p. 39).

2. Idiopathic thrombocytopenic purpura is the commonest cause of a low platelet count in childhood. The disease often appears to be initiated by a preceding minor infection. Purpura may be found in any site but is often seen as large ecchymoses over those sites that children commonly bruise and also as petechiae on the trunk. In most cases the disease is self-limiting. Intracranial bleeding rarely occurs but can be fatal.

3. Drugs, especially sulphonamides, can cause thrombocyto-penia and present as purpura.

4. Leukaemia is a less common but important disease to consider in patients with purpura. Other features to look for are a short history of tiredness, pallor, or limb pain. Hepato-splenomegaly may be found on abdominal examination.

5. Henoch–Schonlein purpura is the commonest non-throm-bocytopenic purpura. There is a vasculitis of unknown aetiology. The earlier skin lesions blanch but soon become purpuric. The purpura is almost always on the lower limbs and there is accompanying oedema which may be quite marked in the scrotum. Another feature is arthritis, affecting large joints, such as the knees and ankles. Most children have microscopic haematuria and in some this is macroscopic. A few children with Henoch–Schonlein purpura have nephritis so the blood pressure must be checked. Abdominal pain is a common complaint and some children pass blood per rectum. There is no specific treatment. All children should be referred to the paediatrician but milder cases may be managed by them as out-patients.

6. Bruises, especially in different stages of discoloration may be caused by child abuse (p. 180).

7. The haemophiliac patient should be managed as described on p. 286.

Common infectious diseases of childhood

• Risk groups

Risk groups

Certain groups of children may be at serious risk from the common infectious diseases of childhood. Children with immune deficiency syndromes or those on immune suppres-sant drugs should be referred to the paediatric department, or advice sought from their specialist if they present with an infectious disease or have been in contact with one. Children with cystic fibrosis can be seriously ill with measles, whoop-ing cough, or chickenpox and should be referred if they have one of these diseases, or have been in contact with one of them.

Neonates are generally immune to the common exanthems of childhood as they have antibodies from their mothers, but if they do develop one of these diseases then they may be seriously ill. Chickenpox is a special risk in this age group. Neonates with an exanthem should be referred to the paediatric team.

Measles (rubeola) This has a characteristic prodromal phase of fever, coryza, conjunctivitis, and a cough. The diagnosis is made at this stage by seeing Koplick's spots—white dots on a red background—on the inside of the cheeks. When the exanthem appears the child's fever rises further as a macular rash starts behind the ears and spreads, becoming papular, over the face, arms, and trunk. Some children have otitis media, pneumonia, or diarrhoea and vomiting. Encephalitis is rare but potentially fatal. Measles can still occur mildly if a child has received measles vaccine. Admission is rarely necessary for a child with measles unless he is very sick or has underlying chronic disease. Infectivity continues for five days after the rash has appeared, and the incubation period is two weeks.

German measles (rubella) Rubella is a much milder infection than measles and its chief health impact is in congenital rubella. The rash is maculopapular, on the face and trunk, and usually disappears over a day or so. Posterior cervical and occipital lymphadenopathy is characteristic. The incubation period of rubella is 14–21 days and infectivity continues until the rash has gone. In older children a transient arthralgia or arthritis occurs occasionally. Treatment is symptomatic.

Roseola infantum This is characterized by a fever with no apparent cause which subsides as a maculopapular rash appears over the trunk and arms, fading within 24 hours. No treatment is required.

Erythema infectiosum or slapped cheek disease The causative agent in this disease is parvovirus B19. The rash begins with bright red cheeks and circumoral pallor. It then appears over the limbs in a confluent or reticular pattern. The disease is self-limiting and benign. In older children arthralgia may occur. In patients with a haemolytic anaemia, such as sickle cell disease or thalassaemia, parvovirus may precipitate an aplastic crisis (p. 285).

Scarlet fever—see p. 200

Chickenpox Chickenpox produces successive crops of itchy vesicles on a red base on the face, scalp, and trunk. Lesions may occur in the mouth, genitalia, or eyes. Treatment is symptomatic, but chloramphenicol or Gentamycin ointment may be used for the eyes as secondary bacterial infection is likely. Complications are uncommon in children, but occasionally a chickenpox pneumonitis occurs for which intravenous acyclovir is used. The disease is infectious from 24 hours before the rash appears until the last crop of vesicles has scabbed. Chickenpox may be fatal in neonates who must be referred to the paediatrician for admission.

Other viruses (such as echoviruses and adenoviruses) These can produce a measles or German measles-like rash in association with fever and upper respiratory tract or gastrointestinal symptoms. Treatment is symptomatic.

Mumps Mumps causes pain and swelling in one or both parotid glands. The swelling is often easier to see than palpate. The angle of the mandible is obscured and the earlobe pushed upward and outward. This is most clearly seen if the patient is observed from the back. In the mouth, redness and swelling around the parotid duct can be seen. Mumps meningitis is quite common during this condition and is the commonest cause of aseptic meningitis. Orchitis is uncommon in childhood. If it is suspected, torsion of the testicle should also be considered as a cause of the testicular pain and swelling. Patients with mumps are infectious until the parotid swelling has subsided, and the incubation period is from 14–24 days.

Hepatitis A Many infections with hepatitis A are anicteric and pass undiagnosed. The prodromal illness consists of fever, malaise, anorexia, and nausea. Jaundice, dark urine, or pale stools are usually the cause for A & E attendance. There is no treatment required for children with hepatitis A, but they should be referred to their GP to be supervized until the jaundice has subsided. Hepatitis A immunoglobulin is not routinely recommended for contacts but should be considered for pregnant mothers and any contact who is chronically ill.

Eye infections

- **Conjunctivitis   Periorbital cellulitis   Kawasaki's disease**

Conjunctivitis (for neonatal conjunctivitis see p. 302)

Red, painful, or purulent conjunctivae, without preceding trauma are infected with *Haemophilus influenzae*, streptococci, or staphylococci or a virus. Some cases of conjunctivitis occur in the course of a systemic viral infection with measles or adenovirus.

Treatment, after a swab for bacterial culture has been taken, is by cleansing the eye with damp cotton wool followed by the installation of chloramphenicol eye drops, two hourly, while the child is awake, and chloramphenicol eye ointment at night. Tetracycline eye ointment 6 hourly is an alternative. Two hourly treatment is usually necessary for only a day or so then 6–8 hourly treatment for three more days will suffice.

Recurrent watery eye is common in infancy and is due to a blocked tear duct. Most improve spontaneously.

Non-infective causes of conjunctivitis include reaction to eye drops already being used, chemical irritation from chlorine in swimming pools, and allergic conjunctivitis. The latter may demonstrate striking conjunctival oedema. Systemic or topical antihistamines may help, but the reaction is usually self-limiting. Occasionally, conjunctivitis is seen as part of a systemic illness such as Stevens–Johnson syndrome (p. 275) or Kawasaki's disease (p. 280).

Periorbital cellulitis

This is a serious infection which can lead to eye damage, cavernous sinus thrombosis, or meningitis.

The child has pain and swelling around the eye and in the eyelid. He is often unwell or pyrexial, but if he is not the condition can be mistaken for conjunctivitis. However, the inflammation is more obvious in the periorbital tissues than in the conjunctivae.

The child should be admitted for intravenous antibiotics effective against staphylococci, streptococci, and *Haemophilus influenzae*.

Kawasaki's disease

This is an uncommon vasculitic disease of unknown aetiology. It is important to recognize, as early diagnosis and treatment in hospital (human immunoglobulin intravenously and oral aspirin) can reduce the risk of late, serious sequelae (coronary artery aneurysm and death).

The diagnosis is considered in a patient who has some, or all, of the following features:

- Prolonged (> 5 days) fever.
- Non-purulent conjunctivitis.
- Cutaneous rash (usually urticarial).
- Dry, fissured lips.
- Red tongue with enlarged papillae.
- Peeling fingers.
- Lymph gland enlargement.
- Arthralgia.
- Thrombocytosis.

Such patients should be referred to the paediatrician.

CHAPTER 13

Blood disorders

Blood disorders

Children with a haemoglobinopathy may develop acute symptoms from their disease or need A & E treatment for another related problem, such as trauma.

Sickle cell anaemia

- **Infection in sickle cell patients   Sickle cell crises Anaesthesia in sickle cell patients**

The term sickle cell anaemia covers a group of disorders which includes homozygous sickle cell disease (HbSS), sickle cell haemoglobin C disease (HbSC), sickle cell–thalassaemia (HbS–Thal), and others. All are characterized by *in vivo* sickling attacks. Symptoms are worse in HbSS cases. Cards have been issued by the Department of Health to indicate what illness patients have. In the UK the disease mainly affects children of Afro–Caribbean origin, but affected patients are also found in the Mediterranean, the Middle East, Greece, and India.

Carriers of haemoglobin S (sickle cell trait) are not anaemic and only rarely develop symptoms. They may develop spontaneous haematuria and sickle with anoxia, for instance during poorly administered anaesthetics.

In a patient with classical sickle cell disease the haemoglobin usually runs between 7–10 g/dl. Jaundice is frequently due to intrahepatic obstruction rather than to simple haemolysis. The spleen is usually large in infancy but atrophies later and is usually impalpable by 5 years of age. Acute splenic enlargement may occur in small children with a rapid onset of anaemia as red cells are trapped in the enlarging spleen. Death may occur from cardiac failure.

Infection in sickle cell patients

Infection is frequently due to pneumococcal disease associated with defective splenic function even in the presence of a large or normal spleen. A seriously ill sickle cell patient probably has pneumococcal or salmonella septicaemia. Urgent paediatric help should be requested and intravenous penicillin or ampicillin given.

Sickle cell crises

Painful crises may occur in any site. They are easily confused with, and may co-exist with, acute infection.

1. Abdominal pain due to sickling in abdominal blood vessels may suggest appendicitis or cholecystitis.
2. Limb sickling may mimic osteomyelitis or acute arthritis.
3. Chest pain and dyspnoea may mimic pneumonia but be due to the acute chest syndrome.
4. Small children develop swelling of the hands and fingers resembling tuberculous dactylitis but with a more acute onset.

Patients should be referred to the paediatrician.

In the treatment of acute episodes it is sensible to assume infection is present and to give antibiotic cover. In view of the frequency of pneumococcal infection, a penicillin should be used. Erythromycin may be used in the pencillin-sensitive patient. Sickle cell patients frequently have impaired renal concentrating ability and dehydrate rapidly, which makes their symptoms worse. Ample fluid replacement, intravenously if necessary, must be the rule. Dextrans and other colloids offer no advance over 4 per cent dextrose and 0.18 per cent saline. Crises may be very painful and demoralizing for patients prone to recurrent attacks. Analgesics must be given regularly and in sufficient dosage to remove pain.

Anaesthesia in sickle cell patients

Anaesthesia in any child with haemoglobin S, including any child with sickle cell trait, needs to be performed with care to ensure good oxygenation and to avoid acidosis. The anaesthetist should always be informed in advance if operation is contemplated. Oxygen is given post-operatively until the child has fully recovered from the effects of the anaesthetic.

Sickle tests should be available to every A & E department and should be used to screen any child of Afro–Caribbean origin with a painful condition or who needs an anaesthetic. A sickle test will not distinguish sickle cell disease from sickle cell trait, but patients with sickle cell anaemia can usually be recognized by their low haemoglobin.

Thalassaemia

The thalassaemias comprise a wide variety of haemoglobin disorders. The only disorders likely to cause problems in the A & E department are thalassaemia intermedia (mild homozygous beta-thalassaemia or haemoglobin H disease) and thalassaemia major due to the usual type of homozygous beta-thalassaemia.

Thalassaemia minor causes a mild microcytic hypochromic anaemia similar to that seen in iron deficiency. It does not predispose to any other diseases, and children with thalassaemia minor do not need different treatment from normal children.

Thalassaemia intermedia produces a mild chronic haemolytic anaemia. Infections, particularly with parvovirus, may exacerbate this anaemia through an aplastic crisis. These patients also develop pneumococcal septicaemia as in those patients whose spleen has been removed.

Thalassaemia major causes a severe haemolytic anaemia with marked hepatosplenomegaly. Lifelong blood transfusion is necessary every few weeks. This leads to iron overload which is treated with regular subcutaneous injections of desferrioxamine, given at home most nights with a battery-powered syringe driver. Some patients develop local erythema at the site of injection but these usually recover spontaneously.

Complications which may develop in thalassaemia major and present to the A & E department include:

1. Overwhelming bacterial sepsis due to splenectomy or a non-functioning spleen. Blood culture should be done and high-dose intravenous penicillin or ampicillin given.
2. Infection with *Yersinia enterocolitica* whose growth is encouraged by the iron overload.

3. Cardiac arrhythmias in older patients with iron overload.
4. Endocrine disorders due to fibrosis secondary to iron overload. These include diabetes mellitus and hypocalcaemia due to fibrosis of the parathyroids.

Patients who have received blood transfusions outside Europe should be regarded as high-risk cases for hepatitis B and possibly HIV infection. Blood should be collected wearing gloves. Samples should be labelled with a 'Risk of Infection' label.

Glucose-6-phosphate dehydrogenase deficiency (G-6-PD)

Patients with a G-6-PD deficiency usually come from Africa, Asia, and Southern Europe. The importance of the condition in the A & E department is that certain drugs can precipitate episodes of haemolysis. Aspirin, nitrofurantoin, and sulphonamides (including co-trimoxazole) may cause haemolysis and should be avoided in patients with G-6-PD deficiency.

Management of the haemophiliac patient

The haemophilias include classical haemophilia (haemophilia A) due to factor VIII deficiency, Christmas disease (haemophilia B) due to factor IX deficiency, and von Willebrand's disease (haemophilia C) due to a defect of the von Willebrand factor, of which factor VIII forms a part. The two former are inherited in a sex-linked manner, the latter is autosomal with both dominant and recessive patterns.

The symptoms of classical haemophilia and Christmas disease are identical and the two diseases can only be distinguished by blood tests.

However, as different clotting factor concentrates are used in their treatment, an accurate diagnosis is essential. Affected patients should be registered at a haemophilia centre and issued with a green card giving details of their disorder. In cases of difficulty the haemophilia centre should be able to give advice about precise diagnosis and the usual treatment. Affected boys bruise easily, and superficial bruises rarely need treatment. Ice-packs applied early will often help a more severe bruise to settle.

Bleeding into joints is the major problem with both diseases. The large joints are usually involved, particularly knees, ankles, and elbows. Early treatment by clotting factor replacement is the rule, in order to prevent joint damage and late osteoarthritis. Affected patients are often able to identify a joint bleed at a very early stage, well before any objective signs are visible or palpable for the doctor unfamiliar with haemophilia. It is unusual for undiagnosed haemophiliacs to present for the first time in an A & E department, so most will be visitors unfamiliar with the local haemophilia centre, patients on home treatment who have used up their supplies, or patients with mild disease who do not normally attend a haemophilia centre. In all cases, do not hesitate to ask the patient or parent what treatment is usually given, which vein is preferred for injection, and what other treatment is needed. These patients usually know a lot about their own disease and it is commonsense to pay attention to their views.

Most joint bleeds respond to a dose of clotting factor which brings the blood level up to 20–30 per cent. Bleeds are usually spontaneous and 80 per cent settle with one injection. Bleeds due to injury need higher doses which may need to be repeated, and the patient should be referred to the local haemophilia centre as soon as possible. The joint may be more comfortable if a crepe bandage is applied. For severe bleeds a plaster of Paris backslab or Robert Jones bandage may be helpful. Plaster should never be applied all around the limb in case further bleeding causes vascular obstruction, and any plaster cylinder should be split. Joint aspiration is rarely necessary, but will relieve pressure, and hence pain, in severe haemarthrosis with a large, hot, tense joint. It must be undertaken with full sterile precautions and further clotting factor subsequently given in an attempt to prevent further bleeding. Aspiration of joints should not usually be carried out by A & E staff.

The dose of clotting factor needed is calculated as follows:

$$\text{Factor dose needed (ml)} = \frac{\text{Weight (kg)} \times \% \text{ rise needed}}{\text{constant (k)}}$$

where for factor VIII $k = 1.5$ and for factor IX $k = 0.9$.

Other bleeds or suspected bleeds which require clotting factor treatment include head injury, bleeding in the floor of the mouth and the neck which could obstruct respiration, and bleeding in the perineum which could obstruct the urethra, Cerebral haemorrhage comes high in the list of causes of death in haemophilia. Affected patients should be given a dose of clotting factor calculated to bring the blood level up to at least 80 per cent immediately and the patient admitted for observation. A CAT scan should be arranged urgently and the neurosurgical team and haemophilia centre contacted at once. Haematomas can be removed and patients may make a full recovery.

Other bleeding complications include bleeding from the mouth and gums, and epistaxis. They can sometimes be stopped by local application of a 50:50 mixture of topical thrombin and 1:1000 adrenalin, but recurrent and resistant bleeds need factor replacement to a level around 25 per cent, which may need to be repeated until the lesion has healed. Tranexamic acid ('Cyclokapron') is helpful for bleeds from the mouth and gastrointestinal tract, but not for joint bleeds. The dose is 250 mg per 10 kg body weight three times daily, both tablets and an elixir are available. Patients with von Willebrand's disease tend to be less severely affected than those with haemophilia A and B. However, some patients are as severely affected behaving like severe haemophiliac boys, with the addition that severely affected adolescent girls may have bad menorrhagia. Joint bleeds may be painful and need analgesia. Paracetamol may be ineffective, and mixtures of paracetamol and codeine are better. Mefenamic acid is often helpful (25 mg/kg/d in three divided doses). Fractures are relatively common in haemophiliacs. Bone rarefaction from disuse and inflammation may be a predisposing factor. Fortunately they heal well. Several days clotting factor replacement is usually recommended. Remember that any plaster should be split. The only exception to this is for a patient who is under continuous observation in hospital, when the distal part of the limb can be observed for circulatory or neurological impairment.

Any laceration large enough to need suturing will need high-dose daily clotting factor replacement until the wound has healed. The blood level needs to be maintained above 50 per cent throughout this time. Wounds heal slowly in haemophiliacs, and even small cuts will break down with the formation of loose jelly-like clots and risk of infection unless covered by replacement treatment. Do not be misled by the fact that the wound has clotted well after suturing; it may break down and bleed up to several days later. When possible, it is sensible to use adhesive strips rather than stitches to bring wound edges together.

Normal immunization can be given in haemophiliacs, but they are better given subcutaneously rather than intramuscularly. Tetanus prophylaxis should not be omitted because of haemophilia.

Bleeding after dental extraction calls for clotting factor replacement. Tranexamic acid is often helpful. Oral penicillin V may help prevent bleeding by depressing growth of oral bacteria which may provoke fibrinolysis. Bleeding from the site of desquamating or recently desquamated primary teeth may be stopped by local pressure and/or topical thrombin and adrenalin (see above).

Haemophiliacs born before 1985 who have been treated with clotting factor concentrates may be infected with HIV or hepatitis B. The products now used are safe, so there is virtually no risk that younger haemophiliacs will have contracted these infections. However, if there is any doubt, it is sensible to treat a haemophiliac patient as potentially infectious. Collect blood samples, treat lacerations, and give injections wearing gloves, and label blood samples with a 'Risk of Infection' warning.

Neonatal problems

Neonatal resuscitation

- **Resuscitation management   Action to take if poor response to resuscitation   When to stop resuscitation Post-resuscitation care**

Occasionally an asphyxiated baby, newly born in an ambulance or at home, may be brought to the A & E department for resuscitation. A baby who is born quickly and unexpectedly and is asphyxiated is very likely to be a preterm baby. Staff in the A & E department should be able to resuscitate such an infant before transferring him to the special care baby unit or neonatal intensive care unit. With modern neonatal intensive care the outcome of preterm birth is likely to be good, even for extremely preterm infants. Surviving infants born at 24–28 weeks gestation have a 70–80 per cent chance of no serious handicap. Surviving infants born from 28 to 31 weeks gestation have a 90 per cent chance of freedom from serious handicap. It is, therefore, appropriate to resuscitate immediately even if the infant appears very preterm. Delayed resuscitation will lead to a poorer outcome.

The equipment and drugs detailed in Tables 14.1, 14.2, and 14.3 will be required for neonatal resuscitation. Some of this will be standard A & E equipment.

Table 14.1 • Equipment for neonatal airway and breathing management

1. Neonatal face mask for oxygen delivery
2. Suction catheter with a soft tip (maximum pressure of 100 mmHg on the suction machine)
3. Infant oral airways sizes 000–1
4. Laerdal infant bag and mask
5. Two straight-bladed neonatal laryngoscopes
6. Endotracheal tubes: sizes 2.5, 3.0, and 3.5 mm
7. A cold fibre-optic light source (optional)
8. Chest drain set

Table 14.2 • Equipment for umbilical vein catheterization

1. Scalpel
2. Fine sterile feeding tube
3. A pair of untoothed forceps
4. Umbilical tape
5. Silk stitch
6. Adhesive tape suitable for delicate skin

Table 14.3 • Drugs for neonatal resuscitation

Drugs	Dose	Route
Sodium bicarbonate, 8.4%	1–2 mmol/kg	i.v.
Dextrose, 10%	2 ml/kg	i.v.
Naloxone	10 μg/kg	i.m. or i.v.
Adrenalin, 1:10 000	0.1 ml/kg	i.v. or i.t.
Atropine	0.02 mg/kg	i.v.
Calcium chloride, 10%	0.5 ml/kg (slowly)	i.v.
Frusemide	1–2 mg/kg	i.v.

A preterm baby is likely to weigh between 1–2 kg.

Resuscitation management

The infant's colour, respiratory effort and rate, and the pulse rate should be assessed.

Paediatric help should be summoned immediately, but the initial resuscitation should be commenced while awaiting the paediatrician.

1. If the baby is pink, active, and crying vigorously, no active resuscitation is required. The baby should be dried and kept warm with warmed blankets and an improvised hat made from tubigrip. Unless the oropharynx is full of meconium or maternal blood the baby should not be routinely sucked out as this may cause reflex vagal bradycardia and apnoea. If the mother is well enough, the baby should be kept with her. If she is unwell or receiving treatment she

should be shown the baby so that she can be reassured that he is well. The baby should be under observation until transferred to the post-natal ward or special care baby unit. If the infant is less than 2 kg, or cold, or unwell a BM stix should be checked. Hypoglycaemia (2 mmol or less) should be urgently confirmed with a venous sample of blood. A hypoglycaemic baby should be fed if asymptomatic or given 10 per cent dextrose (2 ml/kg as a bolus initially) i.v. if he is jittery or convulsing. The feed should be 15–30 ml of a baby milk, but if none is available in the A & E department 10 per cent dextrose will be adequate. Treatment of hypoglycaemia must be immediate and a further BM stix checked to assess response.

2. If the baby is blue, and apnoeic, or gasping, with a heart rate of 100 or above and the tone only slightly decreased, he is in a state of primary apnoea and may respond to peripheral stimulation and facial oxygen or ventilation by bag and mask with oxygen. However, if there is no spontaneous respiration within one minute, or the heart rate starts to fall, then the baby should be intubated by the oral route. A size 3 endotracheal tube is preferred, but below 28 weeks a size 2.5 may be needed.

To intubate the infant, the larynx should be visualized using the infant laryngoscope and any secretions sucked out with a soft tipped catheter. The epiglottis and vocal cords should be identified and the endotracheal tube inserted between the latter. Gentle laryngeal pressure from an assistant may be helpful.

The bag should be connected to the endotracheal tube and gentle inflation of the lungs should commence at 40 inflations per minute. Too vigorous squeezing of the bag may result in a high airway pressure and pneumothorax. The chest should expand, and, on auscultation, air should be heard going into both lung fields. After a few breaths the baby's colour should improve and the heart rate increase. If improvement does not occur, you should check that the lungs are ventilating properly by auscultating again. Also, check that the ET tube is in the right place by laryngoscopy. If in doubt, re-intubate. If ventilation is satisfactory but the baby is not becoming pink, he should be given intravenous bicarbonate and dextrose as described below.

If the mother has had an opiate during labour then the baby may become pink but not start breathing spontaneously. Under these circumstances intravenous or intramuscular naloxone (10 μg/kg) should be given. This is an unlikely requirement in the A & E department as most babies brought here for resuscitation will usually have been born suddenly and unexpectedly.

3. A baby in terminal apnoea is pale, floppy, and apnoeic with a heart rate of less than 80. He may be hypothermic. The baby should be intubated and ventilated as above, and if the heart rate is continuing to slow, an assistant should perform cardiac massage at a rate of 100 per minute. In neonates, the 'hands around the chest' method of cardiac compression produces a better cardiac output than simple sternal compression with the fingers (p. 20). Adrenalin (0.1 ml/kg of 1:10 000) and atropine (0.2 mg/kg) may be given via the ET tube as described on page 20. The umbilical vein should be catheterized. The umbilical tape should be tied loosely around the umbilical cord, and, with a scalpel, the cord should be transected leaving a 1 cm stump. Three vessels will now be seen. Two will be small contracted arteries and the third a large dilated vein. A fine, saline filled, feeding tube can easily be inserted into this vessel and the umbilical tape then tightened to secure it. The tube should be inserted for about 5 cm. It should then lie in the inferior vena cava. Two to five millilitres of 8.4 per cent sodium bicarbonate can be slowly injected into the umbilical vein, this can then be followed by 2-5 ml of 10 per cent dextrose. If there is no response to the bicarbonate then further adrenalin should be given into the umbilical vein. Later the feeding tube may be stitched into the cord. E.c.g. leads should be put on the baby's chest.

Action to take if poor response to resuscitation:

1. Check for technical fault:
- Is the oxygen connected to the bag system?
- Is endotracheal tube in the trachea?—Listen to chest for air entry and observe chest and abdominal movement.
- Is endotracheal tube too far down in a bronchus?—Listen to both sides of chest for unequal air entry.

2. Has the baby a pneumothorax? Auscultate the chest for asymmetry of breath sounds, feel for a displaced cardiac apex and trachea. A cold light source can be used to trans-illuminate the chest. A pneumothorax may show as a hyper-illuminating area (if this test is negative, pneumothorax is not excluded).

If a pneumothorax is clinically thought to be present, a 21 or 23 gauge butterfly needle should be inserted through the second intercostal space at the mid-clavicular line. The end of the butterfly tube should be in a gallipot under saline. If a pneumothorax is present, air bubbles will be seen in the saline. The baby will improve as the pneumothorax is no longer under tension. A confirmatory X-ray can now be done and a properly placed chest drain then inserted by the paediatrician.

3. Does the baby have evolving lung disease, such as respiratory distress syndrome or congenital pneumonia? If the lungs are stiff to ventilate, increased frequency and pressure of ventilation should be tried.

4. Does the baby have a congenital abnormality obstructing respiration, such as a diaphragmatic hernia? This can be diagnosed on a chest X-ray, but only supportive treatment is feasible until the child is transferred to a neonatal surgical unit.

5. Is there profound anaemia? These babies will require exchange transfusion. The procedure should be carried out by the paediatrician.

When to stop resuscitation

If there are no technical difficulties but there has been no effective cardiac activity after 30 minutes resuscitation, then it is appropriate to cease efforts (see also Chapter 16).

Post-resuscitation care

1. Hypothermia is a major hazard for newborn premature babies. Hypothermia will increase acidosis and reduce the chance of a good outcome. The baby should be dried and well wrapped in warm, dry blankets. Make sure that the head is covered as this is a major source of heat loss. The baby's

temperature should be monitored rectally with a low-reading thermometer. If the department has an overhead heater this will be very useful, but care must also be taken to minimize convective losses if the baby is nursed on an open surface.

2. Any preterm, asphyxiated baby is highly likely to develop respiratory distress syndrome, and if there is continuing respiratory difficulty after resuscitation the ET tube should remain in place and ventilatory assistance continued during transfer to the neonatal unit.

3. Oxygen toxicity is a worry in babies of less than 32 weeks. Although the retinopathy of prematurity has probably many causative factors, there is a link with high oxygen levels in the blood. During resuscitation 100 per cent oxygen is necessary and this requirement outweighs any other. After resuscitation, continued high ambient oxygen is usually necessary as there is often evolving respiratory distress syndrome following asphyxia in a premature baby. A pulse oximeter is useful for monitoring oxygen needs and a level of 95 per cent saturation should ensure adequate oxygenation without hyperoxia. Babies should be transferred to a neonatal nursery as soon as possible.

4. The routine dose of vitamin K (phytomenadione 1 mg i.m.) should be given. All medication given should be recorded in the patient's notes.

Congenital heart disease presenting in the neonatal period

• **Neonatal heart disease: management**

There is a trend towards early hospital discharge for mothers and babies who have had an uneventful birth. Some babies with congenital heart disease may, therefore, be discharged from hospital with their heart disease undetected. This is because the haemodynamic changes from fetal to adult type circulation are not completed immediately after birth. In the first week or so of life, as the patent ductus closes and pulmonary arterial resistance decreases, babies with serious congenital heart disease may become symptomatic and present in one of two ways.

Heart failure The main symptom is breathlessness especially on feeding.

1. High output heart failure—caused by a large left to right shunt, as in a large ventricular septal defect, or in complex heart lesions with an overall left to right shunt, such as single ventricle or truncus arteriosus. The physical signs are of a hyperdynamic heart with an enlarged liver and sometimes a triple cardiac rhythm.

2. Obstructive heart failure—this is caused by coarctation of the aorta or severe aortic stenosis. The classical sign of weak femoral pulses in coarctation may not be present in a seriously ill baby with low output heart failure.

Cyanosis The commonest cyanotic congenital heart disease presenting in the neonatal period is transposition of the great vessels. These babies are clearly blue at birth. However, there are some complex lesions in which, because of a large ductal flow, babies are pink in the first few days of life. They become bluer as the ductus closes.

Neonatal heart disease: management

The paediatrician should be called urgently for any baby who is in respiratory distress or who is cyanosed.

Oxygen and a diuretic (frusemide 1 mg/kg i.v.) should be given to the baby in heart failure.

An intravenous infusion of prostaglandin E (0.01–0.05 μg/kg/min) will help keep open the duct of the baby with a duct-dependent cyanotic heart disease until transfer to a paediatric cardiology centre. This drug will usually be ordered by the paediatrician after discussion with the cardiology centre.

A chest radiograph and e.c.g. should be obtained if there is time before transfer and the baby's condition permits.

Neonatal convulsions

Most neonatal convulsions occur in babies who have had perinatal problems and are, therefore, still receiving hospital care. Babies who are likely to present at an A & E department with a neonatal convulsion will probably be those who have a metabolic problem (hypoglycaemia or hypocalcaemia) or neonatal meningitis. Although a neonatal convulsion may be of grand mal type, convulsions in neonates can present just as apnoeic or cyanotic spells.

If a baby is having a prolonged convulsion, intravenous diazepam 0.3 mg/kg should be given, bearing in mind that this may cause apnoea. A BM stix should be done and 10 per cent dextrose (2 ml/kg) infused rapidly if there is hypoglycaemia. A second bolus may be necessary, and a repeat BM stix should be done to check that the blood sugar has risen appropriately. A blood sample for sugar (and calcium) should be taken before this infusion, and all babies who have any suggestion of neonatal convulsion referred to the paediatrician.

Neonatal jaundice

- **Common causes of jaundice in neonates   Neonatal jaundice: management**

Babies may present to the A & E department with jaundice following early neonatal hospital discharge. Jaundice is visible when the serum bilirubin rises above 18 μmol/l. There is a risk of kernicterus from high levels of unconjugated bilirubin, especially in a preterm or ill baby.

Common causes of jaundice in neonates

1. Physiological jaundice—this occurs in the second or subsequent days of life and resolves by 7–10 days. It is rarely a problem except in the very preterm infant.
2. Breast milk jaundice—this is a mild, but prolonged, form of jaundice whose physiology is ill-understood and occurs in babies who are being breastfed. It usually resolves by 2–3 weeks. There is usually no indication to stop breast feeding.
3. Haemolytic disease—Rhesus or ABO incompatibility are the commonest causes of haemolytic jaundice, but rarer

causes, such as spherocytosis, may also occur. Haemolytic disease often presents on the first day of life.

4. Infection of any type often worsens or initiates jaundice.

5. Dehydration worsens jaundice.

Neonatal jaundice: management

All jaundiced babies should be referred to the paediatrician. If the jaundice is mild to moderate and the baby well he will probably be managed as an out-patient. If the jaundice is severe or the baby is unwell then admission for investigation and phototherapy will be likely.

Neonatal infection

- **Neonatal conjunctivitis**

The neonate's immature immune system puts him at risk of serious infection. Septicaemia, meningitis, pneumonia, and urinary tract infection are the most serious problems. Group B *Streptococcus* and *E. coli* are the commonest bacterial pathogens, with *Klebsiella*, *Staphylococcus*, *Pseudomonas*, and *Listeria* spp. occurring less frequently.

Babies with serious signs, such as chest retraction, or a bulging fontanelle, are clearly very poorly and will be admitted for urgent investigation and treatment. However, the early signs of infection in neonates are subtle and non-specific. Serious infection should be considered in babies presenting with the following:

- Pyrexia
- Hypothermia
- Poor feeding
- Irritability
- Drowsiness
- Unexplained jaundice
- Vomiting
- Poor weight gain

Any such baby should be referred to the paediatrician.

Neonatal conjunctivitis

Conjunctivitis starting in the first day or so of life may be caused by *Gonococcus* or *Chlamydia* spp as well as *Haemophilus influenzae*, *Streptococcus pneumoniae*, or a virus. A smear should be taken from the pus and examined in the laboratory immediately. If gonococcus is present the baby needs to be admitted for parenteral penicillin. The eye may be permanently damaged without rapid, effective treatment.

Chlamydia is another maternal genital infection that can cause neonatal conjunctivitis. It is diagnosed by growth of the organism, or demonstration of its antigen, on a swab placed in chlamydia-specific media.

Chlamydia conjunctivitis should be treated with tetracycline eye ointment and systemic erythromycin. The parents should be referred to their GP for treatment. Other bacterial conjunctival infections should be treated with chloraphenicol drops or ointment (see p. 279).

Neonatal skin lesions

1. Milia—these are multiple small white papules particularly seen over the nose and cheeks. They are superficial epidermal inclusion cysts and require no treatment.
2. Toxic erythema—this is a common rash which consists of erythematous macules, sometimes with a central pustular vesicle. They may be quite profuse and occur on the face and trunk in the first 48 hours of life. They usually fade after a week or so. This is a harmless rash but may be difficult to distinguish from an infective rash.
3. Infantile acne—infants sometimes have what appears to be acne over their face. There is temporary overstimulation of the infant's sebaceous glands. It will gradually settle down: regular cleansing will help with the process.
4. Staphylococcal toxic epidermal necrolysis—this is a serious staphylococcal infection of the skin, sometimes known as the 'scalded skin syndrome'. The baby's skin is red

and peels easily. Admission for a parenteral antistaphylo-
coccal antibiotic is necessary.

Other problems

- **The umbilical cord   Sternomastoid tumour   Apnoeic
  spells   Crying baby**

The umbilical cord

Separation of the dried cord at about one week of age sometimes results in a small bleed from the exposed vessels. No
action is required if it has stopped.

A sticky umbilical cord should be swabbed for bacteriological culture and the mother given an antiseptic for cleansing the stump several times daily. Antibiotics are not needed
even if a pathogen grows from the swab, but the information
will be useful if the baby becomes unwell.

Redness around the umbilicus suggests infection and the
baby should be referred to the paediatrician.

Neonatal cephalohaematoma

A cephalohaematoma is caused by bleeding between the
periostium and the skull following the trauma of birth. A
cephalohaematoma is always restricted to one bone, usually
the parietal bone, and does not cross the mid-line. No treatment is required, and, in fact, aspiration is likely to lead to
infection and is strongly contra-indicated.

Sternomastoid tumour

Stretching of the sternomastoid muscle during birth sometimes causes the development of a hard mass in the muscle.
This is a benign condition although it may cause a torticollis.
In most cases symptoms resolve over a few weeks—follow-up
should be by the baby's GP or paediatrician.

Apnoeic spells—see p. 255

Crying baby—see p. 309

Further reading

1. Roberton, N. R. C. (1986). *Manual of neonatal intensive care.* Arnold, London.

CHAPTER 15

Common parental anxieties

Growth and development problems

- **Poor appetite   Poor growth   Poor development**

In addition to concerns about acute injury and illness in children, there are several other areas of child-care which are of concern to many parents. These include their child's difficulties with growth and development, feeding, sleeping, and excretion.

Problems of this type are usually the concern of the patient's general practitioner or community child health physician, but, occasionally, worried parents bring their child with a problem of this nature to the Accident and Emergency department.

More frequently, these general worries surface during the A & E consultation, for example, 'By the way, doctor, he has never been a good eater'—'I think he is hyperactive, he never sleeps and is always on the go.'

It is a paediatric adage that worried parents are ignored at one's peril. The parents' worries should always be thoroughly evaluated, but this will usually involve referral to the child's general practitioner.

The A & E role is to assess whether emergency treatment is required, and, if not, to help the parent gain access to appropriate advice, whether from the general practitioner, health visitor, paediatrician, dentist, etc.

Sometimes, even when history and examination show a clearly healthy child, an anxious parent may not appear to be reassured that no acute problem has been found. It is then worth tactfully enquiring exactly what unexpressed worry the parent has. It may then transpire that the poor appetite was just how a neighbour's child presented with leukaemia, or that the worry about a headache concealed a fear of a brain tumour. More direct reassurance can often then be given.

On occasions when examining a patient for minor trauma or acute illness you may notice poor growth or developmental delay or a physical abnormality. It is important not to worry or upset parents by obvious and unhelpful reference to the problem saying for example, 'He is small for his age, isn't he'—'Hasn't he started sitting up yet?'—'What an odd shaped head he has.' His small size, slow development, or odd shaped head may already be under investigation, and the parents may be upset at constant comment on the problem. Indeed there may be no abnormality as the range of normal growth, development, and individual characteristics is very wide. It is better to enquire about possible abnormalities obliquely, for example 'Do you take him to the Child Health Clinic? Are they happy about his progress?'

If you suspect an unrecognized growth or development problem, rather than dismiss it as not an A & E concern or making an out-patient appointment for several weeks time for the paediatric department (which condemns the parent to weeks of worry), instead a telephone call to the general practitioner or a discussion with paediatric colleagues may solve the problem.

Poor appetite

Poor feeding in infants is an important sign of illness. Recent anorexia in a child is usually caused by acute illness. However, a long history of a poor appetite in an otherwise well and active child is usually a reflection of parental expectation rather than underlying illness in the child. The child should be weighed and measured and the results plotted on a growth chart. A result falling within two standard deviations of the mean can lead to a reassurance that the child is eating sufficiently for his requirements even if not the amount his parents would like. The parents should be advised to consult further with their general practitioner.

The only eating problem in older children that requires urgent referral is when there is suspicion of anorexia nervosa or bulimia. Early paediatric or child psychiatric referral is necessary for this sometimes intractable problem.

Poor growth

Failure to thrive and shortness of stature are presenting features of a vast number of chronic conditions in childhood which it is inappropriate to describe in a text of this kind. If growth charts reveal that the child's weight is below the 3rd percentile for his age, there is documentary evidence of recent weight loss, or the child has physical signs of weight loss with loose skin, particularly around the thighs and buttocks, then he should be referred to the paediatric outpatient department, or if acutely unwell, admitted to the children's ward. Growth charts can be obtained from Castlemead Publications.

Poor development

Babies and children about whose development there is concern, and who are not under supervision for this problem, should be referred to their local child health clinic where experienced community paediatricians, general practitioners, and health visitors can assess the child.

The crying baby

- **Infantile colic   Management of the well, crying baby and his parents   Admission of crying baby**

A common visitor to the A & E department, especially at night-time, is the crying infant with his distraught parents. The A & E doctor has two tasks:

1. To diagnose and treat any physical illness or injury as the cause of crying.
2. To assess whether the parents need help with what may be to them an intolerable situation.

First, a full history is essential. If excessive crying has occurred only in the past 24 hours or so then illness or injury is likely. The baby who has been crying excessively for days or weeks is less likely to have an identifiable cause. Seek a history of any symptoms such as vomiting, diarrhoea, cough, feeding difficulty. Ask how the baby behaves when he is not crying– is he alert and his usual self, or drowsy and disinterested? In the latter event illness is more probable. Has the baby recently been immunized? (Screaming spells after pertussis immunization are described.)

Observation of the baby both when crying and when responding to soothing is helpful in assessing his overall state of health (see Chapter 1). Examination must include all systems. First look for evidence of serious disease, such as meningitis (p. 257). Intussusception or incarcerated inguinal hernia should be especially considered in babies with excessive crying, and the abdomen, genitalia, and rectum examined carefully (see p. 236).

Always examine the baby's ears. Otitis media is a painful disease which may cause inconsolable crying. Remember, however, that a crying baby's healthy eardrums may appear pink.

A careful search should be made for trauma, including threads from clothing wrapped around digits. Look for bruising, a painful or non-mobile limb, a suggestion of fracture, or bone or joint infection. The baby should have a urine specimen examined as infection in the lower urinary tract may be painful.

At the end of history and thorough examination, if any doubt remains about illness or injury being the cause of the baby's crying a paediatric opinion should be requested.

Many babies, however, will have a completely negative examination, appear well, and have no symptoms suggestive of disease. If they have a history of recurrent episodes of inconsolable crying, especially in the evening, this crying is associated with drawing up of the knees to the abdomen, and sometimes the passage of flatus, then the condition known as infantile colic is likely.

Infantile colic

This is a condition of unknown aetiology which affects babies from a few weeks to a few months old. Otherwise well and thriving babies will have paroxysms of crying with a flushed face and drawing up of the legs. In the attack the baby cannot be comforted, and sometimes relief only occurs when the baby passes a stool or wind. Theories of the causation of colic include cows' milk allergy, lactose intolerance, maternal anxiety, and abnormal gut motility. No convincing evidence exists for any theory. No medication now available has clearly been shown to be beneficial.

All babies cry, but medical help is sought by parents who think that their baby's crying is excessive. The definition of 'excessive' will depend on the parents' expectation of their baby's behaviour, previous experience with other babies, and often their social circumstances. A crying baby in a household where a parent is single, unwell, depressed, or has critical neighbours will be more stressful than one in a household with other supportive adults.

Parents have usually done all they can to alleviate their baby's distress. Feeding, winding, changing, cuddles, and play will have been tried, and it is the inconsolable nature of the crying that makes parents anxious that their baby may be ill and at their wits end about what to do.

Management of the well, crying baby and his parents

Many parents will be much relieved by the thorough history and examination which has shown no serious cause for their baby's crying. Relief for the baby often comes from rhythmical motion—parents may have commented that a car ride has a soothing effect. The use of a baby sling so that the infant can be carried around for periods of the day is often helpful. Relatives and friends can be encouraged to take over the baby's care for short periods to give the parents a rest.

The family's general practitioner and health visitor should be informed and asked to provide community support until the crying bouts resolve, which they usually do spontaneously in a few weeks.

Admission of crying baby

Sometimes parents and baby may be so distressed and exhausted by the crying that they cannot go home. Admission for the baby should be offered in such a way as to not make the parents feel they have failed. The parent may want to stay in with the baby, but without compulsion, or they may be encouraged to have a good night's sleep at home.

Further reading

1. Illingworth, R. (1988). *The normal child*, (9th edn). Churchill Livingstone, Glasgow.
2. Modell, M. and Boyd, R. (1988). *Paediatric problems in general practice*, (2nd edn). Oxford University Press, Oxford.

Children brought in dead

Key points in children brought in dead

1 All children brought to hospital who may be dead should be admitted to the resuscitation room and unless contra-indications are very clear, for example rigor mortis or injuries incompatible with life, resuscitation should be initiated.

2 Sensitive and caring management of the bereaved family in the A & E department will aid the long-term grieving process.

3 Ensure that all relevant community health workers are informed of the child's death.

4 Ensure that the arrangements are made for later counselling of the family.

Initial action

- **The parents**

Children who are found suddenly and unexpectedly dead or who have been the victims of a fatal accident are usually brought to the nearest A & E department. All such children should be admitted to the resuscitation room. Unless there is clear evidence of death such as post-mortem rigidity or dependent skin discoloration the A & E staff should start resuscitation. *A paediatric cardiac arrest call should be made* and it will be the leader of the arrest team who decides when resuscitation should cease.

The parents

When the child is taken into the resuscitation room the parents should be taken into a quiet room reserved for their exclusive use. Preferably, it should be near the resuscitation room. They should be accompanied by an experienced nurse who will ensure that they are fully aware of what is happening with their child. The parents' later grieving can be helped by support and understanding from A & E staff at this time.

Parents' needs

- **Breaking the news**

1. Knowledge that an appropriate medical response was made, i.e. 'everything was done'.
2. A private space and sufficient time in which to receive distressing news.
3. The opportunity to be with their dead child.
4. The services of a minister of religion and a social worker if they wish.
5. An understanding of the Law's requirements in a case of sudden unexpected death. Parents should know that the coroner must be informed about their child's death. He will almost certainly order a post-mortem. A police officer will

want to take a statement from them, and may want to visit the home or place of death. An inquest is usual following an accidental death, but is rarely held after death due to natural causes.

Breaking the news

Telling the parents that their child is dead is a difficult and unenviable task. It is usually undertaken by senior staff, such as a paediatric consultant or registrar, or the A & E consultant, but on occasions the task may fall to the A & E SHO if seniors are unavailable.

Once the patient has been certified dead, do not keep the parents waiting in false hope. A direct but sympathetic approach is best. Make sure that you know the child's name. On entering the room sit down with the parents. The parents must be told the news sympathetically, but without euphemisms, using words such as, 'I am very sorry to have to tell you, but despite all that we could do Jason is dead'. Stay with the parents after the receipt of this initial, shocking news. If appropriate and you feel comfortable doing it, you can show sympathy by holding the parent's hand or putting an arm around them. Usually the parents turn away towards each other for a while, but may shortly want to ask questions about the cause of death and what they should do now. If you are asked about the cause of death answer as simply and honestly as possible, but make it clear that some answers are not yet available.

Examination of the child

- **Post-mortem investigations for sudden and unexpected death in infancy**

The child will already have been examined during the resuscitation attempt, but any external features should now be checked and recorded in the notes together with the history:

- Fully undress the child, but save the clothes, including the nappy.

- Note the state of nutrition and hydration.
- Record the child's initial rectal temperature on arriving at the department.
- Note any injuries or rashes.

Although a post-mortem will be carried out, certain investigations are likely to be more informative if specimens are collected in the A & E department. These include investigations which will indicate infection or an inborn error of metabolism as the cause of death. These investigations will usually be done by the paediatrician and the results sent to the duty consultant paediatrician who will later talk with the parents.

Post-mortem investigations for sudden and unexpected death in infancy

1. Bacteriology—swabs should be taken from the nose and throat. Stool and urine samples (suprapubic aspirate) should be collected and blood taken for culture from the right ventricle.
2. Virology—a nasopharyngeal aspirate or throat swab and a stool for culture, should be taken.
3. Metabolic diseases—a urine sample, obtained by suprapubic aspirate (see p. 343), should be sent to the Regional Metabolic Diseases Laboratory as a few sudden and unexpected deaths in infancy are due to inborn errors of metabolism. These diseases are usually inherited in an autosomal recessive manner and the affected family will need genetic counselling. The specimen should be frozen if its transport will be delayed until the next day.
4. A small, full thickness skin sample taken with a sterile scalpel and placed in a tissue growth medium will still contain viable cells. The Regional Metabolic Diseases Laboratory may be able to identify inborn errors of metabolism from cell culture of this material.

A written record in the patient's notes of any procedure, such as suprapubic urine aspiration or skin biopsy, should be made so that the pathologist knows that the injuries were post-mortem.

Helping the family

- Should the bereaved family see the dead child again?
  Follow-up

Should the bereaved family see the dead child again?

Many bereaved parents find that the opportunity to sit with, look at, and touch their dead child in the A & E department makes the reality of death more concrete, and in the long run aids the process of coming to terms with their loss. Parents should be actively and sympathetically encouraged to see their dead child. The child's body should be dressed in his own clothes again and placed in a room where his parents may sit with him undisturbed. At this stage they may wish to be completely alone with their child, but the nurse who has been with them throughout should remain nearby. The parents may want older brothers and sisters and other relatives to be present as well.

Eventually the parents should be ready to go home. The nurse or social worker should ensure that there is someone from their family or neighbourhood who is able to accompany them. If this is not the case the social worker will usually take the parents home.

A few Polaroid photographs of the child may be taken by staff. They should be carefully labelled with the baby's name and the date. Occasionally, parents later tell their bereavement counsellor of their regret that they do not have a photograph of their baby. These photographs may then be welcomed.

The A & E doctor should make sure that the general practitioner and health visitor are informed promptly, by telephone, of the child's death, and know what the parents have been told. The general practitioner will probably want to visit the home later on. If the mother had been breast feeding he may prescribe a lactation suppressant, such as bromocriptine mesylate. A check-list (Table 16.1) is useful for ensuring that no detail is forgotten. Occasionally, as the result of a case of fatal meningococcal disease, prophylaxis should be given to the immediate family (see p. 259).

Table 16.1 • Check list for sudden infant deaths

Child's name . . . . .

Date of birth . . . . . Date of death . . . . .

1.	Registrar or consultant spoken to parents	. . . . .
2.	Brief clinical history taken	. . . . .
3.	Examination/investigations done	. . . . .
4.	Parents offered to be with/hold baby	. . . . .
5.	Coroner informed	. . . . .
6.	Medical social worker informed	. . . . .
7.	GP informed	. . . . .
8.	Health visitor informed	. . . . .
9.	Minister of religion contacted	. . . . .
10.	Advice on registration and funeral given	. . . . .
11.	Pamphlet from SIDS Foundation given	. . . . .
12.	Phone number of local Friends of SIDS given	. . . . .
13.	Consultant follow-up arranged	. . . . .
14.	Social work follow-up arranged	. . . . .
15.	Community physician informed	. . . . .

Follow-up

Some days or weeks later the parents should meet with the consultant paediatrician. The consultant will then have information from the post-mortem and other tests about the cause of the child's death and its implications for the family.

The family should be offered contact with a bereavement counsellor. Depending on local arrangements, this may be a hospital bereavement counsellor, a social worker who has had counselling training, a member of the Foundation for the Study of Infant Deaths (telephone number 071-235-1721), a member of the Compassionate Friends, the patient's own minister of religion, or general practitioner.

Causes of sudden, unexpected death in children

- **Cot deaths   Follow-up of siblings**
- Sudden, unexpected death in infancy (cot death)— including the Sudden Infant Death Syndrome (SIDS).

- Major trauma, for example road traffic accident, fires, choking, drowning, falls from a height, non-accidental injury, poisoning.
- Sudden overwhelming infection, for example meningococal septicaemia, epiglottitis, myocarditis, periotonitis, etc.
- Sudden deterioration in a chronic condition such as asthma, epilepsy, diabetes, or heart disease.

Cot deaths

Cot deaths are sudden, unexpected deaths in infants between the ages of 1 week and 1 year. The incident is 1 in 450 live births, and, in the age group concerned, cot death is the commonest cause of death. Cot deaths occur more frequently in the winter months than the summer months. Boys are at greater risk than girls, and babies who have been preterm, one of twins, or had apnoeic spells in the first week of life are more vulnerable. Statistically, more of these deaths occur in families where the mother is young, unmarried, a smoker, had inadequate antenatal care, and was poorly educated. However, cot deaths occur in families from all walks of life.

At post-mortem some unexpected deaths are found to have a clear cause, such as an overwhelming infection, usually pneumonia. Less frequently, there is a congenital abnormality, such as congenital heart disease or an inborn error of metabolism, particularly of fatty acid metabolism. Very occasionally, accidental or intentional suffocation is considered to be the cause of death. The more careful and skilful the post-mortem, the more likelihood of a recognizable cause of death being found. However, in many infants who have been found suddenly and unexpectedly dead, a careful post-mortem examination reveals no evidence of serious illness. The examination shows either completely normal results, or evidence of only minor illness, such as an upper respiratory tract infection. These unexplained infant deaths comprise the Sudden Infant Death Syndrome (SIDS).

It is generally considered that there is unlikely to be one single answer to the pathology of SIDS. The current hypotheses include:

- An abnormality of the control of respiration.

- An abnormal response to common respiratory infections.
- Hyperthermia, exacerbated by excessively warm bed coverings during a mild illness.
- Some association with the prone position while sleeping.

Follow-up of siblings

If there is a surviving twin, this infant is at increased risk of sudden unexpected death. Also, parents will naturally be very anxious about such an infant. The surviving twin should be referred to the paediatric department who should manage this aspect of care. Counselling and an apnoea alarm may be offered.

Staff distress

Following a death in the department it is helpful for staff to discuss their own feelings of distress. Staff are often helped by the knowledge that sensitive, caring, and supportive management of bereaved families in the A & E department has a profound and prolonged positive influence on the response of the family to the death.

CHAPTER 17

Practical procedures

Circulatory access procedures

- **Intravenous access**   **Intraosseous infusion**   **Arterial puncture**

Intravenous access

Intravenous access may be necessary to withdraw blood for testing, to administer drugs, and to site an intravenous infusion.

Venepuncture The procedure may be difficult, especially in a fat toddler. It is important to prepare all the equipment and obtain the best possible cooperation from the patient as the first attempt is the most likely to succeed.

Equipment needed

- Syringe.
- Needle (usually 21 Gauge).
- Tourniquet.
- Blood bottles (paediatric size if available).
- Skin-cleansing wipes.
- Cotton wool.

Note: 23 Gauge (blue) needles can be used in very small children as the smaller needle may hurt slightly less. This advantage is offset by the longer time needed to withdraw blood.

In toddlers and infants it may be useful to use a 'butterfly' type needle with its attached tubing. This allows the child to move without pulling the needle out of the vein.

Procedure The child should be restrained according to his age. Babies should be held in a parent's or nurse's arms. Toddlers often need to be swaddled in a blanket and held by one or more adults to prevent struggling. School-age children will usually cooperate if they are told exactly what is happening.

Select a suitable site for the venepuncture. As in adults, the antecubital fossa is often the most appropriate. However, small veins on the back of the hand or the foot may also be used. Prepare the syringe. Attach the needle without the child watching. Put a tourniquet around the appropriate limb. Do not tie this too tightly or it may be painful enough to lose the child's cooperation. Cleanse the selected area well with an antiseptic swab. Try to distract the child's attention whilst approaching with the needle. Warn the child when skin puncture is imminent so that the surprise does not cause him to withdraw. Never lie to the child by saying the procedure is painless. Insert the needle through the skin into the vein for a short distance. Withdraw blood into the syringe as needed. Release the tourniquet. Place cotton wool over the needle tip and withdraw the needle (do not use alcohol wipes as they sting). Ask a nurse or the parent to apply continuous pressure over the venepuncture site for about a minute. Remove the needle from the syringe and fill the bottles. These should be labelled immediately.

Problems Sometimes a small vein is entered but collapses as the syringe is aspirated. If the syringe is removed leaving the needle in the vein, blood can be dripped directly into the bottles.

The first attempt may fail. Try a different site and possibly a slightly different technique, i.e. a butterfly needle. If you fail three times call for more senior or paediatric help as further attempts will ruin venepuncture sites and cause the child much distress.

Intravenous infusion The same instructions with regard to handling the child apply as for venepuncture. Remember this is a longer procedure.

Equipment needed
● Tourniquet.
● Cleansing wipes.
● Syringe.
● Cannula.
● Splint.
● Intravenous fluid run through a paediatric drip set (check the burette is filled to a suitable mark, for example 50 ml and the air inlet is open).
● Tape.

Note: Select the cannula according to the size of the child and the site used. Suitable sizes are 24 g for a baby, 22 g for a preschool child and 18 g in an older child. Do not be tempted to use too small a cannula as it will be difficult to push through the skin. A too small cannula will allow an insufficient flow rate for an adequate infusion. Metal 'butterfly' needles can be left in situ for a short period of time in a suitable site (i.e. scalp vein). They are easy to insert and are ideal for short-term use, for example if only a few doses of a parenteral drug are to be administered.

Procedure Select a suitable site. It is preferable that the area can be held flat and still for the duration of the infusion. Ideal areas are the antecubital fossa, the back of the hand, foot, or scalp in babies. The area sould be thoroughly cleansed and shaved if necessary. Apply the tourniquet and prepare the cannula. Insert the cannula through the skin and into the vein. Push the plastic cannula over the introducer into the vein and withdraw the introducer needle.

Attach the infusion line to the cannula. Tape the cannula and line securely. It is useful to tape a loop of the infusion line to the arm to help prevent the end being pulled off. Immobilize the infusion site using a splint. Plaster of Paris can be used to make a solid, well-fitted splint fixing scalp infusions. Check the infusion rate and fluid. Write the in structions for infusion on a chart.

Problems Sometimes the cannula will not advance fully into the vein. This may mean that the cannula has gone through the vein in which case no blood can be aspirated and the cannula should be removed. Sometimes the cannula hits a valve or a branch in the vein and blood can still be aspirated. In this case attach the infusion line and try to advance the cannula while the drip is running slowly. The fluid pressure may make the cannula easier to position. Infusion sites should be checked regularly to make sure that fluid is not escaping into the tissues.

Scalp vein infusion The scalp is a useful site for infusion in small babies, particularly in those under one month. The scalp may need to be shaved to allow the needle to be fixed in properly. Use a butterfly needle or a small cannula. First check the direction of flow of blood in the vein and palpate to make sure it is not an artery. Press on the proximal end of the vein to allow the vein to fill. The cannula can then be inserted as usual. The child should be lying down during the procedure. The cannula can be fixed in place with tape or small strips of plaster of Paris.

Cannulation of the femoral vein In the shocked child it may be difficult to insert a peripheral line. Cannulation of the femoral vein using the Seldinger technique should be attempted. This method is preferred to cannulation of a jugular or subclavian vein as there are fewer possible complications.

Equipment needed
- Skin cleansing wipes.
- Syringe with 1 ml 0.9% normal saline.
- Seldinger cannulation set including needle, guidewire, and cannula (21 gauge needle).
- Infusion set (fully prepared).
- Tape.
- Gloves.

Procedure The child should be lying down as this procedure is usually only carried out on the seriously ill child. The child is likely to be unconscious. If he is not, ensure that the leg and body are held still, and use a local anaesthetic if time permits. Cleanse the area well. This technique should be fully aseptic and gloves should be worn. Attach the syringe to the needle. Locate the femoral vein by palpating the femoral artery. The vein lies adjacent to the artery on the medial side. Keep one finger on the artery to mark its position. Introduce the needle directly over the femoral vein, pointing it towards the patient's head. With the syringe held parallel to the child's leg and directed headwards and posteriorly, advance the needle whilst withdrawing the plunger of the syringe. When blood flows freely into the syringe, stop, and remove the syringe. Put a finger over the needle to prevent blood loss. Insert the guidewire down the needle then remove the needle. Insert the cannula over the guidewire and then remove the guidewire. Attach the cannula to the infusion set. Fix the cannula in place with adhesive tape. The cannula can later be used to measure central venous pressure, if necessary.

Problems There is a risk of puncturing the femoral artery or damaging the femoral vein. Keeping the finger over the artery and entering directly next to it should prevent this. A haematoma may form if the needle goes through the vein. There is a risk of infection which can be reduced by careful asepsis.

Intraosseous infusion

Occasionally a child may be so shocked that it is impossible to cannulate a vein. Intraosseous infusion is a useful technique in this situation and should be used. Fluids delivered into the bone marrow will enter the systemic circulation. Fluid and drugs can be infused to resuscitate the child sufficiently to fill out the veins, thus allowing peripheral venous access, or buy time until more experienced help arrives. It is easiest in babies and small children, but can be performed at any age.

Equipment needed
- Skin cleansing wipes.
- Infusion fluid and giving set (fully set up).
- Cannula—a wide-bore metal needle such as a lumbar puncture needle can be used or a 13/18 gauge bone marrow needle with stilette. There are now specially designed needles also available.
- Tape.
- Syringe with 0.9% saline.
- Three-way tap.

Procedure The child should be lying flat. The site to use is the tibia, approximately 1–2 cm below and 1–2 cm medial to the tibial tuberosity. Clean the leg with antiseptic. Local anaesthetic is not used as speed is vital and the patient usually unconscious. Insert the needle at a right angle through the skin. Using firm pressure and a screwing motion advance the needle until the marrow is penetrated. (At this point the resistance suddenly decreases.) Remove the stilette and, using the syringe, aspirate marrow to confirm placement. Attach the infusion set to the needle using a three-way tap and infuse the fluid. A syringe can also be used to rapidly administer saline, colloid solution, plasma, blood, drugs, etc.

Problems Subperiosteal infusion can occur if the needle fails to penetrate the marrow cavity. Strict attention should be paid to asepsis, as osteomyelitis can occur. Complications are unusual if the infusion site is used only in the emergency situation.

Arterial puncture

Blood gas analysis is required in cases of serious respiratory illness, trauma, or following CPR (if frequent analysis is required, an arterial cannula should be inserted). A pulse oximeter can be used for frequent oxygen saturation measurements.

Equipment
- Heparinized syringe.
- 23 Gauge (blue) needle or butterfly needle.
- Skin cleansing solution.
- Gauze pad.

Procedure Carefully choose the artery to be punctured. The preferred sites are the radial or posterior tibial arteries. Avoid the femoral artery as a thrombosis or haematoma here could compromise the leg circulation. If you use the radial artery check for the presence of an ulnar artery by occluding both arteries at the wrist. Release the pressure on the ulna side. The circulation should return to the hand. If this does not happen it would indicate the absence of an ulna arterial circulation and would contraindicate using the radial artery on that side. Palpate the artery. Ensure the child is suitably restrained and still. Insert the needle over the artery at approximately 45 degrees to the skin. When the artery is punctured blood should pulsate rapidly into the syringe. After collecting the required amount withdraw the needle and maintain pressure on the artery for approximately 5 minutes. Send the blood for analysis immediately, or place it on ice if there is to be any delay. In very small infants it may be easier to puncture the artery, with a 23 Gauge (blue) needle, and to collect blood into a heparinized capillary tube as it fills the well of the needle.

Problems Haematoma formation is quite common and is due to leakage from the damaged artery. This will reabsorb with time and needs simple bandage and splinting to support it.

Chest drain insertion

Indications A chest drain may be needed for the treatment of a pneumothorax (spontaneous or traumatic) or a haemothorax. In most cases the clinical diagnosis is confirmed after an X-ray and the drain can then be inserted. However, if the child is in respiratory difficulties and a haemo- or pneumothorax is suspected, especially after chest trauma, then the drain should be inserted without waiting for an X-ray.

Equipment needed
- Chest drain set (usually available with all necessary surgical instruments).
- Chest drain.
- Underwater seal bottle with connections and filled with the appropriate amount of water.
- 1% Lignocaine in syringe with needle.
- Scalpel blade.
- Silk for suturing the drain in position (e.g. 2.0 silk).

Note: Choose a chest drain of suitable gauge. The larger the number the larger the bore tube diameter. If you suspect blood in the chest the largest suitable size should be chosen (see Table 2.2).

Procedure Select the site for insertion. The ideal site is just anterior to the mid-axillary line in the 3rd/4th or 4th/5th interspace. The 2nd interspace in the mid-clavicular line can be used, but leads to unsightly scarring.

Gown- and glove-up as for a fully sterile procedure, unless the patient is desperately ill when gloves alone will do. If possible, have the patient sat almost upright with the arm held up above the chest and supported by a nurse. At all times the procedure should be explained to the patient. Select the site for insertion (remember the intercostal vessels run just below the rib and, therefore, the drain should be inserted just above a rib). Anaesthetize the skin using the lignocaine. Without withdrawing the needle infiltrate the deeper tissues down to the pleura. Do not worry if the pleura is breached and air enters the syringe. Allow a few minutes for the lignocaine to work.

Using a scalpel, cut through the skin and subcutaneous tissues. The incision should be large enough to insert the chest drain easily. Using forceps or haemostat split the intercostal muscles down to the pleura. Using a gloved finger you should be able to expand the hole and palpate the pleura. Using the forceps penetrate the parietal pleura. Insert the gloved finger again and check that the pleura has been breached and that no organs are in the way of the drain. Then insert the drain into the chest cavity. There is usually a black line on the drain which will show the correct length of insertion. Clamp the external aspect with forceps. Attach the underwater bottle and tubing. Release the forceps and check the water level rises and falls with inspiration and expiration. Insert a purse string suture around the entry site and firmly suture the drain in place. Also fix it firmly with tape. Auscultate the chest to check for air entry. Check the position of the drain with a chest radiograph and see that the lung has re-expanded. (See Table 2.2 for chest drain sizes.)

Problems This method (without an introducer on the chest drain) is less likely to cause damage to a viscus than using an introducer with force. Ensure that the drainage bottle is kept below the level of the patient, especially during transport. The drain should be kept unclamped, especially if there has been a tension pneumothorax.

Local anaesthesia

- **Indications Agents used Local infiltration Digital nerve block**

Indications In every case where a surgical procedure is to be performed, the best method of anaesthesia must be considered. The choice is between local anaesthesia, regional anaesthesia (i.e. proximal nerve block or a Bier's block), or general anaesthesia. Points to consider are:

1. The age of the child—i.e. will the child be able to stay still and cooperate (a small baby may be easier to deal with than a toddler).

2. The site of the procedure—complex facial wounds need particular attention to detail and an unmoving patient, therefore a general anaesthetic may be preferred. Is the area suitable for a regional nerve block? For example a hand wound in an older child may be suitable for a median or ulna nerve block.

3. The length of the procedure—if you envisage spending more than 30 minutes then the child will probably be unable to cooperate for long enough and a general anaesthetic should be used.

4. The nature of the procedure—any complicated procedure should be done under general anaesthetic. If the wounds are extensive and may require an excessive amount of lignocaine then consider that a general anaesthetic is needed.

Agents used Lignocaine is the usual local anaesthetic agent. It is available in 0.5 per cent, 1 per cent, and 2 per cent strengths. One per cent lignocaine contains 10 mg/ml. The maximum safe dose of plain lignocaine (without adrenalin) is 3 mg/kg (see Table 17.1). One per cent lignocaine is usually used, but 2 per cent is useful when small volumes are needed, i.e. a digital ring block. For larger areas of superficial wounds, such as abrasions, 0.5 per cent is useful. Lignocaine is also available combined with adrenalin. Adrenalin causes vasoconstriction and thus provides a bloodless field, it also slows down the absorption of lignocaine and allows a greater amount to be used (maximum 7 mg/kg). Adrenalin must not be used for digital nerve blocks as it could cause permanent arterial constriction leading to necrosis and loss of the digit. Because of the dangers, lignocaine with adrenalin is not recommended for routine use. Other agents, such as Marcain (bupivacaine), have a longer anaesthetic effect than lignocaine. However, in children this is not such a useful property as long procedures will usually be done under general anaesthetic. They may be useful to give post-operative anaesthesia, for example after removal of an in-growing

Table 17.1 • Maximum safe dose lignocaine 1% at different ages (maximum safe dose of lignocaine is 3 mg/kg, 1% lignocaine contains 10 mg/ml)

Age of child	maximum safe dose 1% lignocaine
6 months	2 ml
12 months	3 ml
2 years	3.5 ml
3 years	4 ml
4 years	4.5 ml
5 years	5 ml
6 years	6 ml
7 years	7 ml
8 years	7.5 ml
9 years	8 ml
10 years	9 ml
11 years	10 ml
12 years	11 ml

toenail, maximum dose of bupivacaine is 2 mg/kg, with or without adrenalin.

Local infiltration

Equipment needed
- Lignocaine 1%.
- Syringe.
- Small needle, i.e., 25 Gauge (orange) or 23 Gauge (blue).
- Cleansing agent.

Method Cleanse the wound gently. Thorough cleansing should be left until after the wound is anaesthetized. Check the maximum safe dose of lignocaine for the child. Draw up the lignocaine into the syringe and connect the needle. Insert the needle into the wound at one end and enter the subcutaneous tissues under the skin edge. Insert the needle to its full extent. Draw back to check the needle is not in a vein and then inject a small amount of lignocaine. Gradually withdraw the needle continuously drawing back and injecting. You may then be able to repeat the procedure on the other side of the wound without withdrawing the needle. If the wound is large and requires the anaesthetic to be inserted at a second site, always insert the needle at a previously anaesthetized site. Wait 10 minutes for the anaesthetic to work. (Do not lose the child's confidence by attempting the procedure before full anaesthesia.)

Problems Occasionally the anaesthetic seems ineffective. Check the correct solution and percentage has been used. Allow further time for anaesthetic action. Insert a further dose (remember not to exceed the maximum safe dose of lignocaine). There may be small areas which have not been adequately anaesthetized.

Digital nerve block

Equipment needed
- Lignocaine 1% or 2%.
- Syringe.
- Needle, usually 25 Gauge (orange).
- Cleansing materials.

Method The object is to anaesthetize the digital nerves at the base of the finger or toes to anaesthetize the whole of the digit more distal to the block. The digital nerves run laterally up both sides of the digit. Occasionally there is a dorsal branch of the nerve (especially in the thumb and the large toe) which must be anaesthetized too.

Cleanse the area. Insert the needle into the webspace at the base of the digit to be anaesthetized (see Figure 17.1). Run the needle perpendicular to the finger until you are down to bone. Withdraw slightly. Draw back on the needle to ensure that the artery which runs adjacent to the nerve has not been entered. Infiltrate approximately 1–2 ml of lignocaine around this area. Repeat on the other side. Also infiltrate a small amount of lignocaine dorsally over the base of the finger. Wait at least ten minutes before checking for anaesthesia of the distal digit.

Problems Failure of anaesthesia. Partial failure may be due to incorrect insertion of part of the block. Insert some more lignocaine (remember not to exceed the correct dose). Total failure is unusual. It is worth waiting longer as occasionally the block takes some time to work. It may be necessary to consider some other form of anaesthesia.

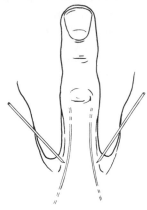

Figure 17.1 • Digital nerve block.

Suturing

• **Suture materials   Procedure   Cleansing agents**

Before suturing check that the wound is suitable for this procedure (see p. 85).

Suture materials The following materials are commonly used:

1. Absorbable—catgut. This loses half its strength in 5–7 days and all its effective strength in 12–18 days. Chromic catgut lasts longer (half strength 17–21 days, loss of strength 28–32 days).
2. Synthetic absorbable materials—for example polyglactin (Vicryl) or polyglycolic acid (Dexon). These are easier to handle than catgut and are less easily absorbed.

Absorbable sutures are useful as they do not have to be removed, and they are suitable for deep tissues or suturing areas such as scalps (also consider glue) or fingertips.

3. Non-absorbable—silk is the traditional suture material. It is very easy to handle and knot. It does tend to leave a scar

(producing a recognizable cross-hatching appearance of the wound), and may be more likely to lead to wound infection as bacteria can grow around the silk.

4. Synthetic non-absorbable sutures—for example polyamide (Ethilon) or polypropylene (Prolene) cause less tissue reaction and, therefore, less scarring. However, they are difficult to handle and knots need extra throws as they may work loose. They are the preferred material where the cosmetic result is important, for example on the face (also consider steristrips).

Gauge of suture—fine thread, i.e. 5.0 or 6.0, with a small needle is suitable for fine suturing on delicate areas, for example the face. Thicker thread, i.e. 4.0 or 3.0, with a stronger needle is needed for areas such as the scalp or a knee.

Equipment needed
• Suture pack—should contain:
    needle holder,
    scissors,
    forceps (toothed or untoothed),
    mosquito forceps.
• Cleansing materials.
• Suture material.

Procedure Anaesthetize the wound (see local anaesthesia). Wash hands well and put on surgical gloves. Although using gloves does not necessarily cut down on wound infections, unless a meticulous 'no touch' technique is used, gloves are preferred. They may also protect the user against blood-borne diseases such as AIDS or hepatitis.

Cleanse the wound. Using forceps evert the skin edge and explore the wound for debris and foreign bodies which should be removed. No traces of dirt should remain. Flush small particles out with normal saline. Check again that no deep structures are involved. Remove any non-viable tissue. Scissors or a scalpel may be needed for this. Hold the suture needle about two-thirds along the circular edge away from the tip with the needle holders which should always be clamped on the needle. Insert the needle perpendicular to the skin through one edge of the wound. Bring the needle fully through. Take another bite through the opposite edge of the wound and again bring the needle through. Tie a knot, cut suture, and repeat along the length of the wound, using the minimum number of sutures to align the skin edges neatly.

Note: It is preferable if the needle enters at an equal distance to the wound on each edge of the skin.

The tension on the suture should be sufficient to oppose the skin edges. Too much tension could lead to tissue necrosis (especially as the wound is likely to swell after suturing has been finished).

Try to produce as neat a scar as possible. Any ragged edges should be debrided. Some wounds may be easier to oppose with adhesive strips.

Removal of sutures If sutures are left in too long the risk of infection and scarring increases. Children heal more quickly than adults and hence sutures are removed at approximately 1–2 days earlier than in adults. The time of removal depends on the age of the child and the area sutured. Typical values are 3–5 days for a face and 5–7 days for a limb. Sutures on knee wounds may need ten days. If sutures are removed early then the wound apposition can be maintained with adhesive strips. Suture removal can be done by district nurses, the general practitioner, or the patient may return to the A & E department.

Problems Sometimes, especially with deeper wounds, the skin folds under and the skin edges, therefore, do not accurately oppose each other. This wound will fail to heal. In his case it may be useful to use a mattress suture. In this stitch a large bite is taken of the skin on either side of the wound, followed by a smaller bite at the edge of the wound which is then knotted.

Small flaps often have a tenuous blood supply. It is preferable to suture adjacent skin and hold the flap in place with adhesive strips.

Cleansing agents The importance of thorough cleansing cannot be over-emphasized. Virtually all wounds seen in an A & E department are contaminated.

1. Soap and water—it is important to clean the whole area close to the wound. Ask the child to wash his hands under a running tap to remove surface debris before the wound itself is cleaned. An older child may prefer to cleanse around the wound themselves, whereas younger children may prefer their parents to perform this part of the procedure.

2. A solvent hand cleaner (such as Swarfega)—may be needed to remove grease and oil deposits.

3. Normal saline—this is a satisfactory cleanser. The wound is cleansed by mechanically removing the dirt. A syringe can be used to irrigate with normal saline.

4. Chlorhexidine solutions, for example Hibitane and Savlodil—these are commonly used. They have a disinfectant action which will help to destroy bacteria and other contamination on the skin surrounding the wound. Do not use on the wound itself as they may cause tissue damage.

5. Hydrogen peroxide—this agent is no longer recommended for wound cleansing. It has been shown to be cytotoxic. The benefits of the oxygen released on application of the peroxide to tissues are dubious.

6. Iodine solutions, for example povidone-iodine (Betadine)—have an antiseptic action for skin surrounding the wound. Check before use that the patient is not sensitive to iodine. They can cause some stinging on application.

7. Alcohol—this stings and is not an effective antiseptic. However, it is useful for skin cleansing of injection sites, and as it removes grease from skin and then evaporates it is useful for drying the skin, especially prior to application of dressings, etc.

Incision and drainage of abscess

Indications Most abscesses are extremely painful and require a general anaesthetic for proper incision and drainage. However, some very small abscesses (or large boils) may be treated under local anaesthetic. The abscess should be 'ripe' for drainage, i.e. the pus should be pointing. This is easily determined if there is redness with a yellow head on top. Other pointers are pain and fluctuation on palpation. For incision under local anaesthesia the abscess must be superficial.

Equipment needed Incision pack which should include:

Scalpel.
Forceps (toothed and untoothed).
Artery forceps.
Sinus forceps.
Curette.
Scissors.
Wound probe.
Wick.
Liquid solution, for example proflavine to soak the gauze in.
Local anaesthetic.

Procedure Cleanse the area. Anaesthetize the area to be incised using either a regional block or local skin infiltration with lignocaine. Using the scalpel incise through the centre of the abscess. Take a wound swab for bacteriological analysis. Express as much of the pus as possible. Curette the walls of the abscess until fresh bleeding occurs. Loosely insert a wick soaked in proflavine. Put a dry dressing on top of this. The patient should be reviewed the following day and the wick removed. The wound can then be further dressed with dry dressings.

Problems Occasionally the abscess refills. In this case, using the bacteriology report as a guide, oral antibiotics may be needed. Confirm the aetiology of the abscess. In particular note whether there may be a foreign body which will have to be removed before the abscess will settle. The abscess may also be an indicator of an underlying health problem, for example drug abuse, diabetes, poor immunity. These should be excluded in recurrent or resistant abscesses.

Cricothyrotomy

Indications This is required when the child's airway is blocked and an endotracheal tube cannot be inserted. The commonest reason is an inhaled foreign body. It is also needed in severe facial trauma, oropharyngeal haemorrhage, epiglottitis, or fracture of the larynx. In such cases a needle cricothyrotomy must be performed. This will allow oxygenation until a formal tracheostomy can be arranged. By attaching the cannula to an oxygen line the patient can be ventilated for 20–30 minutes. Because exhalation is inadequate carbon dioxide tends to build up and, therefore, this method should not be used for longer periods of time.

Equipment needed
- 12 or 14 Gauge over the needle cannula.
- Cleansing swabs.
- Paediatric (3.0 mm or 3.5 mm) endotracheal tube adapter.
- Y connector and oxygen tubing.
- Syringes.

Procedure The child should be lying flat with the neck and head supported. The child is likely to be unconscious when this procedure is being carried out. Palpate the cricothyroid membrane which lies anterially between the thyroid cartilage and the cricoid cartilage (Figure 17.2). In small infants the membrane may be difficult to identify and tracheal puncture may be the alternative. Get someone to hold the head securely with the neck extended.

Cleanse the area. Attach the cannula to a syringe. Puncture the skin in the midline directly over the cricothyroid membrane. Direct the needle at 45 degrees towards the chest and carefully insert the cannula, aspirating via the syringe. When air enters the syringe the needle is in the trachea. Withdraw the needle whilst advancing the cannula into the trachea. Attach the cannula to a Y-shaped connector, one end of which is connected to an oxygen supply. For adolescents the flow rate should be 15 litres/min. However, for younger children this flow rate may be too high and a flow rate of 7–10 litres/min should be tried first.

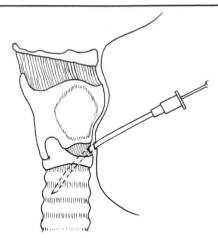

Figure 17.2 • Cricothyroid membrane puncture.

Ventilation is achieved by intermittently occluding the open end of the Y-shaped connector. Occlusion should be for one second for inspiration, and non-occlusion for four seconds for expiration. Chest compression may be necessary to assist expiration through the small gauge cannula. Alternatively, attach the cannula via a syringe to a paediatric endotracheal tube adapter. Ventilation can be achieved then with a bag and reservoir with 100 per cent oxygen. Inspiration should be for one second and expiration for four seconds. Chest compression may be necessary to assist expiration. If expiration is difficult, the bag device should be disconnected from the patient during expiration. Auscultate the chest to check ventilation is occurring. Secure the cannula in the correct position. Get help as soon as possible. It is possible to ventilate a patient for several minutes by this technique.

Problems Asphyxia may occur whilst the procedure is being carried out. As the tube inserted is not large enough to occlude the trachea, aspiration of stomach contents is possible. Bleeding from damage to a thyroid artery or other vessels may cause problems. It is possible to perforate the posterior tracheal wall or oesophagus. This is prevented by proceeding slowly whilst aspirating. When air appears in the syringe do not advance the needle further, just the plastic cannula. Ventilation may not be adequate. Proceed to skilled tracheostomy as soon as possible. Prepared cricothyrotomy sets are now commercially available.

Suprapubic aspiration

This method for obtaining a sterile urine specimen is suitable for under 1-year-old infants, in whom the bladder is an abdominal organ. Palpate the abdomen to ensure that the bladder can be felt. Restrain the infant in a supine position and cleanse the skin above the pubis. Keep a sterile bowl to hand as the abdominal palpation or skin preparation may induce urination and a clean catch specimen can be obtained. In a sick baby in whom speed is important, no local anaesthetic is used but if time permits, a local anaesthetic cream should be applied under an occlusive dressing for an hour before the procedure.

Prepare a 21 gauge needle with a 5 or 10 ml syringe attached. The needle is inserted into the abdomen, 0.5–1 cm above the pubic bone, and advanced backwards and caudally aspirating continuously until urine is aspirated. A depth of 2–4 cm is usually required.

This technique is virtually free from serious complications. Occasionally, a few red cells may subsequently appear in the urine.

Further reading

1. Ferguson, D. G. and Lord, S. M. (1986). *Practical procedure in accident and emergency medicine*. Butterworths, London.

CHAPTER 18

Legal aspects

Key points in legal aspects

1 If there are complaints about your management of a patient, full and accurate medical records are usually the best defence.

2 Ensure medical confidentiality.

3 Parental consent is not necessary for the emergency treatment of a seriously ill or injured child.

Police involvement

Police involvement is commoner in the A & E department than in most other hospital departments because some patients have suffered violent injury, either accidental or non-accidental, for example road traffic accidents, assault, or child abuse. The police and other agencies may require information and subsequently legal action may be taken.

Complaints

Medical complaints are more frequent in A & E departments than in some other hospital departments for three reasons. Firstly, the demands of an open door service, where patients' injuries and illnesses range from the trivial to the life-threatening, can stress all staff and render mistakes and misunderstandings more likely. Secondly, the problems with which patients present range across the whole spectrum of medicine requiring a broad basis of knowledge and experience from doctors who may be relatively inexperienced. Thirdly, patients and their relatives attending an Accident and Emergency service are often anxious and frightened. This can impede the doctor–patient relationship.

The chances of making a mistake can be minimized by keeping the following in mind:

- Examine the patient properly.
- Ask for help if you are uncertain.
- Be aware of your own limitations and do not take on anything which you are not confident to do.
- Follow departmental guidelines if available.
- Only tackle one problem at a time. It is easy to become distracted by frequent demands.
- Make good notes.

Notekeeping

The importance of making adequate notes at the time of the

incident cannot be over-emphasized. Firstly, many legal cases take years to come to Court or settlement, and the accuracy of memory cannot be relied upon. Secondly, if there are any complaints about your management of a patient, well-kept records can often exonerate you, but actions cannot be defended if they are not documented.

It is useful to start your notes with the time and date when you have seen the patient. Note who is accompanying the child and from whom the history is taken. Relevant positive and negative features of the history should be noted, and the examination notes should document the salient clinical findings. Particular note should be made of describing the absence of a relevant important sign. Injuries should be described in full stating size, site, and description of the lesion. A diagram of the injury is invaluable. Remember to note the side of injuries, and to name fingers rather than number them. Finally, give a diagnosis, describe the treatment ordered, and the eventual disposal of the patient. Always sign the notes, and also print your name if the signature is illegible. A new act *Access to Health Records Act 1990* came into force in November 1991. This establishes a right of access by patients to manually held health records, and provides for the correction of inaccurate health records. In the case of a child patient a person with parental responsibility may apply for access to the record, if either the child has consented or (in the case of a child incapable of understanding) if the access is in the child's best interests.

Confidentiality

In a busy department it is sometimes difficult to ensure the patient's privacy. Medical records may be left in different parts of a department awaiting procedures, and confidentiality may be breached. It is important to keep in mind the patient's rights to privacy.

Information about the child can be disclosed to medical and paramedical colleagues who need to be aware of the clinical findings, for example general practitioners, dentists, physiotherapists, etc. There is also a statutory requirement to disclose information in certain cases, for example notification of infectious diseases and notification of births and deaths.

In the case of a child attending without a parent, the parent should usually be informed of the details of the child's visit to the hospital. This may be done by relatives or school teachers who have come with the child. Occasionally in the case of an older child, the child may request that the parents are not informed. In this case the general practitioner and a senior doctor should be consulted and a decision made as to whether the information can justifiably be withheld.

Difficulties may arise in relation to police requests for information. The doctor has a duty to the patient of confidentiality, but also a social obligation to the community. Information should not be released to the police without signed informed consent from the patient or parents. However, in serious cases, social responsibility may override the need for confidentiality and information can be released to the police. In this case, first ask for senior advice or call the Medical Defence Union or Medical Protection Society.

As A & E departments are becoming computerized users must be aware of the *Data Protection Act*. If medical information is held on a computer file then the patient has a right to see that information unless some part of it is thought necessary to be withheld from the patient. This decision is taken by the consultant in charge of the case.

Consent to treatment

Consent may be implied or express. In most cases in the A & E department implied consent is given by adults on behalf of children by bringing them for treatment and allowing procedures to be undertaken after due explanation. Express written consent should be obtained, after an adequate explanation, for any procedure requiring general or regional anaesthetic.

Consent may be made on behalf of the child by a parent or other adult 'in loco parentis', such as a teacher, relative, or adult friend.

Sometimes children attend A & E without any accompanying adult. It is sensible to attempt to contact the parents before examining and treating the child. However, if the child has a sufficient understanding of what is proposed he may consent to a doctor making an examination and giving treatment. The doctor must be satisfied that any such child has sufficient understanding of what is involved in the treatment which is proposed. A full written note should be made of the factors taken into account by the doctor in making his assessment of the child's capacity to give a valid consent. In practical terms this usually means that children over 12-years-old can have minor treatments performed, such as minor wound care. However, for radiographic investigations and drug treatment an adult responsible for the patient should be contacted. Consent over the telephone may be acceptable, but this must be written on the A & E record. Sometimes the social work department or police can be helpful in locating a parent.

In an emergency, if a child is seriously ill and needs urgent life-saving treatment and investigations, then these can proceed without parental consent. Any immediate action which is necessary to preserve life or to prevent a serious and immediate danger to the patient or other people can be undertaken. The treatment should be sufficient to bring the emergency to an end.

There may be situations when a parent refuses to allow certain treatments or procedures to be performed (for example blood transfusion in a Jehovah's Witness). Senior help should be obtained and, if necessary, the consultant and social services department would attempt to make the child a Ward of Court.

For children who are in the care of the Local Authority, the relevant social services department is able to give consent to treatment.

Child Abuse

The Children and Young Persons Act of 1933 made it a criminal offence for anyone over 16 who has the custody, charge, or care of a child under 16 wilfully to ill-treat, neglect, or abandon that child, or expose him or her to unnecessary suffering or injury to health.

If a child is thought to have been physically or mentally abused, sexually assaulted, or neglected, then the perpetrator can be prosecuted under the above law. It may be necessary for the child to be removed from his home to a place of safety, which may be hospital or a foster home, for his own protection until the full details of the case can be assessed. *A Place of Safety Order* would then be obtained from a magistrate by the social services department or the police.

Section 28 (1) of the Children and Young Person's Act 1969 gives authority to a Justice:

to detain the child in a place of safety if there is a reasonable cause to believe that his/her proper development is being avoidably prevented or neglected or his/her health is being avoidably impaired or neglected or he/she is being ill-treated.

A new wide ranging act, The Children's Act 1989 came into force in October 1991 and supersedes the previous acts. As far as child protection is concerned, the new act emphasizes partnership with parents and aims at the prevention of abuse. However, immediate power to intervene to protect children is given in the *Emergency Protection Order*, which enables a child to be made safe when he or she may otherwise suffer harm. Anyone may apply to the Court for such an order on behalf of a child, although it will usually be obtained by a Local Authority. The order lasts for a maximum of eight days.

Police statements

You may be asked by the police to provide a statement about the injuries sustained by a patient whom you have seen in the Accident and Emergency department. It is necessary to obtain consent from the patient or parent, as appropriate, to release such details, and the police will usually already have obtained this. A police statement is a statement of fact and should only contain information which you yourself can verify, i.e. physical findings. No mention should be made of the history which is hearsay. Never dictate a statement to a policeman but write it yourself, or if possible have it typed and check it carefully. Ask your consultant for advice if you have any problems. Always keep a copy of the statement and your A & E notes in case you are asked to appear in Court. A fee is usually paid for a police statement.

Giving evidence in Court

If a case later comes to Court, you may be asked to appear as a professional witness. This does not happen often as usually your police statement will suffice. As a witness you will be called into Court and guided to the witness box. You will be asked to swear an Oath or an Affirmation. The first few questions will be your name, address, and occupation. You will then be asked to give a factual account of the patient's injuries. Direct your answers to the Bench. You may refer to your notes, but ask the Court's permission first. You should not give any opinion as to the causation of the injuries, as such opinions should only be provided by someone of experience who would be called as an expert witness.

It is unlikely for an A & E SHO to be required to attend Court in the case of child abuse as this role will probably be taken by the paediatrician. The A & E SHO might, however, be invited to a case conference.

Further reading

1. Gee, D. J. and Mason, J. K. (1990). *The Courts and the doctor.* Oxford University Press, Oxford.
2. Livesey, B. (1988). *Giving evidence in Court.* British Association for the study and prevention of child abuse and neglect, Rochdale.

Index